"The ultimate Darin reference book...Darin was an artist of diverse talents who proved to be ahead of his time in many ways...This bio provides in-depth coverage and analysis of his evolution as a multi-talented artist."

— *Billboard*

"A meticulously chronological and openly affectionate musical biography...A study of the music done in the clear belief that's the meat of any Darin discussion."

— *New York Daily News*

"Bleiel has researched well...His details about Darin's recordings are unimpeachable."

— *Pittsburgh Tribune-Review*

"Straightforward and laudably unsensationalistic...The book concentrates principally on Darin's professional activities, providing informed commentary on virtually every Darin recording."

— *Goldmine*

"An articulate, thoughtful, and sympathetic overview of Bobby Darin's hectic performing career...Bleiel makes a strong case for Darin's lofty place in music-making history...Well worth reading."

— *Popular Music and Society*

The book is far more than a simple reference, and in fact proves to be an entertaining page-turner...There is much in the text that gives readers a view of Darin's near-obsessive drive, his professionalism and perfectionism...Through Bleiel, Darin at last receives his due as a rock and roll pioneer."

— *Association for Recorded Sound Collections Journal*

"When you finish reading *That's All*, you'll conclude that Bobby Darin was a true one-of-a-kind."

— *Dick Clark*

THAT'S ALL
BOBBY DARIN

ON RECORD, STAGE AND SCREEN

REVISED AND EXPANDED SECOND EDITION

THAT'S ALL
BOBBY
DARIN

ON RECORD, STAGE AND SCREEN

REVISED AND EXPANDED SECOND EDITION

Jeff Bleiel

Tiny Ripple Books
P.O. Box 1533
Cranberry Township, PA 16066

Published by:
Tiny Ripple Books
P.O. Box 1533
Cranberry Township, PA 16066
www.tinyripple.com

ISBN 0-9675973-4-X
Library of Congress Control Number: 2004094091
Printed in the United States of America

Contents

Foreword to the First Edition

by Dick Clark

Through the years, I've been asked hundreds of times to reflect on my favorite artist of all time. Having dealt with thousands of performers, I've never been able to adequately answer. Quite frankly, I've always been afraid of offending the artists I didn't name. Having been asked to write a foreword to this book, I didn't feel as constrained. I've always admired Bobby Darin tremendously.

Bobby had a voracious appetite for variety. He wanted to do everything. As it turned out, he did it and he did it well in a much-too-short lifetime. He is one of the most versatile performers I've ever met.

That's All: Bobby Darin on Record, Stage & Screen is a work that surveys the career of my friend Bobby Darin. Jeff Bleiel has purposely emphasized the professional side over the personal side of Bobby's life. But let me add a personal note. Bobby was one of the most complicated and interesting people I've known. You didn't always "get what you saw." He could be equally tough and gentle. He was autocratic and at the same time very democratic. He was generous to a fault.

There were things I always knew about him. If I were in trouble, no matter where he was, he would find me and come to my aid. Had I needed it, he would have given me money. I never asked for money but, like everybody else, I had my share of emotional setbacks. Bobby was always there to advise and console me. It was a reciprocal arrangement. I can illustrate the kind of friend he was with an example....If ever your home or family are put in danger, the person who shows up to help put out the fire and take care of the kids is really a friend. I could always count on Bobby Darin. He knew he could count on me.

My appraisal of his extraordinary talent and contributions may be colored by my love for him. I hope that when you finish reading *That's All: Bobby Darin On Record, Stage & Screen,* you'll conclude that Bobby Darin was a true one-of-a-kind.

Dick Clark (1993)

Acknowledgments

I wish to acknowledge and express my appreciation to the 22 professional associates of Bobby Darin who were gracious in sharing their remembrances with me. Thanks to Dick Bakalyan, Richard Behrke, Glen Campbell, Ernest Chambers, Bob Crewe, Quitman Dennis, Steve Douglas, Geoff Edwards, Ahmet Ertegun, Saul Ilson, Carol Kaye, Charles Koppelman, Brent Maher, Billy May, Roger McGuinn, Terry Melcher, Tom Morgan, Walter Raim, Don Rubin, Bobby Scott, Alan Thicke, and Nik Venet.

Thanks also to Bobby Darin's long-time friend and associate Harriet Wasser for sharing her insights and memories with me.

I also wish to thank Al Aronowitz, Fred Dutton, Tim Hauser, Robert Hilburn, Georges LaForge, Jack Newfield, and John Stewart for providing their comments.

Also thanks to the following for their assistance and/or encouragement: James Austin, Virginia Boles, The Carnegie Library, Dick Clark, Al DiOrio, The Federal Bureau of Investigation, Erik Jacobsen, Gary Levine, The Library of Congress, Richard Lorenzo, Frank Mankiewicz, Marlene Miller, The Museum of Broadcasting, Tom Schultheiss, Jeff Tamarkin, Ted Venetoulis, Allen Wiener, and Mike White.

Most special thanks to Judy Bleiel, Doris Diethorn, Laura Bleiel, and Nicky Bleiel.

Jeff Bleiel

Prologue

Comments about Bobby Darin's talent and legacy, from professional associates who were interviewed for this book:

"I thought he was a terrific rock'n'roll artist. He understood and appreciated Chuck Berry. He loved that music, but he also loved Cole Porter and Sinatra. And he could do both quite handily."

— *Ahmet Ertegun, President, Atlantic Records*

"He was one of the greats. He was like a mentor to me. He convinced me that rock'n'roll was where it was at."

— *Roger McGuinn, singer, guitarist,*
founder of The Byrds, Darin guitarist 1962-1963

"In the record business in those days, nobody in their twenties used to produce. Young singers used to be an instrument of someone else. Darin did what nobody did in those days. He picked everything. It always had his thumbprint on it."

— *Nik Venet, Capitol Records producer*
(Darin, The Beach Boys, Lou Rawls, Linda Ronstadt)

"He was one of the greatest performers I ever saw on the stage. I've worked with a hell of a lot of singers, and I don't think any of them had Bobby's essential performing ability."

— *Bobby Scott, jazz pianist, arranger, composer ("A Taste Of Honey," "He Ain't Heavy, He's My Brother"), Darin arranger and accompanist*

"The thing I always respected about Bobby was that I totally believed every phase he was in. I believed his rock'n'roll phase, I believed his Vegas phase, and I believed his folk phase."

— *Alan Thicke, actor ("Growing Pains"), writer for "The Bobby Darin Show"*

"I've worked a lot with Frank Sinatra. Bobby was similar. When he came on in Vegas, he owned it. He was probably the best performer ever to play Vegas."

— *Dick Bakalyan, actor (appeared with Darin in* Pressure Point, *"The Bobby Darin Show")*

"Thinking back, he was probably one of the most talented, gifted entertainers I've worked with."

— *Saul Ilson, television producer ("The Smothers Brothers Comedy Hour," "Tony Orlando & Dawn"), co-producer of "The Bobby Darin Show"*

"He was able to go in so many different directions. People, on the radio level in particular, like to be able to characterize an artist. He was going from Buddy Holly to Frank Sinatra. He liked it all."

—*Terry Melcher, record producer (The Byrds, Paul Revere & The Raiders, The Beach Boys), Darin co-writer and associate*

"He was very helpful in the studio. He cut right down to the core of the matter and knew just what to do. He was an incredible professional and an incredibly great singer."

— *Don Rubin, co-producer of two Darin albums*

"He was one of the greatest singers that I ever worked for. I equate him with Ray Charles as far as the amount of talent he had."

— *Carol Kaye, studio musician (played bass and guitar on numerous 1960s sessions for Darin, The Beach Boys, Phil Spector, others)*

"In Memoriam"

Bobby Darin's entertainment career lasted only 18 years, from 1956 through 1973. He was not the most popular, most revolutionary, or most remembered entertainer of his era, but he may well own the most interesting career of any performer of the second half of the 20th century.

Rock and Roll Hall of Famer. Oscar-nominated actor. TV variety show host. Preeminent Las Vegas entertainer. Songwriter. Musician. Music publishing executive. Teen idol. Record producer.

Some people working in the same business as Bobby Darin can claim one, or a few, of the identifications above. The truly great or ambitious ones may claim a handful. But Bobby Darin claimed them all.

Darin earned his fame while popular entertainment was mirroring the era's incredibly swift social and technological changes. He was alternately of his times, ahead of his times, and behind his times. Part of him belonged on a turn-of-the-century vaudeville stage with a megaphone. Part of him belonged in front of a bank of amps at Woodstock.

He opened for both Buddy Holly and George Burns. He wrote songs with both Johnny Mercer and Randy Newman. He did television specials with both Eddie Cantor and Stevie Wonder. He sang at The Apollo Theatre and at The Royal Albert Hall; at sock hops in high school gymnasiums and in showrooms in hotel casinos. He admired Sophie Tucker and understood why audiences liked her. He admired The Rolling Stones and understood why audiences liked them.

Musically, Darin performed and recorded rock'n'roll, pop standards, jazz, R&B, country, and folk music. For fans devoted solely to any one of those styles, it was too easy to ignore him or think of him as insincere or calculating. It is precisely because he is uncategorizable that he is often overlooked when it comes to discussing the musical greats of the two decades which coincided with rock'n'roll's nascence.

For a long time, the simplistic, but too-widely-held historical take on Darin's career was that he used a couple of authentically good 1950s rock'n'roll hits as a springboard to traditional show business success. But it takes a truly comprehensive career overview to discover Darin's artistic genius – not only consistently great work, but also the capacity to continually surprise.

In retrospect, it's hard to recall how sharply divided the lines in pop music once were. Now it is considered perfectly normal to have both Frank Sinatra and Jimi Hendrix CDs in your collection; in fact, you can be accused of being close-minded if you don't. But go back to 1962. Pop music had its old school, and its new schools. There was no co-mingling among them.

Their own individual audiences knew where Chuck Berry stood, where Tony Bennett stood, where Joan Baez stood. It was clear that while they were all in the same business, they were working different sides of the street. Privately, the performers may have appreciated styles they weren't practicing, but only Bobby Darin had the inclination to break through the barriers. In the 1960s, there were no Vegas nightclub singers who were also writing protest songs. Except Bobby Darin. There weren't any folk club performers who were also dancing with a top hat and cane on television. Except Bobby Darin.

These laudable qualities ironically made it much more unlikely that Darin would be cited as an obvious influence on performers of subsequent generations. While it was very easy to identify all of Chuck's children, or a slew of "new Dylans," there were no Bobby Darin disciples. It has turned out to be his attitude, his risk-taking nature, more than his music, which has emboldened some later rockers to defy the expectations of their audiences.

Most noteworthy, Neil Young has acknowledged that his genre-shifting, if not exactly inspired by Darin, was at least validated by the example of Darin's kindred career.

"I used to be pissed off at Bobby Darin because he changed styles so much," Young told *Rolling Stone* in 1988. "Now I look at him and I think he was a fucking genius."

Previously, there has been little consideration given to Bobby Darin as a significant musical artist of his time. There has been little to flag his artistry, his songwriting ability, his experimentation, and the genre-busting and expectation-confounding nature of his career. That is why this book is written.

There isn't a single sentence about Bobby Darin in *The Rolling Stone Illustrated History of Rock & Roll*. Indeed, some questioned why a performer who was opening for George Burns in Las Vegas in 1959 was inducted into the Rock and Roll Hall of Fame alongside The Who and The Kinks. But dozens of his recordings show Darin to be a true rocker, not just in his pre-"Mack The Knife" days, but throughout his career.

Any temptations to dismiss him as a "second rate Sinatra" or hip lounge lizard fly out the window upon hearing how Darin handled popular standards and jazz-tinged material. He could swing with authority, and there was a latent respect for Darin in the jazz community.

Whispers that Darin's forays into country or folk music were commercially-motivated bandwagon hops are belied by the understanding he displays for the essence of those genres in both his studio recordings and in surviving audio and video recordings of his live performances. Had he recorded only his six folk-oriented albums and then disappeared, he would no doubt be regarded as a cult favorite in folk circles today.

The differing styles displayed in his recordings is obvious, but his legacy as a songwriter is perhaps even more indicative of his unique ability to successfully cut across varying styles of popular music.

Fellow Rock and Roll Hall of Fame inductees Elvis Presley, Buddy Holly, Rick Nelson, Dion, Gene Vincent, Jerry Lee Lewis, The Coasters, Ruth Brown, LaVern Baker, and Duane Eddy have all recorded Darin-written songs. On the other end of the musical spectrum, so have Barbra Streisand and Wayne Newton. Darin has also been covered by cult folk artist Tim Hardin, country greats Johnny Cash, Sonny James, and Conway Twitty, and British Invasion bands The Searchers and Gerry & The Pacemakers.

He didn't merely get lucky with one or two hits which got a lot of covers. Darin wrote or co-wrote more than 150 songs, including nine of his own hits, and over 35 different songs which have been recorded by other artists. This track record led to his induction into the National Academy of Popular Music's Songwriters Hall of Fame.

Darin also displayed a limited, but nevertheless impressive ability as a musician. On stage, he played piano, guitar, vibes, drums, and harmonica. No less an authority than Henry Mancini called him "a very, very fine musician."

Darin's reach also extended into other areas beyond the music field (where he tallied 41 hit singles, of which 22 made the Top 40, and ten of those reached the Top 10). As an actor, Darin appeared in 13 films, playing prominent roles in 11 of them, and earned a Golden Globe Award and an Academy Award nomination. On television, he briefly had his own series, he headlined three specials, and he made nearly 100 guest appearances on other programs.

But the most rewarding thing about researching Darin's career is the continual surprises one encounters: the shock of seeing a "teen idol" chillingly portray a bigoted Nazi in *Pressure Point*; the jarring musical juxtaposition of albums such as *In A Broadway Bag* and *Commitment*, where a blindfolded, unknowing listener would never guess that they were the product of the same artist; the respect evident in the remembrances of figures as diverse as folk-rock pioneer Roger McGuinn of The Byrds and television actor Alan Thicke, both of whom referred to Darin as a "mentor"; the discovery of his largely unpublicized activity in the social and political causes of his time.

Then there is the story of the personality behind this unique life and career. Darin earned, even cultivated, a reputation for being a brash, cocky (some go so far as to say obnoxious) individualist. But nobody who worked closely with Darin remembers him that way. His good friend Dick Clark told *Rolling Stone*, "I used to laugh when people told me how Bobby was an arrogant little son of a bitch. But if you knew him, he was the kindest, gentlest person."

Likewise, each of the 26 Darin associates interviewed for this book remembered him with respect and affection. Their recollections and anecdotes provide fascinating insight into the motivations that fueled Bobby Darin's fire.

However, the emphasis of this book is on Bobby Darin's professional career, rather than his personal life. This is not intended to be the definitive biography of Darin's life, but rather a detailed, comprehensive account of his work, complete with background, anecdotes, analysis, and the remembrances of numerous professional associates.

Some comments on Darin's character and personality are included, as are details on some personal events in his life. But a reader looking for gossipy tidbits about his marriage to Sandra Dee, or other items about his romantic or family relationships is advised that those matters will not be covered in these pages.

The main goal of this overview is to give Bobby Darin's career proper historical due. He was so much more than a teen idol, a pop star, or a showbiz icon. He was an artist. He had the ability to make a rock fan appreciate "Mame" and a Sinatra fan appreciate "Roll Over Beethoven." He brought Bob Dylan songs to Las Vegas and Rodgers & Hart songs to rock'n'roll caravan tours. No other artist of the past 50 years followed a similar career path. Because he was one of a kind, he was the last of a kind.

"Long Ago And Far Away"

The Early Years

The two constants of Bobby Darin's youth were sickness and poverty.

He was born Walden Robert Cassotto on May 14, 1936. Bobby Cassotto was a frail, sickly child. At age three, he fell from a chair and broke his leg. When he was eight, he had his first attack of rheumatic fever. Before he was 12, he would have three more attacks. Each night, members of his family would take turns checking in on the sleeping young boy to make sure he was still breathing.

Doctors told his mother that he probably would not live to be 16. Years after he outlived that prediction, he would talk of how, when he was a baby, neighbors would stop his mother on the street and say, "Why do you want to wheel that thing around for? It's gonna die."

"My earliest recollections were of being in bed, stiff, hurting," the adult Bobby Darin would recall. "I used to read or do coloring books. I couldn't do what everybody else was doing."

He grew up without a father in a series of East Harlem and Bronx tenements. His mother, and a sister, born 19 years earlier, raised him. "We were poor, on relief-type Bronx people," Darin would explain. "It was a poverty very hard for me to describe."

––––––––––––––––––––––––––––––––

Bobby's parents were Saverio "Sam" Cassotto and Vivian "Polly" Walden Cassotto. Sam was the son of an Italian immigrant tailor. A cabinetmaker by trade, Sam Cassotto was reported to be close friends, and even partners in a bar, with Frank Costello, reputed head of the New York Mafia.

Convicted for participating in a pickpocket scheme, Sam was sent to Sing Sing prison in 1934. While there, he died of pneumonia.

While completely distancing himself from his father's shady connections, the adult Bobby Darin was not at all shy about relating the story of Sam Cassotto to the press. It made good copy, and in many ways, served the image Darin wished to create.

Vivian Polly Walden had show business in her blood. As a teenager, she ran away from home to join a road show. Using the stage name of Paula Walden, she later landed a featured role in a vaudeville revue. On a trip to Chicago, Sam saw her on stage and sent her flowers. Soon she was off the vaude-ville circuit and heading to Harlem as Sam's wife.

Nineteen years before Bobby came along, Sam and Polly had a daughter, Vanina (Nina) Cassotto. In 1936, it was the unmarried, teenage Nina who gave birth to Walden Robert Cassotto.

Not until he was about 30 years old did Bobby Darin learn the truth about the circumstances surrounding his birth – that Nina, whom he thought was his sister, was his natural mother, and that Polly, whom he called his mother, was his natural grandmother. Nina took the identity of Darin's biological father to her grave.

Because throughout his life, in every known interview or biographical profile, Bobby Darin referred to Sam and Polly as his parents and Nina as his sister, that is how they will be designated in this book. The true story was not made public until long after Darin's death.

A few years after Bobby's birth, Nina married Charlie Maffia, who moved in and helped support the family – and pay Bobby's medical bills. Years later, Maffia would work as a valet, chauffeur and road manager for Bobby Darin.

Bobby was always encouraged by his mother. "You don't belong in a tenement," she would tell him. Indeed, an IQ of 137 enabled him to excel in school. He was an A student at Clark Junior High in the Bronx, and he did well enough to get into the respected Bronx High School of Science.

"I enjoyed doing homework," he would recall. "That made me a freak to the kids on the block. My neighborhood was not geared to things scientific and scholastic. I was going to a fine school, then going back to a neighborhood where an education didn't mean a damn."

Despite his academic potential, Bobby was more interested in performing and entertaining. He loved the attention. At one point, he thought comedy was his calling, but he also picked up on music. He learned to play rudimentary piano by ear.

Toward the end of his junior year at Bronx High School, some musically inclined friends of Bobby's decided to form a band. The Eddie O'Casio Quintet consisted of Eddie O'Casio on piano, Richard (Dick) Behrke on trumpet, Walter Raim on guitar, and Steve Karmen on saxophone. They needed a drummer, so that's what Bobby Cassotto became. He had never played before, but in three weeks he became proficient enough for the band.

"We were all learning our instruments, really," recalled Walter Raim. "Bobby was a talented, musical kid. He decided that he would be the drummer, then he learned to play afterwards. He was untutored. He just learned the drums himself."

Drumming was an unusual, potentially dangerous physical activity for Bobby. Even in high school, he was excused from calisthenics and had a special pass to use the school elevator. But he decided that playing music was worth the risk to his health. He also knew that he'd have to test his strength to follow another of his dreams, becoming an actor.

"When we met him, he was hell-bent on being an actor," said Raim. "At the time we got involved with the band, he was trying to learn French, because he was trying to get a part in a play with a French-speaking company. He wanted to be an actor. Music was just another creative activity he thought would be fun."

The band played gigs like high school dances, private parties and lonely hearts clubs. Then in the summer of 1951, they got a job playing at a hotel in the Catskills called Sunny Land. For the princely sum of 35 dollars a week, they got to be the house band by night, bus boys by day.

"We were a real old-fashioned dance band," Raim recalled. "We played stock arrangements that you could send away for – three or four-part band arrangements of standards from the '30s and '40s. It was the pop music of the time, which was the Frank Sinatra-Perry Como era."

The band repeated the engagement the following summer, another season of "Fools Rush In," mambos, and waltzes. Their wildest number was "When The Saints Go Marching In." But with high school over, so was the band. However, this modest little group produced an impressive musical legacy. Bobby Cassotto became Bobby Darin. Both Walter Raim and Dick Behrke would go on to successful careers as musicians, often working with Darin. Steve Karmen would later write popular commercial jingles, including "I Love New York." Such potential, of course, wasn't so readily apparent in 1952.

"At the time, I thought we were a fine band," said Walter Raim. "If I heard a recording now, I don't know what I'd think."

Following high school, Bobby enrolled at New York's Hunter College, intending to major in theatre arts. He appeared in productions of *Hedda Gabler*, *The Valiant*, and *The Curious Savage*, but only lasted one semester. Later, he would explain that he was not interested in learning the technical side of the theatre, which was to have been the focus of his second semester.

He then spent some time on the road with a touring children's theatre company, performing in *Kit Carson*. Back in New York, he and Dick Behrke shared an apartment at West 71st Street, and the duo occasionally played at an off-Broadway bar called Club 77.

"We would ad lib performances there," Behrke recalled. "Jazz, cabaret stuff. There was a blind guitar-player named Chuck, and he would let us sit in. By that time, Bobby had spent a summer in the mountains as a singing waiter. He'd be doing comedy and singing."

At age 18, Bobby had one additional professional – and personal – experience which, in early interviews, he would cite as having a profound influence on his life. A 31-year-old dancer invited Bobby to join her on the road and play bongos for her act.

The relationship turned out to be more romantic than musical, and it ended with the dancer dismissing the naïve teenager. He had fallen hard, and he was crushed. "Before I met her, I was just a kid in the Bronx," Darin later told *Life* magazine. "Afterward, I was the most disillusioned human being in the world. But I was no kid."

The bitterness of the experience stayed with him for a long time, but he found a way to make it work for his career. "I know what I'm singing about," he would say.

"I Have Dreamed" 3

In 1956, Bobby Cassotto became Bobby Darin. With his sights set on breaking into the music business, he decided that a stage name would beneficial.

Two stories exist about how the name "Darin" was chosen. One is that Bobby picked it out of the phone book. Another is that it came to him when he was passing a Mandarin restaurant, with the neon letters "M-A-N" burned out the flashing sign.

Early that year, Darin started writing songs with another former Bronx High School student, Don Kirshner. The duo copyrighted their first song, "Bubble Gum Pop," on January 17, 1956. Their earliest efforts included commercial jingles such as "The Rogers Cha Cha" for a local furniture store.

The co-writers were also making the rounds to music publishers to plug their songs. Their demos featured Darin's voice. One day, they took a song called "My First Real Love" to George Scheck, the manager of Connie Francis. Though her first hit, like Darin's, would be almost two years away, Francis had a contract with MGM Records.

Scheck was impressed by both the song and the demo. With his name (as George M. Shaw) added to the songwriters' credit, "My First Real Love" became Francis' fourth single. The backing group credited on the record, The Jaybirds, was in fact Bobby Darin. Though it fell short of becoming a hit, "My First Real Love" was a well-constructed beat ballad with a typical 1950s rock'n'roll arrangement, including doo-wop-style backing vocals.

A romance also blossomed between Darin and Francis. In her biography *Who's Sorry Now*, Francis describes Darin as her "first real love and a man I would love 'till the day he died and beyond." She reports that Darin proposed to her in the days before either of them became famous. However, their romance was opposed by Francis' domineering stage father, who, to prevent the young couple from seeing each other, reportedly once went after Darin with a gun on the set of "The Ed Sullivan Show."

Meanwhile, George Scheck helped Darin get a contract with Decca Records. His first single, the Leadbelly folk/blues classic "Rock Island Line," was an ill-advised, unnatural choice for Darin. The record opens with approximately one minute of spoken-word introduction before Darin begins to actually sing. Even then, his singing was interspersed with his off-key impression of a train whistle.

If material and performance were problematic, so was timing. The record was released only after British skiffle star Lonnie Donegan's version had already begun its ascent up the charts (where it would eventually reach the Top 10). The fact that the release was too late was mentioned in *Billboard* magazine's review of the single, which nevertheless noted Darin as a "new artist (who) shows solid promise."

The single's flip side was a Darin-Kirshner (and Scheck) original, "Timber." It was another work-type song, and though not very good, it is noteworthy that one of Darin's earliest songs would fall into that genre.

An early publicity photo

Four days after the "Rock Island Line" recording session, Scheck and Decca arranged for Darin to make his first television appearance, a performance of the single on the program "Stage Show," hosted by the Dorsey Brothers and produced by Jackie Gleason.

Darin gave a very energetic, dynamic performance on the program, but again, unfortunate timing worked against him. Having only learned and recorded the song four days earlier, Darin expected to be able to read the lyrics off cue cards when performing the song on "Stage Show." When he was told that cue cards would not be provided, he wrote the lyrics on his hands, only to see the words perspire away.

"I went out cold, scared to death, and sang 'Rock Island Line,'" he told *TV Guide* later. "It bombed."

That was an apt description of all of Darin's Decca recordings. For his second single, Darin dove into the rock'n'roll market with a novelty-style original called "Silly Willie." Credited to Bobby Darin and The Jaybirds, *Billboard* called it "a fast and furious bit of nonsense." It was not quite hit material, but the song's bridge, which featured an energetic big beat and rock saxophone, showed potential.

Darin's next two Decca singles veered away from rock'n'roll. On these tracks, Darin's vocals sound unlike his singing on any other record of his career, almost as if he were trying to impersonate another singer. Only "Dealer In Dreams," a Darin-Kirshner beat ballad with big band horns, rose above the mediocre level. Calling the track "reminiscent of Johnny Ray," *Billboard*'s review noted that Darin "projects strong emotion in a vigorous, outgoing way."

Darin went on the road for the first time, performing in small nightclubs with Kirshner backing him on guitar and acting as his manager. The two also continued to write songs, and managed to place a few with other singers. A seasonal novelty, "I Want To Spend Christmas With Elvis," was recorded by Little Lambsie Penn in 1956.

A more impressive list of singers would record Darin-Kirshner songs in 1957. Rockabilly great Gene Vincent cut "Wear My Ring," R&B legend LaVern Baker recorded "Love Me Right" and jazz singer Bobby Short took "Delia." But Darin was still trying for a hit of his own. When Decca dropped him, the outlook grew dimmer.

While on the road in Nashville in May 1957, Darin paid for a recording session himself. He recorded two songs he and Kirshner had written – "Wear My Ring" and "Talk To Me Something" – and two others, "Just In Case You Change Your Mind" and "I Found A Million Dollar Baby (In A Five and Ten Cent Store)," the latter an old Billy Rose standard. Influenced and inspired by Elvis Presley's success, Darin produced all in the rock'n'roll idiom.

Back in New York, Darin and Kirshner took the masters to Atlantic Records. The tracks impressed Herb Abramson, who had helped Ahmet and Nesuhi Ertegun found the R&B-oriented label a decade earlier. Abramson oversaw the company's Atco label and he purchased the four masters from Darin.

Atco released "I Found A Million Dollar Baby" as its first Darin single. It was a respectable rock'n'roll effort with an appealing electric guitar sound and big beat drumming. The single received favorable reviews in both *Billboard* ("a hefty, rocking commercial reading") and *Cash Box* (which designated it as "Sleeper of the Week" and called it "a stepping stone to a promising future"). But, backed with Darin and Kirshner's affected rock'n'roll ballad "Talk To Me Something," the record flopped.

Darin still wasn't entirely comfortable or confident as a rock'n'roll singer or songwriter. This was evident on his second Atco single, recorded on August 21, 1957. It was another pair of Darin-Kirshner originals, "Don't Call My Name" and "Pretty Betty." Both were certainly rock'n'roll in style, but the former was a rip-off of Fats Domino's "Ain't That A Shame" while the latter echoed Little Richard's "Ready Teddy."

Though a hit still hadn't arrived, Atlantic stood behind Darin, and their backing helped him achieve significant exposure. In July, he jointed Chuck Berry, Frankie Lymon and Andy Williams on Alan Freed's TV show, "The Big Beat." He also got a spot in a Freed rock'n'roll revue playing at New York's legendary Apollo Theatre.

In a 12-minute segment, Darin sang a few of his Atco songs, Larry Williams' "Short Fat Fannie," and medleys of songs by Fats Domino and Ray Charles. Trying to please the Apollo audience was a tough assignment for any white performer, let alone an inexperienced one like Darin. "He patterns himself after Fats Domino," said a *Variety* review, "and the contrast is quite glaring. White singer is not in that class."

In December, Darin made his first appearance on "American Bandstand," performing "Don't Call My Name." His finger-snapping style was already in place and, chatting with Dick Clark, Darin proved to be a polished, natural TV interview. "I want to congratulate you on a really great thing," the smooth Darin told Clark. "Every city I've visited throughout the land, you know they said the best show on television in the afternoon is Dick Clark's 'American Bandstand.'"

Darin and Clark struck up a close friendship which would last throughout Darin's life. Clark has called Bobby Darin "my all-time favorite performer" and "probably my closest friend in the business."

Atco tried another track from the Nashville session, "Just In Case You Change Your Mind" as a single in early 1958. It was another forced attempt at copping the Elvis sound, even to the point of employing a Jordanaires-style backing group. Darin still sounded unnatural in the role.

It was three misses and no hits for Bobby Darin at Atco, and for Herb Abramson's money, that was enough. Then Ahmet Ertegun stepped in.

"When Herb said he was going to release Darin from his contract, I said, 'No. If you don't want him, I'll take him over,'" Ertegun recalled.

Darin and Ertegun had developed a friendly relationship in the Atlantic office. Ertegun's office was right next to the waiting room, where Darin would sometimes pass time before his appointments with Abramson. There was a piano in the waiting room and Darin would catch Ertegun's ear with his piano noodling.

"On that piano, he would play music totally different from the masters Herb had purchased," Ertegun said. "I heard some terrific things."

"Splish Splash"
1958

On April 10, 1958, Atlantic Records had scheduled a recording session for jazz singer Morganna King. Ahmet Ertegun told Darin to show up with some of his new songs.

Ertegun quickly produced two tracks for King. He wanted to use the remaining two hours to record three songs with Darin. To warm up, they decided to cut the weakest song first. It was the non-Darin song "Judy, Don't Be Moody," co-written by Ben Raleigh (who had earlier co-written Nat King Cole's hit "Faith Can Move Mountains" and would later co-write the appealing Lesley Gore pop hits "She's A Fool" and "That's The Way Boys Are"). Ertegun, Darin (who played piano), and the pickup band got a suitable version by the fourth take.

They then moved on to a song that Darin wrote from an unusual inspiration. Since signing with Atlantic, he had become friends with legendary New York City disc jockey Murray Kaufman, better known as "Murray The K." Kaufman's Portrait Music subsequently published several of Darin's compositions. One day, while visiting Kaufman's home, Darin met the disc jockey's mother, who suggested that "Splish Splash, Take A Bath" would make a great title for a song.

Twelve minutes later, Darin had finished writing "Splish Splash." Because she had suggested the title – and because having half a songwriting royalty go to the mother of a famous disc jockey could only help airplay – Jean Murray received co-writing credit for the song.

Darin and the band's first run-through of "Splish Splash" in the studio was good, although the song's lyric and arrangement were not yet fully formed.

"I'm not happy from here," Darin said after the first take. Ertegun suggested a different sax solo and instructed the drummer to keep the cymbals from ringing.

Darin, again playing piano and singing simultaneously, was much more assured on the second take, and the idea to have the track fade out was agreed upon. While this take was a possible keeper, Ertegun and Darin decided to try a few more times. Darin flubbed the lyrics on the next few takes.

"That's all right man, don't rush," Ertegun said. "We've got all the time in the world."

The pounding piano, big beat, wailing sax, and rough-edged vocal were coming together to create a bonafide 1950s rock'n'roll classic. Darin molded his vocal so that it echoed the styles of Jerry Lee Lewis (the exclamatory "hey-yea") and Fats Domino (the way "door" became "doe" and "floor" became "flo"). Darin's lyrics were full of clever rock'n'roll references – Peggy Sue, Lollipop, Good Golly Miss Molly.

After messing up again midway through Take 6, Darin asked if he and the band could just resume from the point of the mistake, and edit the takes together later.

"No, let's do it all the way through," Ertegun said. "I wanna do it all the way through if it kills you."

Two takes later, "Splish Splash" was completed.

"Let's go on to the last number," Ertegun yelled.

Darin immediately began working out his piano introduction to another new song, "Queen Of The Hop." A bass singer was to accompany Darin throughout the song, intoning the title phrase repeatedly. Darin instructed him on where to come in. The track struggled to come together through numerous takes. Ertegun instructed the saxophone player to refrain from playing in the introduction, allowing Darin's piano to be more prominent. The bass singer was wisely dropped.

Darin remained very confident and in-charge throughout the entire recording process. Finally, after more than ten takes, "Queen Of The Hop" was in the can. Ertegun was convinced that Darin's "last chance" would pay off.

Atco released "Splish Splash" (with "Judy, Don't Be Moody" on the B-side) in early June 1958. Atlantic engineer Tom Dowd grafted a "bubbling water" effect onto the beginning of the record, and it was this sound that introduced Bobby Darin to the young American record buying public that summer.

The track's energy, rocking beat, and semi-novelty lyric (aligning it with "Hound Dog," "Good Golly Miss Molly," "Bony Maronie" and other '50s rock classics) struck a chord with the teenage audience. "Splish Splash" hit #3 in August and went all the way to #1 on *Billboard*'s R&B chart.

In fact, Darin's performance was so convincing that some listeners assumed he was a black R&B artist. The fact that Atco was an R&B label contributed to the misconception.

"Thank God we didn't have video then," Atlantic executive Jerry Wexler told author Joe Smith in *Off The Record*. "Nobody knew he was white."

Before "Splish Splash" took off, however, Darin wasn't entirely confident about the record's hit potential. After all, he was 0-for-7. With only two weeks left before his Atco contract expired, Darin felt he needed some professional insurance.

In case Atco dropped him, Darin wanted to have a record to sell to another label. He went into the studio and produced and recorded "Early In The Morning," a new song he'd written with Woody Harris.

Murray Kaufman sold the master to Brunswick Records. But when "Splish Splash" caught on, Atco renewed Darin's contract. A month after "Splish Splash" charted, Brunswick released "Early In The Morning" under the name The Ding Dongs. Atco was not fooled. Darin was now hot property, and they would not allow another label to release a Bobby Darin record.

Atco secured ownership of the master and, not wanting to compete with the still-climbing "Splish Splash," released the record under the name The Rinky Dinks. Decca countered by rush-releasing Buddy Holly's cover of "Early In The Morning" one week after the Rinky Dinks disc charted. In the chart battle that ensued, the Darin version (#24) edged out Holly's cover (#32). Darin's record also became a sizeable R&B hit, reaching #8.

Ertegun was upset, but understanding of Darin's action, given the conflicting status reports the singer was getting from Atco. "Herb (Abramson) probably told Darin we were going to drop him. I told him we weren't."

Likewise, Darin was very conciliatory when the press picked up on the fact that he was The Rinky Dinks.

"I thought there was a chance Atco wouldn't pick up my option," he told *Billboard*. "We were accused of all kinds of underhanded tricks, but no kidding, we didn't mean to hurt anybody. We were just trying to protect our own interests so we would have somewhere to turn."

The public also caught on when Darin appeared on Dick Clark's weekly prime-time show on July 19. After presenting Darin with a gold record for "Splish Splash," Clark announced that Darin would perform his follow-up hit, "Early In The Morning." Atco then started labeling the single as "Bobby Darin with The Rinky Dinks."

Lost in the shuffle was a fine flip side, "Now We're One." Featuring a prominently-strummed, loud-for-its-time electric guitar, the song was also covered by Buddy Holly (as the B-side of his "Early In The Morning").

Also in July, Atco issued Darin's first album, *Bobby Darin*. In addition to "Splish Splash" and "Judy, Don't Be Moody," the album included the six flop sides which preceded the hit, and the Nashville session leftover "Wear My Ring."

Two tracks recorded in New York in January 1958 stood out. A Darin-Woody Harris collaboration, "Brand New House," found Darin sounding much more comfortable in the R&B mode. And "Actions Speak Louder Than Words" was a fine R&B ballad co-written by future Motown founder Berry Gordy, Jr.

Darin also helped out Atlantic out with his songwriting ability. In September, "This Little Girl's Gone Rockin'," which Darin wrote with Mann Curtis (who would later pen the lyric for "Let It Be Me"), became a pop and R&B hit for legendary R&B singer Ruth Brown. It reached #7 on the R&B charts and became one of only two Top 40 pop hits Brown would ever score.

In September, "Queen Of The Hop" was released as a single and quickly shot into the Top 10, becoming another Darin rock'n'roll classic.

Through the years, writing credit for "Queen Of The Hop" has often gone to Woody Harris. But in 1987, when Warner Special Products released *The Ultimate Bobby Darin* CD, songwriting credit for the track was given to "Darin-Harris."

A search of copyright records at the Library of Congress showed that "Queen Of The Hop" was copyrighted three times. Twice, in August and September 1958, the copyright credits Darin and Harris. A November 1958 copyright cites only Harris. However, in his introduction to the song in live appearances in early 1959, Darin said, "I had the pleasure of penning this song."

Given the above information, and the nature of the song, it is highly likely that Darin did indeed co-wrote "Queen Of The Hop," despite the fact that Harris' name continues to show up alone in many places. As with "Splish Splash," the song's lyric is replete with clever rock'n'roll catch phrases ("Bandstand" and "Sweet Little Sixteen" were added to Peggy Sue and Miss Molly), a distinct element of Darin's early writing style.

The Darin-Kirshner writing team was back with the single's flip side, "Lost Love," which found Darin, for the first time, singing in the restrained manner which he would later use to great effect on his folk recordings. The track sounds eerily similar to the classic hits Roy Orbison would record a few years later, proving that Darin and Kirshner were ahead of their time.

On December 5, 1958, Darin entered the Atlantic studio for the last session of the year in which he'd cut rock'n'roll material. Though he had racked up two major and one minor hit to this point – each co-written by Darin – for this session he was supplied two songs written by Doc Pomus and Mort Shuman, the team responsible for R&B classics such as Ray Charles' "Lonely Avenue," Big Joe Turner's "Boogie Woogie Country Girl" and The Coasters' "Young Blood."

Despite its pedigree, the material was not up to the quality standards Darin's initial hits had set. The first song recorded, "I Ain't Sharin' Sharon," was a pleasant but unremarkable semi-novelty rock'n'roll number. The second song, "Plain Jane," was based on the 1800s popular song "Buffalo Gals."

Darin had trouble with the song in the studio, needing 14 takes to achieve a satisfactory version. Along the way, he

27

tinkered with the song's lyrics, length, and arrangement. The released version, which was sped up, is rather slight, but Darin's work in the studio improved it from its initial origins. Released as a single in January 1959, it only climbed to #38 on the *Billboard* charts.

Darin also cut some other fine rock'n'roll records in 1958, including two more Woody Harris songs ("I Want You With Me" and "Pity Miss Kitty"), and "All The Way Home," written by early rock songwriting great Otis Blackwell ("Great Balls Of Fire," "Don't Be Cruel," "All Shook Up") and future Shirelles svengali Luther Dixon. Another impressive track was Neil Sedaka and Howard Greenfield's "Keep A Walkin'," which rocked far harder than the duo's songs that were recorded by Sedaka himself. If either it or "All The Way Home" had been released as singles, they almost certainly would have become hits. However, Atco did not release these tracks for almost two years.

This suited Darin just fine, because after three rock'n'roll hits, he was already getting antsy. Just two weeks after the "Plain Jane" sessions, he went back into the studio to cut decidedly non-rock material with a big band, tracks that Atco would hold for about four months.

In press interviews at the time, Darin stressed that he did not want to be confined to the rock'n'roll genre, and wanted to reach an adult audience.

"I sing rock'n'roll because it sells records," he told *Billboard* in September 1958. "The young kids like it and want it and I can do it. But I try to be versatile. It's the only way to build a future in this business. In the night clubs, I lean to other things, ballads done fairly straight, special bits, etc. I even do 'Mack The Knife' from *Threepenny Opera*."

In fact, Darin seemed downright perturbed that he was derisively labeled a rock'n'roller on the basis of "Splish Splash." "I have a rock'n'roll hit," he said. "That makes me one of a thousand other guys. Now I've got to prove I can sing."

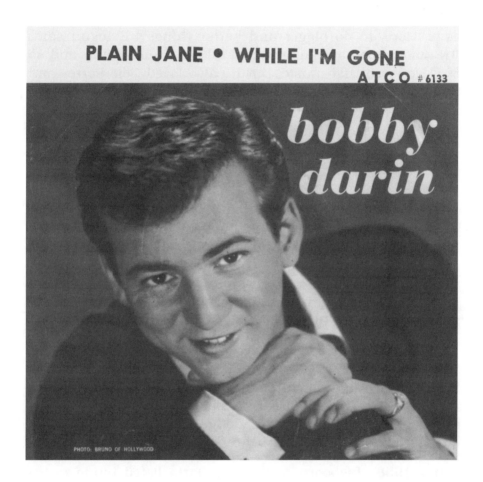

Ahmet Ertegun was not surprised that his label's first successful white rock'n'roll artist intended to move toward a more adult style. In fact, Ertegun believed Darin could successfully make the transition.

"I thought he was a terrific rock'n'roll artist, but he had aspirations to do bigger and better things," Ertegun said. "He understood and appreciated all the Chuck Berry and so on. He loved that music, but he also loved Cole Porter and Sinatra, He liked the glamour of Las Vegas, The Copacabana, and all of that. He wanted to do it all."

Over the years, many music industry observers have contended that Bobby Darin didn't really like rock'n'roll music, and that he simply "used" the music as a springboard to traditional show business stardom. Such contentions were justified by the often-contradictory statements Darin made about rock'n'roll during the first years of his career.

On the pro-rock side, Darin never failed to praise Ray Charles. "I put Ray Charles on a pedestal," he said. "Ray Charles is the greatest thing since Beethoven." While Charles always made his list, the 1958 Darin would speak enthusiastically about other rock'n'roll stars, while the 1960 Darin would lean toward pop standard bearers.

In a 1958 *Billboard* interview, Darin listed his favorites as Fats Domino ("a great artist, with the sound of the Delta"), Little Richard ("a wonderful church-type blues artist"), and Elvis Presley ("I'm crazy about Presley's understanding of what he does").

Speaking with *Down Beat* magazine in 1960, Darin changed his tune: "Rock'n'roll? I love *some* of it," he said. "There are only three singers who move me emotionally: Peggy

Lee, Frank Sinatra and Ray Charles. These three people are my Rock of Gibraltar." He also discussed his admiration of Bing Crosby and Sammy Davis, Jr.

Darin's comment on Pat Boone in the *Down Beat* article was telling: "Boone was using rock'n'roll as a device – which is all well and good; it's exactly what I did."

In examining the question of whether Darin liked rock'n'roll, two things should be remembered. Darin seemed to change his mind as often as he changed his style, which was quite often. And Darin had a habit of telling interviewers what they wanted to hear, especially when it came to how he wanted to present himself to a particular audience.

His best rock'n'roll records speak for themselves; suffice to say that he made some great rock'n'roll records and performed credible live rock'n'roll intermittently throughout his career. His public leaning toward the Vegas style may have been more of a commercial career decision than a reflection of his personal taste.

"Nobody likes the good authentic early rhythm and blues any better than I do, but it's not right for me," Darin told the British music publication *Melody Maker* in early 1960.

In fact, Darin's personal taste in music was, as might be expected of anyone who experimented as much as he did, quite eclectic. But an appreciation of rock'n'roll was always there.

"He liked rock'n'roll music," asserted record producer Nik Venet, who would work extensively with Darin in the 1960s. "I traveled cross-country in a train with him, and we sure didn't play Sinatra. We played R&B stuff like The Five Keys, what they used to call race records. He could sing anything that the Keys did. He knew more about rock'n'roll than most people in rock'n'roll."

Despite his imminent move away from rock, Darin hit the rock'n'roll caravan tour circuit in late 1958. In October, he joined a tour that included Buddy Holly & The Crickets, Frankie Avalon, The Coasters, and Clyde McPhatter.

He fit in well with the artists he toured with. One tour included Duane Eddy & The Rebels, the hit instrumental group. During the tour, the band would occasionally back Darin on stage.

"He was a dynamite guy," said Rebels saxophonist Steve Douglas, who would later work with Darin in the 1960s. "All those things they say about him being cocky were certainly true."

On a tour with Dion & The Belmonts, Jimmy Clanton and Jo Ann Campbell, Darin became close friends with Dion DiMucci, the legendary rock'n'roller. "Even then, you could tell he had more on his wish list than just being a teen idol," DiMucci wrote about Darin in his autobiography *The Wanderer.* "He was a great person to be around – positive, fun and extremely ambitious."

Entertainment critics who usually scorned or ignored rock'n'roll hitmakers began to take notice of Darin's versatility. A *Variety* review of Darin's December 1958 performance at Brooklyn's Town & Country called him "a promising performer" and a "singer of considerable savvy."

"Darin is a subscriber to no particular school," the review continued. "Although he works in an idiom closely resembling rock'n'roll, he can steer his catalog into a ballad or he can do a rhythm number in a manner that seems to be a lot of fun."

One of the few people not impressed with Darin in 1958 was Uncle Sam. Amidst all the excitement of Bobby Darin's career taking off, Walden Robert Cassotto forgot to report for his induction for military service with the Selective Service Board in New York.

It took an investigation by the FBI to finally track down the missing Walden Robert Cassotto. He told them he had not intentionally sought to avoid military service and that he failed to show up for induction because he had never received his induction notice.

The United States Attorney decided not to prosecute Darin if he would agree to immediate induction. Darin agreed, knowing he would never pass the physical. Indeed, Darin was rejected for induction due to his rheumatic heart condition.

"The Right Time"

1959

In January 1959, Darin played Australia as part of a rock'n'roll package tour. His four-song set consisted of "Splish Splash," "Queen Of The Hop," "Early In The Morning" (which had become a big hit in Australia), and "Plain Jane."

Audio recordings from the tour show Darin's performances to be very enthusiastic and rocking. He is very much at ease with the audience and very professional, but not Vegas slick.

In March, Darin was back in the studio in New York to cut one of the best records of his career. Of all the songs Darin ever wrote, "Dream Lover" is the one that has stood the test of time and become a true pop standard. It has been recorded by Rick Nelson, Glen Campbell, Dion, Tony Orlando, Johnny Nash, Don McLean, and The Paris Sisters, among others.

Darin explained the songwriting process behind his most often-covered and commercial songwriting effort: "I had just discovered the C-Am-F-G7 progression on the piano," he said. "I stretched them out and I liked the space I felt in there, and the words just flowed."

In February 1959, while making a tour stop in Seattle, Darin recorded a two-channel stereo demo of "Dream Lover" at the J.F. Boles Studio. Dick Behrke and Darin signed the studio log ("The pleasure was all mine. Hope we can do it again – Bobby Darin.") This minimalistic demo, featuring only Darin's vocal and an electric guitar, serves the song very well. (This tape languished in the Atlantic vaults until 1995 when it was discovered during the pre-production of the *As Long As I'm Singing* box set.)

In the Atlantic recording studio, "Dream Lover" was given a big production – strings, heavy percussion, male and female background vocalists, and piano (supplied by Neil Sedaka). The single reached #2 in July and was an incredibly important transitional record for Darin. It still had something of a rock'n'roll feel, and it was still the teenage audience which made it a hit. But it also gave Darin the opportunity to croon, to show off the more traditional singing style he was using in his nightclub act.

Increasingly, adults started to take notice of Bobby Darin. When he performed "Dream Lover" on "The Ed Sullivan Show" in May 1959, the audience saw a suave entertainer snapping his fingers, twirling, and shrugging his shoulders with the beat of the song. He came across with the confidence and polish of a showman twice his age.

The "Dream Lover" single was aided by a tremendous flip side. Although it did not become a hit, "Bullmoose" (another Darin original) is arguably the finest pure rock'n'roll record Darin ever made. It features a loud, Holly-like electric guitar, absolutely wild piano playing, and exuberant vocals from Darin and the background singers. "Bullmoose" could actually qualify as a great lost '50s rock'n'roll gem, and those who doubt Darin's credentials as a rock'n'roller should give this side a listen.

But Darin still had his sights on nightclubs and traditional show business stardom. His biggest break came in

May 1959, when George Burns invited Darin to be his opening act at Harrah's in Lake Tahoe.

Darin sang "Splish Splash" and two songs from his newly-issued Atco album of standard pop material, *That's All* – "Mack The Knife" and "Some Of These Days." Together, he and Burns did a vaudeville-style soft-shoe routine on the song "I Ain't Got Nobody."

Sharing the stage with Burns gave Darin the chance to exchange shtick with a veteran show business professional. "The old-timers in show business have given me some good tips," Darin would quip to Burns on stage. "Elvis helped me out a lot."

Personally, Darin grew very close to Burns. "I love the man," Darin told an interviewer. "My father died before I was born. If I had to pick a father, it would be George Burns. I'd work with him anytime he wants me."

When Burns' show moved to Las Vegas, Darin went along. "George Burns taught me more in six weeks in Las Vegas than twenty others could have done in ten years," Darin said. In addition to dispensing show business advice, Burns also looked out for Darin in other ways.

One night, after Darin lost $1,600 gambling, Burns was so angry that he refused to shake Darin's hand on stage. After Darin begged for the customary handshake, Burns told the audience the story and made Darin promise from the stage that he's never gamble again.

Jazz pianist and arranger Bobby Scott, who was about to start working with Darin, saw the Burns-Darin show in Vegas, and was knocked out by Darin's opening set.

"By the time Burns came on stage, that audience was so warm and so delighted with what Bobby had done that they were in George's hands," Scott recalled. "Bobby knew he was the opening act, and he prepared the audience for

George. He took them to the limit; they were really primed. That's no mean accomplishment."

Darin impressed the show business establishment on his first foray into the big-time showrooms. Don Hearn of *The Washington Daily News* wrote, "He has the amazing quality of being able to handle any kind of tune with remarkable success, presenting each with a fresh approach that displays his versatility. A star has been born."

Many celebrities, including Burns, were on hand for Darin's opening as headliner at The Cloister in Hollywood in August. "His presentations have a surety that belies the performer's youth," wrote *Variety.*

Even the jazz publication *Down Beat* was laudatory: "Self-assured, almost cocky in manner, young Bobby Darin cradled a sophisticated house in the palm of his hand...and made his bid as leading contender to the title Young Sinatra. Clearly, Bobby Darin has emerged from the juvenile rock and roll league and is now preparing to carve himself a hefty slice of adult big time."

In October, Darin became the youngest performer to ever headline at The Sands in Las Vegas. *Variety* called him "one of the most versatile, polished young performers around today."

Darin brought a trusted friend on the road with him. His old high school bandmate and West 71st Street roommate Dick Behrke acted as his pianist and conductor, a role Behrke would retain in Darin's stage shows for years.

Darin was now performing nearly the entire *That's All* album in his act, and his acceptance on stage was enhanced by the fact that the album was starting to take off on radio and in record stores. With brilliant, exciting arrangements by Richard Wess, the album featured full string and horn sections and a clever selection of songs. (Among the members of the big band assembled for the sessions was future

George Burns (left) with Darin
(Las Vegas News Bureau)

"Tonight Show" bandleader Doc Severinsen.) The pairing of Darin's go-for-broke singing and Wess' arrangements was inspired.

"Dick (Wess) seemed to be so perfectly suited to Bobby because they were both very blunt and basic," said Dick Behrke. "Bobby was that kind of singer, a very hard, rhythmic singer. There wasn't really the sophistication that a Sinatra or a Bennett had, but there was much more drive. Dick was always keyed into that."

Darin's snappy, frantic-tempo reading of the title song, recorded by many other vocalists (including Nat King Cole) as a ballad, was a classic. On this, as well as other superb tracks such as "I'll Remember April" and "Softly As In A Morning Sunrise," Darin showed an absolute mastery of the "swingin'" style associated with Frank Sinatra.

Another highlight was Darin's lone songwriting contribution to the album, "That's The Way Love Is." The melody was a bit too close to Sinatra's (Cahn and Van Heusen-penned) "Love Is The Tender Trap" for comfort, but who would have expected – in the middle of *That's All*'s collection of established standards – that young rock'n'roll star Bobby Darin could write a song which fit in so well with its surroundings?

Throughout *That's All,* with a big band swinging behind him, Darin was given the opportunity to project his youthful personality onto older popular standards. Brash, loud, hip, alive – all could be used to describe *That's All.* Darin was giving pre-rock music a shot in the arm. Sure, he had made great rock'n'roll records. But *That's All* was a great *Bobby Darin* record – there was no separating the success of the songs from the style of the delivery.

The acceptance was so encompassing that in the summer of 1959, only six months after "Queen Of The Hop," Darin was invited to sing at the Hollywood Jazz Festival. But even as Darin was wowing them there and in Vegas, Atco had yet to release a single from *That's All.*

The hesitation was understandable, as the next single would follow-up "Dream Lover" and *That's All* had no track with such obvious youth appeal. But the choice was made by radio, which did not sit back and wait for a single, but jumped on the album's lead track, "Mack The Knife."

"Moritat" or "Mack The Knife" was written by Kurt Weill and Bertolt Brecht for *Threepenny Opera*, then enjoying a successful off-Broadway revival. The English lyric was written by Marc Blitzstein. The song had already been a hit for numerous others, as five different instrumental versions (including records by Lawrence Welk, and Les Paul & Mary Ford) charted in 1956. But the version which most influenced Darin was a '56 vocal hit by Louis Armstrong.

Atco released Darin's "Mack The Knife" as a single in August. Although it was a radical departure from the rock'n'roll style which had garnered Darin five Top 40 hits (three in the Top 10) over the previous year, Ahmet Ertegun knew there was something special about the track.

"I knew it could not miss," Ertegun said. "Once in a while you hear something and say, 'That's it. The magic is there!' Bobby worked out the arrangement with Dick Wess and it was fabulous. We put together a great band. It was just one of those forever records."

The single entered the *Billboard* charts on August 24, 1959. Six weeks later, it was the number one single in the country. It stayed there for nine weeks, making it the third biggest hit to that point in the rock era, which began in 1955. Only Presley's double-sided "Hound Dog/Don't Be Cruel" and Guy Mitchell's "Singing The Blues" stayed at number one for more weeks. Even after 32 years of rock (the span of 1955-1987), "Mack The Knife" was the sixth biggest hit of the era, according to Joel Whitburn's *Top 1000 Singles*.

"Mack The Knife" became Bobby Darin's signature song. Instantly, he was accepted by adults. But the record also received heavy airplay on the same youth-oriented stations that played "Dream Lover" and "Splish Splash." Teenagers knew it wasn't rock'n'roll, but they could sense – and relate to – the hip attitude inherent in Darin's performance. "Mack" was almost the very definition of an "across the board" smash. The single sold two million copies.

Darin's performance on "Mack The Knife" is one of the most famous vocals of all time – instantly recognizable, eternally dramatic, simply immortal. Outswinging all competition, Darin used every measure of Richard Wess' arrangement to his advantage. His "eek," "Ho! Ho!" and other stylistic improvisations with the song are now as embedded in the popular culture as the lyrics themselves.

In fact, the vocal was such a *tour de force* that few of the millions who bought the record ever stopped to think about what the song was about. In Darin's hands, the song's lyrics were strictly a vehicle, something he could stylize.

The lyric Darin sang, which was similar to the one in Louis Armstrong's version, was much lighter than a literal translation of the original German lyric in the *Threepenny Opera*. MacHeath, "Mack The Knife," is a murderer, not the swingin' character depicted by Darin. In fact, many *Threepenny Opera* and Brecht-Weill purists ridicule Darin's "Mack The Knife" because it is a complete bastardization of the song's original *mise en scene.*

So, in essence, Darin created a new "Mack," one that would be forever his. In a nice touch, one of the names Darin drops in the lyric is Lotte Lenya, Kurt Weill's widow, who was then starring as Jenny in the revival of *Threepenny*. Unbeknownst to Darin, Lenya has suggested to Ahmet Ertegun that some Atlantic artists should record her late husband's songs.

"I told her we were not a general record label, that we just did R&B and rock'n'roll," Ertegun said. "But I said I'd think about it. I didn't have the opportunity to mention it to Bobby. So when he came up with 'Mack The Knife,' I said, 'I can't believe it – three days ago I had lunch with Lotte Lenya and I was going to suggest it to you.'"

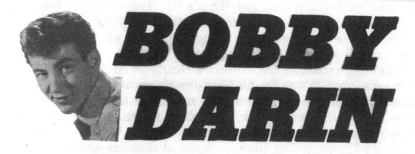

As "Mack" made him a true star, Darin was candid about jumping off the rock'n'roll bandwagon. "I had to go beyond rock'n'roll," he said. "'Mack' introduced me into the adult world."

"My record, which is completely away from rock'n'roll, came at a time when tastes were shifting," he told *Melody Maker* in 1960. "It was perfectly timed and turned out to be the luckiest thing I ever did. It's the sort of thing I intend to concentrate on, because adults like it as well as the kids."

The same week "Mack The Knife" hit number one, *That's All* finally cracked *Billboard's* album chart. It would eventually climb to #7 and remain on the best-seller chart for 52 weeks.

Big-time television also came calling. In September, Darin showed up on the special "An Evening With Jimmy Durante," performing "Mack" and "That's All," as well as two duets with Durante. Two months later, he reprised his nightclub shtick with George Burns in "George Burns In The Big Time." Big time, indeed: Burns' other guests were legends Jack Benny, Eddie Cantor and George Jessel.

Darin even had a chance to return to the dramatic acting he had given up years earlier. In October, he appeared on the CBS series "Hennesey," portraying a young entertainer unhappily serving a stint in the Navy.

But the high point of the year would come on November 29. The music industry's second annual Grammy Awards ceremony was held at the Beverly Hilton Hotel in Los Angeles. Darin and "Mack The Knife" were up for four awards.

Richard Wess' arrangement of "Mack" was nominated for Best Arrangement, an award which went to Billy May for Frank Sinatra's "Come Dance With Me." The same two records also paired off in the Best Vocal Performance, Male category, with Sinatra taking the award.

For the first time, a Best New Artist award was given. Darin's competition was Edd Byrnes, Mark Murphy, Johnny Restivo and Mavis Rivers. In (speaking in retrospect) one of the few times the Academy would get this award right, Darin was the winner.

The nominations for Record Of The Year were "Mack The Knife," Sinatra's "High Hopes," Elvis Presley's "A Fool Such As I," Andre Previn's "Like Young" and The Browns' "The Three Bells." The winner was "Mack The Knife."

Darin had not only performed "Mack" on the show (tele-cast by NBC), but also received two Grammys – heady "establishment" recognition for a singer who was dismissively labeled a "rock'n'roller" nine months earlier.

It was the ultimate night of triumph for Bobby Darin. But the next day, the press would be awash with news not of what Darin did, but what he said.

""Two Of A Kind"
Darin vs. Sinatra

"I hope to surpass Frank in everything he's done."

Frank, of course, was Sinatra. And the above quote, reportedly uttered by Bobby Darin on Grammy night, would follow – and help define – Darin until his death.

The Darin-Sinatra comparison was an easy item for the press to pick up on in the wake of Darin's singing (and swinging) style on *That's All.* And the fact that the two singers and their records shared Grammy nominations made comparisons almost inevitable after Darin took two awards.

So after *UPI*'s Vernon Scott asked Darin about challenging Sinatra, Darin's "hope to surpass" quote was picked up off the wire by hundreds of newspapers in the following days. It caused a stir and painted Darin as a brash, cocky kid whose accomplishments had yet to match his bravado.

Such a portrayal wasn't entirely inaccurate. But Darin spent the next year denying and clarifying the remark, especially in an effort to offer an olive branch to Sinatra, who reportedly did not appreciate the upstart's boldness.

Darin claimed he was misquoted. He told *The New York Post* that he actually said, "There's no question of beating

Sinatra. Please don't use the comparison. I want to do everything that anybody's ever done, but better."

Vernon Scott stuck by his story: "I don't blame him for denying it," Scott told the *Post*. "It wasn't the brightest thing in the world to say. But he didn't say it spitefully. He just said it exuberantly, flush from the victory of his awards."

There *was* good reason to compare Darin and Sinatra, and the comparisons would have come up even if Darin had been silent on Grammy night. But to counter the perceived brashness of his comment, Darin would spend almost every interview of the next two years talking respectfully about Sinatra.

"It's an insult to Frank to compare him with a 24-year-old punk like me," he told *The New York Post*. "I don't want to be a second Frank Sinatra. I want to be a first Bobby Darin."

Even as late as 1962, Darin still occasionally found himself having to fend off charges of riding Sinatra's coattails. "I'll admit Frank's vocal style influenced me – but so did Bing Crosby, Louis Armstrong, Eddie Fisher and a lot more," he told *Melody Maker*. "In the future, somebody might be as great as Frank Sinatra. But never greater than him."

Of course, these treatises on Sinatra only helped Darin. As *New York Post* writers Alfred G. Aronowitz and Jack D. Fox put it, "The aura of controversy which has followed Sinatra throughout his career now hovers over Darin like a halo." Darin himself acknowledged that, publicity-wise, the quote "did an awful lot of good."

But Darin eventually tired of the matter. In a 1962 interview with *Newsweek*, he said, "The biggest single fallacy that has been built up (about me) is that I think the sun rises and sets on Frank Sinatra."

Indeed, the furor over Darin's statement overshadowed the important issue – the ways in which Darin the entertainer was influenced by the master.

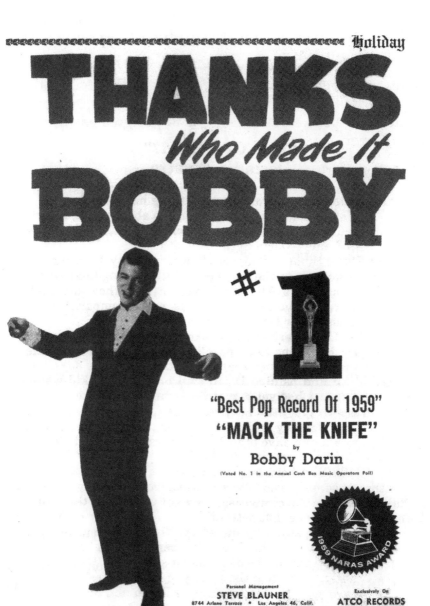

"It is Sinatra as a person more than Sinatra as a singer that has influenced me," Darin told *Down Beat*. "His outlook on the business and his attitude to performance are the important things.

"My approach to singing is not the same," he continued. "Sinatra has a clipped speech. I'm a slurrer. But let's face it, he's the boss. Frank Sinatra is the greatest living lyric interpreter."

But some critics were starting to suggest what Darin himself would have gotten slammed for saying – that comparisons to Sinatra were absolutely valid.

"Darin today is unquestionably the only young pop singer who handles standards with something approaching the polished intensity of Sinatra," wrote *Down Beat's* Gene Lees in May 1960. "To those who would offer the rejoinder that Darin does not have Sinatra's vocal finesse and musicianship, it would be adequate to point out that Sinatra is 42 while Darin is 23."

The New York Post's Aronowitz and Fox wrote, "Like Sinatra, Darin generates an in-personality which lights up a nightclub floor beyond the wattage of other show business dynamos. Like Sinatra, Darin makes every performance a command performance and it is Darin who is always in command."

Sammy Davis, Jr., who authored a laudatory telegram about Darin which was reprinted on the back cover of *That's All,* commented on Darin-Sinatra similarities in a 1960 interview.

"I think what people really compare is their attitudes on stage," Davis said. "Certainly Bobby's style is more physical than Frank's ever was."

An interesting perspective on the comparison of the two singers came from musician and arranger Bobby Scott, who worked with many of the giants of jazz, as well as more contemporary vocalists such as Darin, Aretha Franklin and Marvin Gaye.

"Bobby belonged, as a performer, in the age that produced a Sophie Tucker, an Al Jolson," Scott observed. "He was in the great performing tradition, and I kind of think of him as the last hurrah of the preceding Golden Age of Performing.

"I don't put Sinatra in that category," Scott continued. "Sinatra is a product of the record industry. Had Sinatra been born earlier and tried to perform during the vaudeville era, we'd have never heard of him. I don't think Bobby was a product of the record industry. If Bobby had never made a record, but had secured some kind of employment where he could perform, he would have become a star in any case.

"I think Sinatra needed a band. I don't think Bobby ever needed a band. I think Sinatra had to learn things that were inherent in a guy like Bob."

Despite Darin's reverential comments about Sinatra subsequent to the Grammy night quote, Sinatra never publicly complimented Darin. This led to lingering speculation that there was an official (and lifelong) "feud" between the two singers. Credence was given to this theory by a report that Sinatra and Dean Martin were seen tossing darts at a picture of Darin after the Grammy comment.

In reality, however, it appears unlikely that there was ever serious animosity for Darin on Sinatra's part. Though Darin and Sinatra were never seen publicly together, Darin was openly accepted in the Sinatra circle in a way that would have been impossible if Sinatra harbored any true resentment.

Throughout his life, Darin was close to Sinatra's daughter, Nancy. He was also close friends with other members of the so-called "Rat Pack" – including Dean Martin and Sammy Davis, Jr.

Record producer Nik Venet, who worked with Darin in the 1960s, was also friends with Nancy Sinatra, and worked with her first husband, singer Tommy Sands. Venet dismissed any notion of a Sinatra-Darin feud.

"That was all bullshit made up in the papers," Venet said. "Sinatra never snubbed Darin. I think he respected him. I think the 'feud' was something made up in the trades. Those two names rang a bell, they got a response, and the press just ran with it."

Still, it would not be until 1984 (11 years after Darin's death) that Sinatra made what appeared to be his first complimentary gesture toward Darin – a recording of "Mack The Knife" in which he respectfully alluded to Darin's earlier version.

Some reports to the contrary, Darin was not crushed by any thought of a Sinatra "rejection" of him. In fact, he went so far as to express admiration for one particular Sinatra swipe at him.

When, shortly after the controversy began, Sinatra was asked what he thought of Bobby Darin, he replied, "I sing in saloons. Bobby Darin does my prom dates."

Calling that "one of the greatest lines of all time," Darin told *Down Beat* "All I can say is that I'm only too happy to play his prom dates...until graduation."

"Actions Speak Louder Than Words" 7
The Personality

"It is impossible not to like the guy."

—Gene Lees, *Down Beat*, 1960

"In person, Bobby Darin is fully as offensive as he is in public."

—Richard Gehman, *TV Guide*, 1961

The Frank Sinatra comment was not the first time Bobby Darin's personality and attitude attracted as much attention as his skills as a singer and entertainer. Even the liner notes to *That's All,* released before Darin had broken into big time show business circles, referred to his reputation as an "Angry Young Man."

By the time Darin reached star status with "Mack The Knife," the press was ready to shine the white hot spotlight on Darin's personality. It made great copy.

In the wake of "Mack," Darin's Grammy success, and his appearances on a number of TV variety shows, Darin was profiled with major articles in *TV Guide, Life,* and *Down Beat* magazines. When he played The Copacabana in September

1960, Darin was the talk of New York: both *The New York Post* and *The New York Journal-American* ran multi-part, in-depth, hometown-boy-made-good profiles.

The articles would inevitably focus on Darin's brashness, cockiness or ill manners. And that appeared to be precisely the way Darin wanted it. He knew what it took to make a good story – to separate himself from the hundreds of other entertainers who were written about constantly – and he played the role to the hilt.

"I like people who don't know me to dislike me," Darin told the *Journal-American's* Anita Ehrman, who described Darin's life as "a series of temper tantrums punctuated by laughter."

"It gives me a great pleasure to get bum-rapped," Darin said. "I thrive on it."

"When you write about me, make it tough," he told the *Post*. "Ruin me."

But most writers, while relating every detail on how Darin rubbed people the wrong way, couldn't help but admire their quotable, candid subject. "The white heat of his temper has become part of the glow of his charm," wrote *Post* reporters Aronowitz and Fox.

Darin's life story read like a legend in the hands of the New York press. The poverty and sickliness of his youth were submitted as sympathetic counterbalances to the excesses of his star personality.

But the Darin persona was built far more on ambition than arrogance. The defining statement of Darin's career, one that would literally follow him to death (it was part of most obituaries) came from Shana Alexander's *Life* profile of January 11, 1960.

There, Darin bluntly expressed his goal – "To establish myself as a legend by the time I'm 25." An instant headline.

Darin at The Sands
(Las Vegas News Bureau)

"I want to make it faster than anyone has ever made it before," he said. "I'd like to be the biggest thing in show business by the time I'm 25 years old."

Rather than being taken at face value – as the honest ambition of a talented young performer who was newly-rich, in great demand, and being acknowledged as a potential giant by his peers – the comment was perceived as a prediction. Darin might as well have said "I *will* be a legend by the time I'm 25."

So the statement was viewed as another example of Darin's gall. It fit in nicely with other stories making the rounds, such as Darin ordering noisy nightclub patrons to behave during his act. Or refusing to go on stage until a certain record industry executive who had snubbed him in his pre-fame days was removed from the club.

Not all of the negative appraisal of Darin's personality could be chalked up to misconception, or a carefully-orchestrated publicity front on Darin's part. He did often court trouble.

Before Darin left Hollywood to go to New York and open at the Copa, Nancy Sinatra and Tommy Sands planned an elaborate send-off and good luck party for him. Angered over a minor oversight (a friend of his was left off the guest list), Darin skipped the party.

Darin's reputation was well-known in the show-business community. "I've never seen someone so disliked," Paul Anka told the *Post* in 1960.

In a brutal January 1961 *TV Guide* profile ("The Astoundingly Brash Character of Darin"), Richard Gehman made his intense personal dislike of Darin explicit – "He does not merely talk rudeness, he lives it." Yet, even Gehman could not pronounce Darin completely unappealing.

"There is more than a suspicion in my mind that the extreme cockiness is merely a device for attracting attention," Gehman wrote. "All I can report is that for all his

faults and offenses...Bobby Darin still is somehow an appealing, interesting fellow...There is a single-minded honesty about him and a candor that is all too rare in the strange show-biz world he inhabits."

Darin did not often publicly discuss his concern about his health – surely the most justifiable explanation of his impatience and lack of regard for the usual show business niceties. But occasionally he would drop a telling tidbit to the press.

"I have the feeling I'm going to die young," he told *The Los Angeles Times* in 1959. "So I've got to do what I'm going to do now."

"He didn't expect to make it through his twenties," rock'n'roll tour companion Dion recalled in a BBC Radio 2 interview. "He said, 'Boys, I got a lot to do in a short period of time, and I'm going to accomplish it.'"

"The whole key to Bobby's personality was his illness," said Darin's friend Harriet Wasser, who first met him in 1957 and did some publicity work for him early in his career. "If it wasn't for his illness, he probably never would have done what he did. He could be really obnoxious. He did things that I felt were just unnecessary. But by the same token, he had this attitude which was, 'If the only way I can get to be a star is to be Mr. Nice Guy, I don't want it.' It was more important for him to make an impact than to live a long life.

"He wasn't sickly, in the sense that he was home a lot, in the hospital, etc.," she said. "But he couldn't take the subway because he couldn't walk up all the stairs at the station. There were certain things that he couldn't do, but he didn't let everybody see those things."

Wasser was with Darin in September 1959 when he became very ill after a rehearsal for his appearance on "The Ed Sullivan Show." "He grabbed my arm and I thought he was going to collapse backstage," she recalled. "I mean the guy was ready to die." Darin's friends became accustomed to this.

"Bobby would always get wiped out by a show, he would always recover, and this was life," said Dick Behrke, who was Darin's on-stage bandleader from 1959 through 1963. "It was that way since we were kids. On stage, he seemed to show unbounded energy, and afterward he would just collapse in the dressing room."

Pianist/arranger Bobby Scott recalled Darin telling him "I'm not going to be around here very long." Scott also believed that the specter of death was Darin's principal motivation.

"It colored his existence and his personal life," Scott said. "To those who didn't know about his ailment, there was no chance they'd understand what motivated him. He made a bargain with himself: The world was going to know he'd been here."

Scott met Darin in 1959 and began working closely with him in the studio – as the arranger and pianist for three albums – in 1960. Scott's musical credentials were impressive. He previously worked with jazz greats such as Gene Krupa, Lester Young and Stan Getz, and even scored a pop hit of his own, "Chain Gang," in 1956. (Scott would later compose two pop standards, "A Taste Of Honey" and "He Ain't Heavy, He's My Brother.")

In addition to their close professional ties – Scott would also play piano for many of Darin's live dates in New York City and would later work for Darin's publishing company – these two products of the Bronx struck up a close personal relationship. But Scott remembered that his initial meetings with Darin were tense.

"We had a little bit of trouble at first," Scott recalled. "On the first couple of arrangements I wrote for him, he wanted to change this, and change that. I told him, 'Why don't you learn to write your own goddamn arrangements?'

"He did not suspect that I would be proprietorial about what I wrote," Scott said. "He thought that since he paid for it, he owned it. I said, 'Oh no you don't. You don't fuck up my music because my name goes on it too.'"

Legendary arranger Billy May also found his initial contacts with Darin to be difficult. May, who played with Glenn Miller's orchestra and arranged classic '50s recordings by Frank Sinatra and Nat King Cole, among others, did not appreciate Darin's manner of challenging the orders of older music industry veterans.

"He really was a smart-ass little kid in those days," said May. "He came in and started telling us how to do it. I figured if the record company hired me, they knew that I knew what to do, and I didn't need him to help me.

"I'll tell you what got me off on the wrong foot with Bobby Darin," said May, recalling their first session together. "The first number involved a bright tempo and there was about eight bars of band, and then a drum break. So we started running it down. The drummer played the break, and Darin stopped the band and went over and started to tell the drummer how to play the break. I thought, 'Who the hell is this?'"

May, whose work with Darin included arranging two albums plus music for a TV special, eventually grew more tolerant of Darin as their work together became less strenuous.

"Everything was amicable, you know," he said. "I took his suggestions. A couple of times, we had cross words, but we never really got into any beefs or anything. It's just that he was more difficult to work with than other people. But as he grew older, he became a little more knowledgeable. He turned out to be a pretty good guy. He was friendly and we got along very well."

It didn't take Bobby Scott long to soften his initial impression of Darin. He became a Darin confidante. "I got to know him on a level that other people did not, in that he was never evasive with me," Scott said. "He leveled. He liked my calling a spade a spade. And I enjoyed the way he kicked the usual music business procedures in the butt.

"If I served him at all, I believe it was through being as honest as I could be with him," Scott said. "I may be patting myself on the back, but I think it was refreshing to him, considering all the 'yesses' he was hearing."

For that reason, Scott's remembrances of dealing with Darin professionally and personally offer insights into Darin's character that are often missing from the public record promulgated by the press (and, in some cases, Darin's own publicists).

"I know he had the reputation of being an arrogant bastard, but I don't think so," Scott said. "I think he was like a whole lot of other people: He was a bright enough guy that he did not suffer fools easily.

"I'm a Bronx kid," Scott continued, "and there's a certain kind of belligerency in people that come from the Bronx. Bobby had a hell of a lot of that. Bobby was not the kind of guy that somebody mugged – you might mug him, but you'd get a broken jaw, too. He was enough of a street kid for that."

But Scott also saw another side of Darin, a friendly nature apparent to friends and associates, but rarely relayed in the press.

"I'm not putting a halo on his head; he deserves no halos," Scott said. "But if you run across somebody that really paints him out black, you can best believe they didn't know him.

"He was put down by almost everyone I'd met in the business," Scott said. "But I never met anyone who had a decent idea about who and what he was. The reason I found this contempt odd was that Darin was a remarkably convivial fellow."

Darin was also a loyal friend. When Scott's wife was in the hospital delivering their first child, Scott was broke. When it came time to bring his wife and newborn daughter home, the hospital wouldn't accept his check, essentially holding his family until he could come up with some cash.

"Bobby Darin came to the rescue," Scott recalled. "He offered to give me money with no strings attached. He gave me enough work – arranging and accompanying – over the next couple of weeks to tidy everything up for us financially.

"The first gift my daughter got – delivered to the house by messenger when the baby got home – was from Bobby," Scott said. "He beat the relatives."

Darin's loyalty was also evident to other friends, such as actor Richard (Dick) Bakalyan, who appeared with Darin in the 1962 film *Pressure Point*, and later on Darin's television series.

"Bobby was one of the guys, one of the boys," Bakalyan said. "He'd go to the wall for you if there was trouble.

"I'd heard that he was a cocky guy and this and that," Bakalyan recalled. "He was far from that. He was a gentleman and he treated everyone with great respect and they responded in same."

Studio musician Carol Kaye, who played on numerous Darin recording sessions, also recalled that the Darin personality she experienced was different from the reputation which preceded him.

"People have asked me, 'Wasn't he mean?'", she said. "I never saw that in him at all. He was the opposite – a real sweetheart.

"He was a very nice guy," she said. "Very intense, and very fast. He spoke fast. He did things fast. He knew exactly what he wanted out of life. He knew exactly what he wanted on his records. He was on a mission to get things done right. We all liked that in the studio, because you don't want to be around a wishy-washy guy."

Bobby Scott concurred that what sometimes seemed like impatience on Darin's part was really quality-control.

"He insisted on holding all the aspects of his performing life in his own hands, and in making all the decisions," Scott said. "He was correct in assuming that if you wanted things done right, do them yourself.

"But he was not a malicious person," Scott continued. "Not at all. A lot of people thought he was a smart aleck; he wasn't. I think he threw up a lot of defenses and gave the wrong ideas to people. I think he was, at core, really a very, very good person.

"If I told Bobby I needed something, he got it for me," Scott said. "If I said, 'Six strings ain't gonna work, I want twenty,' twenty would have been there. He was as good as his word in all those departments."

Darin's intense ambition carried over from his career to his personal life. Never forgetting the poverty of his youth, the adult Darin relished the discovery of "finer things" such as great literature, art, and classical music. He delighted in the opportunity his fame provided him to associate with important people.

"He used to come to my house for dinner," recalled Ahmet Ertegun, whose father had been the Turkish ambassador to the U.S. "I'll never forget the first time he came, he saw photographs that were given to my father by Roosevelt, Truman, the president of Turkey, and so on. He said 'My God.' He came from a very poor background, and he loved the big life."

Many of Darin's associates attested that his personality was not changed by fame.

63

In his book *Rock, Roll & Remember*, Dick Clark wrote: "After his success, people asked me, 'When did he turn into such an egotistical son of a bitch?' I'd laugh and say 'He was always that way.'"

"A lot of people think Bobby changed with success," said Atlantic Records' Nesuhi Ertegun. "He was exactly the same character when he was totally unknown with five dollars in his pocket as when he was the biggest star in America."

So despite the intense dislike some members of the press felt for Darin – and described to the public – there would be the occasional writer, such as *Down Beat*'s Gene Lees, who would portray Darin as a disarming young man.

Of course, it is not unusual for press descriptions to fail to completely capture all aspects of a celebrity's personality, especially those qualities most apparent to insiders such as friends or close professional associates.

In looking back at what was written about Darin in the early '60s, hindsight also comes into play. The combination of Darin's youth and brashness understandably rubbed some members of the mainstream entertainment press the wrong way. Ten years later, after the rock explosion and some of the personalities it spawned, Darin's early behavior would seem almost gentlemanly.

There was also the recognition that it was the temperament of an artist. As the years went by, and Darin dispelled any "flash in the pan" notions, it became obvious that his talent transcended that of a mere rock'n'roll hitmaker or Vegas crooner. What was initially perceived, as cockiness became confidence, a badge of artistic honor.

Los Angeles Times writer Estelle Changas summed it up best in a 1972 portrayal of Darin:

"Early in his career, Darin was branded brash, cocky and arrogant, labels which clung tenaciously for years," she wrote. "Though intended as insults, they really served to confirm the disquieting candor Darin refused to relinquish, an individuality which became increasingly visible."

"Beyond The Sea"

1960

"I want to be in the upper echelon of show business to such an extent it's ridiculous," Darin told *Life* magazine in 1960.

As the year dawned, it appeared as if that upper echelon was only a short step away for Darin. Professional acceptance poured forth from his peers and the press.

"Do you realize you're alone in your generation?" Jerry Lewis told Darin. "Sammy, Dean and I are all ten years ahead of you. Unless you destroy yourself, no one else can touch you. You're alone."

Influential music critic Gene Lees of *Down Beat* called Darin "probably the most fascinating singer to watch on this side of the Atlantic...With his combination of excellent movement and intense, driving singing, Darin is one of the most stimulating and vital acts in show business today."

As Lees alluded to, as much focus was placed on Darin's performing style – his on-stage movements – as on his voice. Darin told *Life's* Shana Alexander that he strove to be regarded as "a singer who moves like a dancer. That is my billing, and I intend to sell the hell out of it."

"I'm not just a singer," Darin told *Newsweek*. "I really try to sell my personality. For me, it's got to be a salesmanship job, not just a good voice. Singing isn't enough. Spontaneity and personality are the things."

Darin discussed the selling of another commodity with Gene Lees: "The sex element is the most important in this business," he said. "The fact remains, you must sell sex. It must not be conscious, however. You're either sexy or you're not. I don't know whether I am. I will know, 15 years from now."

From the stage, accompanist Bobby Scott analyzed Darin's performing genius. "Bobby danced through his numbers," Scott said. "An arrangement was very important to him if he could use it – for his feet, a turnaround here, a turn there.

"He viewed arrangements for their extramusical value," Scott said. "No singer I knew made more performing use of brass syncopations and licks than did Bobby Darin. He'd drop the mike and catch it to coincide with a brass burst, or turn himself around when the musical materials did so. He would even stop a song if the band tempo wasn't in accord with his idea of what it ought to be.

"He knew how to read an audience. He knew how to use his hands. He knew how to use his clothes, even to loosen his tie," Scott observed. "He knew things it took other singers 20 or 30 years to gather.

"I've worked with a hell of a lot of singers, and I don't think any of them had Bobby's essential performing ability," Scott concluded. "I mean, he could come on hoarse and carry off the show. He'd have been dynamite in vaudeville. He was one of the greatest performers I ever saw on the stage."

Darin continued to be a ubiquitous presence in the media. In December 1959, he was the subject of TV's "This Is Your Life." Murray The K, George Burns and Sammy Davis, Jr. joined Charlie and Nina Maffia, Don Kirshner, Dick Behrke and other old friends for the tribute. In January 1960,

Darin was reunited with old flame Connie Francis on "The Ed Sullivan Show." The pair sang charming duet versions of Cole Porter's "You're The Top" and Sinatra's "You Make Me Feel So Young."

Ed Sullivan had become an ardent Darin champion, introducing him at various times as "the best rhythm singer in the country" and "the best beat singer since Sinatra."

Like most rock'n'roll hitmakers, Darin couldn't avoid having his name brought up in the payola scandal. On December 4, 1959, Darin, along with Les Paul and Mary Ford, was questioned by the New York district attorney about payola and his radio appearances on Alan Freed's show. He denied paying Freed. (Apparently, Darin's relationship with Murray Kaufman never came under question.)

Darin saw the payola scandal for the political charade it was. "What is it going to do?" he said in an interview at the time, "win a few new senatorial seats?"

With an artistically and financially successful year behind him – his 1959 gross income was reported to have been $250,000 – Darin began the new decade on the right foot.

His first single of 1960 – his follow-up to "Mack The Knife," – was "Beyond The Sea," another *That's All* track. Darin's vocal moved him even closer to Sinatra territory (this one was a little harder for the rock'n'roll crowd to get into) and Richard Wess' arrangement brilliantly alternated between the gentle and the blaring.

"Beyond The Sea" proved that "Mack The Knife" was no accident: Darin was a bona fide stylist. As with "Mack," the song wasn't new and it wasn't his. But Darin turned it into his second straight standard, another definitive reading. The record reached #6 in February.

In May 1959, long before *That's All* had taken off, Darin and Wess went into the studio to record a follow-up in the same style. The result, *This Is Darin*, was released in

Darin with Dick Clark

Darin with Connie Francis and Ed Sullivan

February 1960. While the album lacked any bursts of glory as bright as "Mack" or "Beyond The Sea," it was a very successful effort.

In many ways, the album, highlighted by standards such as "Caravan," "The Gal That Got Away," and "I Can't Give You Anything But Love," opened more eyes to Darin than its predecessor, which cynics had been inclined to regard as a fluke. Now that Darin was starting to be mentioned in the same breath as Sinatra, it seemed as if a gauntlet had been thrown down, challenging Darin to keep up the quality. *This Is Darin* satisfied the doubters.

Down Beat exclaimed, "Darin can sing and he can swing. He may even be the heir apparent to Sinatra's mantle...If Darin can become the big thing among our teenagers, perhaps all is not lost."

New York Times reviewer John S. Wilson was even more effusive in praising the album. Calling *This Is Darin* "the most striking instance of the renaissance of showmanship" on pop records, Wilson wrote, "Any doubts that Mr. Darin can stand up on his own are dissipated...[his] musical personality comes across in electrifying fashion...This is a disk that belongs with the best work of such masters of the genre as Bing Crosby and Frank Sinatra."

This Is Darin peaked a notch higher than *That's All,* reaching #6. The album's single, Darin and Woody Harris' reworking of the chestnut "Clementine," hit #21. The track was again designed to subjugate the song in order to showcase Darin's show-stopping style. While it succeeded at that, it was a little too forced to match the appeal of "Mack The Knife" or "Beyond The Sea."

"'Clementine' was meant to be another 'Mack The Knife,'" said Dick Behrke, who played piano on the album. "That was the full intent of it. You can't go home again like that, but still, in the nightclubs, it was always a rouser."

A strange Darin single appeared shortly thereafter. "Moment Of Love" and "She's Tanfastic" were two Darin-penned rock'n'roll songs recorded in February 1960. It appeared to be an effort to reach out to the young audience left behind by the past two LPs, but to avoid confusion with an "official" single release, Atco labeled it as a "special premium record" with the cryptic credit "Produced by Ferron, Inc."

In March, Darin traveled to Britain to headline a concert tour with rockers Clyde McPhatter and Duane Eddy. During his opening night show in Lewisham, Darin was surprised to be greeted with boos when he began "My Funny Valentine." A small, but vocal percentage of the audience (Teddy Boys who, according to most accounts had been pumped up by Duane Eddy's music) had come expecting 100% rock'n'roll. Though Darin brushed off his hecklers with "I thought you people lived on the other side of town," the boos dogged Darin throughout the tour.

It became a major controversy when *Melody Maker* bannered "Darin Slams Back At British Rock Fans" on the front page of an issue during the tour. Darin told the publication "I'll never tour Britain again in a rock'n'roll package show."

Back home, Darin's next single was another re-working of an old public domain workhorse, "Won't You Come Home Bill Bailey." On February 2, Darin had recorded an entire album with a small jazz combo and arrangements by Bobby Scott. The session was over when Darin and Scott started messing with "Bill Bailey."

"We got rid of a few musicians and we ended up with just a rhythm section: bass, drums and piano," Scott recalled. "It was an afterthought."

The restrained jazz arrangement contrasted nicely with the big band swing of Darin's previous three hits. "Bill Bailey" reached #19. Its flip side, Darin's ballad "I'll Be There" (recorded in July 1959), also became a minor hit. In time, the song would come to be regarded as one of Darin's top pop songwriting efforts: Britain's Gerry & The Pacemakers scored a Top 20 hit with it in 1965, and it was later recorded by Elvis Presley.

For a performer of Bobby Darin's ambitions, the mecca was not Carnegie Hall, but The Copacabana. The major showrooms of Vegas, and clubs like The Cloister in Hollywood were prestigious bookings, but the Copa was the crowning achievement. It unquestionably placed a performer in the upper strata of nightclub stars.

For Darin, a Bronx kid, headlining at the Copa was an even sweeter triumph. He could, for a few days, rule his hometown. And Darin did rule, as the New York press excitedly hyped his return, building up anticipation for his appearance. Previews pegged Darin as "the potentially greatest talent in the business."

The Copa timed Darin's debut for June in order to bring in a younger crowd during the prom season. But Copa boss Jules Podell found out he didn't need to hedge his bets with Darin. The club was standing-room-only every night.

As *Variety* pointed out, "The premiere audience was composed almost entirely of adults, and it's these clients that seem to swing along more robustly than the youngsters."

In addition to clicking at the box office, Darin's show received rave reviews. "Darin's finger-snapping, jazzy and extremely hep delivery has its moments of humor, ease and at all times, a singular brand of charm that make it big at this particular scene," commented *Variety*. Laudatory reviews also appeared in the New York newspapers *Journal-American, Mirror, Post,* and *World Telegram & Sun.*

Darin's Copa repertoire consisted of a few hit singles ("Mack The Knife," "Clementine" and "Bill Bailey"), a handful of numbers from the two hit Atco albums, some standards not yet recorded by Darin (a couple of Cole Porter songs, Rodgers & Hammerstein's "I Have Dreamed") and traditional material such as a medley of "Swing Low Sweet Chariot" and "Lonesome Road."

Darin also took turns on the vibraphone, drums and piano. "He would, just with total nerve and gusto, pull it off," Dick Behrke said of Darin's on-stage instrumental endeavors. "Just by sheer personality and guts. He had an incredible amount of nerve, because he really had only a rudimentary knowledge of all the instruments."

There were a few quick nods to his early rock'n'roll roots. Darin played piano on a credible version of Ray Charles' "I Got A Woman." "Splish Splash" and "Dream Lover" were also included in the 19-song set, though it was fairly obvious that Darin was performing them in an almost obligatory manner.

"He didn't like to do those hits," explained Bobby Scott, who often played piano for Darin's Copa shows. "At the time, he had moved on to a new area and they kind of stuck out like a sore thumb, and he knew it. He did them because there were people out there who had bought the records. But he did them a little bit tongue-in-cheek."

To compound the excitement of the Copa dates, the June 15 and 16 shows were recorded for a live album. *Darin At The Copa* became his third straight Top 10 album, climbing to #9 in the fall. The entire Copa show was documented, with the exception of three songs which were edited from the release, "Birth Of The Blues," "My Funny Valentine" and "Splish Splash."

The album gave listeners a taste of Darin's show-business *savoir-faire,* which was knocking out nightclub audiences. But in retrospect, Bobby Scott felt Darin's subsequent Copa performances were superior and he believed the live album was rushed out too soon.

"The recording was so bad in there," Scott observed. "They just did not get the band. The sound was horrible. I don't think they should have done it. I think it was a little early in his career for a live album."

Reminiscing about Darin's now-legendary early '60s appearances at the Copa, Scott most remembered the sense of excitement that surrounded Darin in those days.

"I remember in between shows, in the apartment in the Hotel 14 above the Copa," Scott recalled. "Jesus Christ, it was like a show business pantheon. Everybody came out. I remember Judy Garland bringing Liza Minnelli in. I remember Lee Remick complimenting Bobby on his show.

"There were so many people who wanted to see the show," Scott said. "The crowds were so large that they filled the stage area and Bobby sang about three feet from me, pressed up against the grand piano. Bobby was at the height of his performing abilities. They were really great times."

One of Darin's biggest boosters at the time was Walter Winchell, the influential and nationally syndicated *New York Mirror* columnist. A regular attendee at Darin's shows at the Copa, the Cloister, and Washington, D.C.'s Casino Royale, Winchell dropped Darin's name into his column frequently.

"The Winchell thing happened quite unexpectedly," Darin explained to *The New York Post*. "He saw me working, he liked me, and he came down to tell me. The next night, he and I had an argument about a certain individual in politics. The net result of that argument was a very close friendship."

While Darin was playing in D.C. in May, Winchell telephoned the office of his friend, FBI Director J. Edgar Hoover, to request an FBI tour for himself and Darin. Although Hoover did not accompany them, Darin and Winchell received a special tour of FBI facilities.

All the while, Atco continued to pump out the product. Strangely, in September, an instrumental single, "Beachcomber" (credited to "Bobby Darin at the Piano") was released.

Although *Billboard*'s review gave Darin credit for "interesting boogie work against solid string backing by Shorty Rogers," the song barely dented the charts at #100.

A quick follow up single, "Artificial Flowers" from the musical *Tenderloin*, found Darin swinging about a poor, dead orphan girl. While the song became a hit and has many fans, others consider it the nadir of Darin's "style over substance" swingin' phase.

"I remember an attempt to make that in the same vein as 'Mack The Knife,'" recalled the song's arranger, Dick Behrke. "Let's do this, and let's modulate, and let's keep modulating. I actually hate that arrangement. It got to be so busy. In the interest of trying to write in someone else's style, I just kept throwing more and more in. It was a forced idea from the beginning."

Its flip side, "Somebody To Love" (which also charted), was recorded in 1959 at the same session as "I'll Be There" and was decidedly more youth-oriented than any Darin hit since "Dream Lover."

Along those lines, Atco released an album in September called *For Teenagers Only*, a title indicative of the label's marketing strategy for Darin. The album package included a photo spread and pull-out poster. With the exception of "Somebody To Love" and "You Know How" (another track from the July 1959 session), the entire album consisted of leftover material from 1958. For the most part, teenagers stayed away; the album did not chart.

Atco's bad habit of keeping Darin material in the can increased in 1960. Two entire albums were shelved and held from release until 1963 and 1964. The label did have some understandable concern about the glut of Darin product, and the commerciality of the material in question. Atco released four Darin albums in both 1960 and 1961, so finding a hole in the schedule would have been difficult.

But by burying the albums until after Darin had left the label and his record sales were in a down-cycle, Atco virtually insured that two of the greatest albums of his career would go largely unheard. The label didn't know what to make of the albums, and it was easier to throw together a greatest hits album, a collection of unreleased rock'n'roll for teenagers, or a *Live At The Copa* than to take a chance with the material Darin recorded in January and February of 1960.

"We just thought at the time we would go with things that were more commercial," acknowledged Ahmet Ertegun about the shelved LPs.

The first of the rejected albums was *It's You Or No One*. The concept was Darin's, right down to the album's artwork, which featured a bright color picture of a smiling Darin on the front, a black and white shot of a forlorn Darin on the back. The photographs symbolized the style of the album: upbeat songs, arranged by Torrie Zito, on Side 1; melancholy songs, arranged by Bobby Scott, on Side 2.

Featuring jazz-style arrangements, the album was heavily orchestrated, with Darin's reading of Sammy Cahn and Jule Styne's title track standing out. Acclaimed jazz guitarist (and future Phil Spector session stalwart) Barney Kessell played guitar on the Side 1 tracks.

Bobby Scott's arrangements for Side 2 were unique in that the accompaniment consisted solely of a string quartet, a flute, a clarinet, French horns, and bass. Neither guitar nor drums were utilized. Slow versions of Duke Ellington's "Don't Get Around Much Anymore" and Irving Berlin's "How About Me" were highlights.

"I think Bobby did a wonderful job bringing them off," Scott said of the material. "But Atlantic didn't like it at all. They thought it was so esoteric."

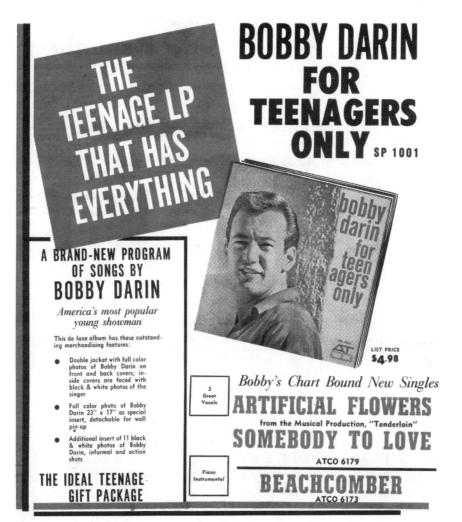

An even better album resulted from sessions held a week later, on February 1 and 2 (the session that produced the "Bill Bailey" single). Ten of the fourteen other tracks were finally released on the 1964 Atco LP *Winners.*

Winners was a true jazz vocal album, as Darin shone in a swingin' style, but with more relaxed instrumentation than found on *That's All* or *This Is Darin.* Scott assembled a great small jazz combo: he played piano, with Howard Roberts on guitar, Joe Mondregon on bass, Ronnie Zito on drums, Larry Bunker on vibraphone, and Carlo Vidal and former King Cole Trio member Jack Costanzo alternating on congas. The six-piece band's restrained arrangements provided a new, effective showcase for Darin's singing. Here, Bobby Darin was a jazz singer, although arranger Bobby Scott was not fond of that term.

"I don't believe that there is such a thing as a jazz singer," Scott said, "but I would call Bobby a jazz singer as much as I call Ray Charles kind of a jazz singer. Bobby easily went over that line, and had that relaxed thing, and could improvise, certainly much better than Sinatra, or Vic Damone, or the 'straight up' singers. He was much better at improvising and moving things around. Bobby was ingenious. He could come up with some interesting phrasing."

A few of the session's tracks rank among the best of Darin's career, particularly "When Day Is Done," "What A Difference A Day Made" and "Easy Living." The latter stood out in Bobby Scott's mind.

"'Easy Living' is a classic record," Scott said. "Bobby sang beautifully on it. That record holds up today. A lot of people who are good singers today would have been proud to make that record."

Regarding Darin's rendition of Dinah Washington's classic "What A Difference A Day Made," writer Ken Emerson, who penned the liner notes to the 1991 CD compilation *Mack The Knife: The Best Of Bobby Darin, Volume Two,* raved

"(Darin) murmurs with tender intimacy, an almost feminine delicacy you'd never expect from a performer with Darin's range...Darin was multi-faceted, but here is yet another side of him that he seldom revealed."

George Burns dropped by the sessions for the only guest vocal on a Bobby Darin album, providing the "Ho-Ho's" on George and Ira Gershwin's "They All Laughed."

In August 1960, Darin, again with Scott as arranger, began work on a project which would be released that fall – a Christmas album called *The 25th Day of December.* The seasonal theme not withstanding, Darin viewed the project as a gospel album.

Thus, most of the songs sported a gospel feel and Darin was able to display his R&B roots more decidedly than in most of his recent pop efforts. There was some shouting, and a definite edge in Darin's voice. The album contained no secular seasonal fare; in fact, only two selections – "Silent Night" and "O Come All Ye Faithful" – could be called traditional Christmas material.

In a strange marketing move, Darin's 1960 Christmas single, "Christmas Auld Lang Syne," was not included on the album. This track, using the "Auld Lang Syne" melody with new Christmas lyrics, charted at #52 that December.

On October 3, 1960, Darin joined Patti Page and Joan Crawford as guests on Bob Hope's TV special. Darin performed "Artificial Flowers" and "Lazy River" (slated to be his next single), as well as duets with Page and Hope.

He also took another crack at TV drama, appearing on "Dan Raven" that fall. The series revolved around a detective whose beat was the supper clubs and jazz spots on the "Strip." In the series' very first episode, Darin played himself.

But Darin also had his sights on the big screen. In the *Down Beat* profile in May, Darin reported that he had already received "20 or 25 scripts," but turned them down. "I want the right roles," he said. "I don't want to do an exploitation picture. I want to do drama, light comedy, and the whole range. And someday, I want an Academy Award."

Darin's first motion picture appearance was in *Pepe*, released in December 1960. In the three-hour, fifteen-minute bomb, Darin cameoed in a nightclub scene, singing "That's How It Went All Right." The track was released by Colpix Records as a single, but received even less attention than the movie.

But in the summer of 1960, Darin was cast in his first major big-screen role. *Come September*, starring Rock Hudson and Gina Lollobrigida, began shooting in Rome in the late summer.

Darin's received fourth billing in the role of an American student who, while vacationing in Italy, falls in love with another young American tourist. The love interest was played by Sandra Dee.

Dee was already an established film favorite, having starred in two smash 1959 movies, *Gidget* and *A Summer Place*. She had been a child model, moved into television, and landed her first film role before she was 15. Known for playing innocent young girls in the throes of romance, Dee was very popular among teenage movie audiences. Her previous credits also included *The Reluctant Debutante*, *The Restless Years*, and *Portrait In Black*.

Darin and Dee were inseparable on the set. The pair fell deeply in love and after a whirlwind, brief courtship, Bobby Darin and Sandra Dee were married on December 1, 1960, only a few weeks after their return from Italy.

The ceremony, planned on the spur of the moment, was held at 3:00 a.m. in the living room of Don Kirshner's apartment in Elizabeth, New Jersey. Darin borrowed a ring from Kirshner's father-in-law, and Richard Behrke stood as the best man.

America had a new teen idol dream couple.

"Multiplication" 9

As Bobby Darin looked into the NBC cameras in January 1961 and sang the opening lines of "I Got Rhythm," one could not help but think he was describing the state of his own life. Who could ask for anything more?

A finger-snapping medley of "I Got Rhythm" and "I Got Plenty Of Nothing" opened another milestone in Darin's career: his own television special. Produced by Bud Yorkin and Norman Lear, "Bobby Darin & Friends" aired on January 31, 1961.

Anyone who had heard Darin's albums, or seen his night-club act, would not have been surprised that his showman-ship could successfully carry an hour of television variety. Still, the savvy that the 24-year-old displayed during this prime time showcase was impressive.

The opening medley segued into a dance number and Darin nicely hoofed his way through some rudimentary choreography. His comic acting skills were evident in a cute musical skit with guest Joanie Sommers, in which the couple played shy high schoolers (with Darin as the prototypical nerd).

Darin also had the chance to perform a vaudeville routine with a master of the form, Bob Hope. Though Darin over-did the mugging slightly, it was obvious that the pair was having a great time with the loosely-scripted bit, and their comic rapport appeared quite genuine.

In addition to his finger-snapping, swingin' style on num-bers such as "Some People," Darin (accompanied by Billy May's orchestra) also played the ultra-smooth balladeer on "I Have Dreamed." Other musical highlights included a long duet number with Sommers, and a Darin-Hope-Sommers soft-shoe through "Bill Bailey."

"Darin works with the aplomb of a stage-scarred veteran," said *Variety's* review of the special. "The whole performance [was] super-charged with his self-assured air. He used his talent to the hilt and gave this variety hour the benefit of his sharp personality edge."

Executive producer of the special was Steve Blauner, who became Darin's manager (the fifth in five years) in 1960. The headstrong Blauner, who had earlier been instrumen-tal in securing Darin's gig with George Burns, immediately produced results, such as the TV special, regular Copa book-ings, and a new Las Vegas contract – three years at The Flamingo at $20,000 per week.

"It's a great pairing," Darin said of his teaming with Blauner. "I know where I want to go. Steve knows how to get me there."

Darin's single version of "Lazy River" made the charts in February, eventually reaching #14, his biggest hit in a year.

"Lazy River" completed the trilogy, begun with "Mack The Knife" and "Beyond The Sea," of older popular songs which came to be regarded as "Bobby Darin standards." The song was first popularized by its co-writer, Hoagy Carmichael, in 1932. In 1956, Roberta Sherwood had a minor hit with it. But Darin made the song uniquely his own with another

show-stopping vocal. This time, the arrangement, which built from simple bass and acoustic guitar to a full big band fury, was courtesy of Dick Behrke, with a large assist from Darin himself.

"The basic rhythm figure was worked out largely due to Bobby," Behrke acknowledged. "He had the bass figure in mind, and the whole arrangement was built around it. He was geared to singing the song around that riff."

Darin's first album of 1961 was *Two Of A Kind,* a collection of duets with the legendary Johnny Mercer, one of the finest popular song lyricists of the 20th century. Unfortunately, the project was misguided in several respects. Though billed as a "Bobby Darin & Johnny Mercer" album (probably for commercial reasons), Mercer dominates nearly every track.

Mercer's considerable catalog of classics was largely bypassed in favor of (as the liner notes mention) "some of the long neglected corners of Tin Pan Alley." But if the album was conceptualized as a rediscovery-of-lost-gems musical project, the amount of humorous banter Darin and Mercer exchange calls attention to their rapport – not the songs – as the album's centerpiece.

The pairing did produce one masterpiece in the title track, a Darin-Mercer writing collaboration. Darin's true "standard" melody and Mercer's typically clever lyric combine for a wonderful song which singing duos should be performing for ages.

Darin was very proud of the project, which was another example of his acceptance in the community of pre-rock musical greats. During Darin's Copa engagement that year, he coaxed a reluctant Mercer on stage with him for a song.

"Bobby forced Johnny to come on stage and sing a tune," recalled Bobby Scott. "Johnny hated being thrown into the lights. He and Bobby carried it off, as consummate pros will, but John was still blushing when they finished."

Two Of A Kind did not chart, the third consecutive Darin album which failed to do so. There was a glut of Darin LPs on the market and each of the previous three had been a "special project" – the duet album, the Christmas album, and the collection of unreleased rock'n'roll for teenagers. Thus, Darin's momentum as a record-seller slowed, making it easy to second guess about what might have happened if Atco had released the stronger *It's You Or No One* or *Winners* collections.

The next Atco LP, however, was a can't-miss. *The Bobby Darin Story* collected Darin's 12 most popular recordings, evenly split between rock'n'roll and standards. It marked the first album appearance for many hit singles such as "Queen Of The Hop," "Dream Lover" and the concurrent hit "Lazy River." The album sold well, reaching #18 and staying on the charts for nearly a year.

Darin was back in the swingin' mode for his next album, the tasteful *Love Swings.* This album concentrated on often-recorded standards to an even greater degree than *That's All* or *This Is Darin*, with songwriting credits full of luminaries such as Rodgers & Hart, Ira Gershwin, Jerome Kern, Hoagy Carmichael and yes, Johnny Mercer.

With arrangements by Torrie Zito (whose younger brother Ronnie played drums for Darin from 1959-1963), Darin turned in very stylish readings of "It Had To Be You," "Skylark" and "I Didn't Know What Time It Was." He updated "How About You" with contemporary references to JFK, Sandra Dee, and rock'n'roll.

The album did not include his latest single, a remake of the Nat King Cole standard "Nature Boy." The track's production was oriented toward the younger Top 40 crowd, and indicated Darin's decision to gravitate back to rock'n'roll.

"You Must Have Been A Beautiful Baby," his next single, was indeed a standard (with lyrics by Mercer), but Darin gave it a pounding rock'n'roll arrangement (later appropriated by

The Dave Clark Five) and put the edge back in his voice. It became Darin's biggest hit single since "Mack The Knife" two years earlier.

On August 9, nearly a year after filming began, *Come September* opened in Minneapolis. While Hudson and Lollobrigida were still major box-office attractions, Darin and Dee's standing as Young America's Sweethearts helped attendance.

"I can't go wrong," Darin told Bobby Scott when the film opened. "The box office people will come out to see the stars, they'll see me, and maybe I can build something out of it."

Darin's reviews were relatively promising for a newcomer. "Darin does a workmanlike job, and gives evidence he'll have more to show when the parts provide him with wider opportunity," wrote *Variety*.

Darin composed two songs for the movie, including the instrumental title theme, released as a single under the name "The Bobby Darin Orchestra." It only reached #113, but three months later, Billy Vaughan and His Orchestra fared a little better with the song, taking it to #73 on the pop chart and #18 on the Easy Listening chart.

Bobby Scott remembered the occasion when Darin first played the song for him on the piano. Scott told him that he considered the melody's pseudo-classical aspirations to be pretentious.

"He laughed and told me to play it," Scott recalled. "His piano playing left a little to be desired. So I played it, cleaning up the harmonic design. He leaned over the keyboard and said, 'There, now it's so pretentious, it works.'"

The second Darin-penned number, which he performed in the film, was "Multiplication," a clever pop song in the loose novelty style of "Splish Splash." Although it was released as a B-side, it still became a fair-sized hit, reaching #30.

Sandra Dee

(It was a bigger hit internationally, reaching #5 in Britain and #1 in Australia.)

The A-side of that December 1961 single was "Irresistible You," a horn-driven rock'n'roll number whose appeal lived up to its title. Darin's "Let's twist awhile" exclamation at mid-song drove home that the record's intended audience was the nation's twist-crazy teenagers. "Irresistible You" reached #15.

Darin's not-so-subtle move back into the rock'n'roll arena was intentional, said Ahmet Ertegun. "No pop singer was having a series of hits then, including Tony Bennett, Sinatra and so forth. Their records weren't big pop records. Darin was trying to get back, to find something that would go both ways. It was the right thing to do, because those records became hits."

Both sides of the hit single and "You Must Have Been A Beautiful Baby" were included on *Twist With Bobby Darin,* the first Darin rock'n'roll album which sold well. The remainder of the album was filled out with old tracks such as "Bullmoose," "Queen Of The Hop," the Rinky Dinks singles, and a few tracks recycled from the *For Teenagers Only* album.

Though it can't be considered a true album project because it was a mish-mash of old tracks, *Twist With* is one of Darin's most enjoyable albums. It's a great party record which could almost serve as a time capsule capturing the joys of '50s rock'n'roll.

The year 1961 was capped off with another personal milestone for Bobby Darin. On December 16, his son, Dodd Mitchell Darin, was born at Cedars of Lebanon Hospital in Hollywood.

10

"Look At Me"

"Bobby Darin is not yet the biggest thing in pictures, but he is just about the busiest." So proclaimed a *Newsweek* story on Darin in April 1962.

If any newcomer to the silver screen ever ran the risk of wearing out his welcome, surely it was Darin in 1962. His work in *Come September* had earned him a 1961 Golden Globe Award as a "New Star of the Year," and building upon that momentum, Darin corralled prominent roles in five movies that year.

"The pictures are my first love," Darin now announced to *Newsweek*. "I've attacked the movies with the same ferocity I did other things."

For critics who were used to pop or rock stars taking on bubbly roles in inconsequential fluff, Darin was a welcome change of pace. "He is good," *Newsweek* exclaimed with apparent surprise. "Singer Darin belts out his material with elaborate gusto, but actor Darin's style is as natural and understated as that of Bing Crosby or Frank Sinatra."

Darin's first film of the year was *Too Late Blues*, for which he shared top billing with Stella Stevens. The film was directed by John Cassavetes, making his first Hollywood picture after receiving acclaim for the low-budget, independently-produced *Shadows*. *Too Late Blues* premiered in Paris in November 1961 before a January 1962 U.S. opening.

Darin portrayed John "Ghost" Wakefield, a pianist in a small-time jazz combo. His acting was low-keyed and sophisticated, entirely appropriate for his character. "Darin is effective," said a *Variety* review. "His flaccid, unformed face and his fumbling idealism fuse well." The *New York Times* concurred: "An arrogant punk of a hero [is] played to perfection by Mr. Darin."

Unfortunately, the film's reviews were deservedly negative. Without a linear plot, the narrative intended to be a character study, but development was nil and motivation was unfounded. As the *Times* review began, "All that *Too Late Blues* needs to make it one of the best movies ever about jazz musicians is substance."

Darin's next film was his first and only true musical, *State Fair*. The 1962 version, which also starred Pat Boone, Ann-Margret and Pamela Tiffin, was the second remake of the venerable Rodgers & Hammerstein favorite.

Darin portrayed Jerry Dundee, a fast-talking, worldly television announcer involved in a mating ritual with Tiffin's small-town girl. Darin sang "This Isn't Heaven," a new song written for the film by Richard Rodgers, and participated in an ensemble number, "It's A Grand Night For Singing." The film's soundtrack album was a sizable hit, reaching #12 in the summer of 1962.

However, Darin found himself in another film panned by critics, and this time, their barbs didn't stop at the story. "Pat Boone and Bobby Darin emerge rather bland and unappealing," wrote *Variety*, while the *New York Times* called Darin "rather awkward as an actor." Though critics almost unanimously agreed that the whole idea of the remake was miscalculated,

Darin (center) in Too Late Blues
(Paramount Pictures Corp. publicity photo)

Darin (second from left) in Hell Is For Heroes
(Paramount Pictures Corp. publicity photo)

the film was a commercial success, finishing 23rd on *Variety's* list of "Big Rental Pictures of 1962."

Critics were kinder to Darin's next film, *Hell Is For Heroes*. Although Darin received second billing, his role in actuality was merely supporting. When first introduced in the movie, Darin's character (Private Corby) shoulders the role of comic relief, although later Bob Newhart steps in and Darin becomes just another soldier.

Except for Steve McQueen, none of the actors were given much character to work with. Again, Darin did well with what he was given, as *Variety* noted – "Bobby Darin has a colorful role of a battlefield boarder which he portrays with relish."

The movie was ultimately confusing and often sluggish, with battle strategy and battle scenes all portrayed at length on screen. Nevertheless, *Hell Is For Heroes* was a solid, if unspectacular, box office hit, finishing at #39 on *Variety's* tally of the top films of 1962.

Darin's next role would not only elicit his greatest on-screen performance, but also result in the finest, most thought-provoking film of his career, *Pressure Point*. Sharing top billing with Sidney Poitier, Darin portrayed a character simply referred to as "The Patient," a prison inmate under the psychiatric care of Poitier's "The Doctor."

A black and white film set in 1942, *Pressure Point* finds Darin as a racist, anti-Semitic Nazi sympathizer arrested for subversive activities in the German American Bund. Considering Darin's image, it was a fascinating role for him to take on.

He convincingly put across the character's hatred, insulting FDR and donning a Nazi uniform. But he also superbly handled scenes in which the roots of his character's sickness are explored. One of the best is the scene in which Darin's character attends his first Bund meeting. As the

Darin in Pressure Point
(United Artists publicity photo)

audience sings "The Star Spangled Banner," and Darin eventually, reluctantly joins in, the confusion and doubt on his face is convincing.

Though the film did not attract audiences, Darin's performance gained wide recognition. "Bobby Darin gives a strong performance, delivering a believable, natural characterization," said *Variety*. "He plays with a frighteningly realistic attitude of distrust and psychopathic fear." Even the usually reserved *New York Times* was complimentary: "As was intended, Mr. Darin's portrayal should make anyone recoil."

The New York Herald Tribune wrote of Darin: "That this usually light, romantic young man undertook such a vicious portrayal is evidence of his seriousness. That he brings it off with such ghastly sureness of touch underlines his talent with unexpected incisiveness." Darin's received a Golden Globe Award nomination in the category "Actor in a Leading Role, Dramatic" for his performance in *Pressure Point*.

One scene showcasing The Patient's anti-social nature depicted a Darin-led gang terrorizing a bar. Eventually the members go so far as to play tic-tac-toe on the body of the owner's wife (played by actress Mary Munday). For this scene, actor Richard (Dick) Bakalyan joined Darin. During the shoot, Darin and Bakalyan played chess every day, and the two struck up a lasting friendship.

Darin and Poitier also became close. (Ironically, given the film's anti-bigotry message, *Pressure Point* was the only film of 1962 to feature a black actor in a lead role.) Just as Darin admired Poitier's consummate professionalism as an actor, Poitier admired Darin's musical integrity. Once, Poitier stopped by one of Darin's recording sessions.

"Poitier had come fully assuming he was going to hear a guy singing 'My Funny Valentine,'" recalled producer Nik Venet. "Darin, myself, an engineer, and one of the violin

Darin in If A Man Answers
(Universal International publicity photo)

players were the only four white people at the session. Poitier was stunned. He couldn't believe that he was coming to a session that was so funky."

After proving his mettle as a serious dramatic actor, Darin returned to the expected for his fifth film of 1962, *If A Man Answers*. It was the first vehicle concocted especially for the Darin-Dee team. *Time* summed up the critical consensus with "Actor Darin and Actress Dee, who are Mr. And Mrs. in real life, just sort of stand there like Tweedle Dumb and Tweedle Dee [sic]. And the production is in the cheapest kind of expensive bad taste."

But the box office appeal of Dee was still strong, and the film was a moderate hit. More than any of his previous, more respected efforts, *If A Man Answers* placed Darin, albeit briefly, in the exclusive category of "movie star."

Darin was riding high. The film opened shortly after he signed his lucrative new contract with Capitol Records. His first single for the label was the movie's title song, the first record he made with Capitol producer Nik Venet.

A few nights before the film's opening, Darin, Dee and Venet were taking a late night cab ride down Broadway, driving past the theater where the movie would premier. The theater had just erected 30-foot-high cutouts of Darin and Dee to hang above the marquee. To savor the moment, Darin asked the cab driver to pull over just across the street. Darin and Venet got out.

"In the privacy of the night, we stood there in total awe," Venet recalled. "He said to me 'Can you believe this?' For two guys who came from parents who didn't have much, it was amazing."

The cab driver, who did not initially recognize any of his passengers, finally concluded that there was a celebrity in the back seat of his car. The driver turned to Darin and said, "Your friend looks like somebody."

"He sure is somebody," Darin replied.

"I knew it," the driver replied, turning to Venet. "Mr. Mineo, can I have your autograph?"

"Sal will do anything for you," replied Darin. Venet obligingly signed Sal Mineo's name on a piece of paper. When time came to pay the fare, Darin told Venet, "Sal, the guy recognized you, give him a big tip." Darin yanked a fifty dollar bill out of Venet's wallet.

"Darin and I laughed our asses off," said Venet. "That's the kind of sense of humor he had. He didn't say 'But I'm Bobby Darin' to the driver, he went along with the gag."

Darin on stage at The Flamingo, August 1962
(Las Vegas News Bureau)

"Things"

Despite Darin's full slate of film projects in 1962, he devoted just as much time to his music as ever. Before jumping labels in July, Darin capped off his Atco stint in grand style.

One of the most intriguing albums of his career was *Bobby Darin Sings Ray Charles,* recorded in November 1961 and released in the spring of 1962. Darin tackled 11 songs written by or associated with Charles in very impressive fashion. Driving versions of "The Right Time," "Hallelujah I Love Her So" and "Leave My Woman Alone" showed that Darin hadn't lost touch with his R&B roots.

Some impressive help was on hand. Jimmy Haskell arranged the album. Saxophone was supplied by future Phil Spector session ace (and soon-to-be "Deep Purple" hitmaker) Nino Tempo. Background vocals were provided by The Blossoms, whose Darlene Love stepped up to the microphone for some wicked solo vocal parts on "The Right Time."

Darin's four-minute version of "What'd I Say" was split in half and released on both sides of a single. "Part 1" reached #24, while the album reached #96. Ahmet Ertegun, who produced the sessions, considered the album too ahead of its time to succeed commercially. Darin himself was ambivalent about the results.

"It wasn't the greatest LP I've ever made," he told *Melody Maker* later that year, "but I had to get it off my chest. It seems to be the fashion now to admire Charles. I'm proud to have been admiring him for a long time."

Darin's version of "What'd I Say" received a Grammy nomination for Best Rhythm & Blues Recording. In entirely appropriate irony, Ray Charles won the year's award for his rendition of the country classic "I Can't Stop Loving You."

—————————————————————————————

Rumors about Darin working with legendary producer Phil Spector have popped up in many published accounts of Spector's career, and they are usually placed at about this time period – 1962. The assertion that Spector produced some tracks for Darin is presented as fact in a number of rock history tomes, with no specification or documentation, despite the fact that no Darin single or album bears a Spector production credit and no track has an obvious "Spector sound."

Atlantic chief Ahmet Ertegun, who served as supervisor (sometimes solely, often in tandem with brother Nesuhi and/or Jerry Wexler) for all of Darin's Atco sessions – a role which over the years ranged from actually producing to acting as "executive producer" – said that Spector had no involvement in Darin's Atlantic records.

However, Ertegun reported that he intended to have Spector work with Darin, and arranged for the two to meet.

"By that time, Bobby had married Sandra Dee and was living in Beverly Hills," Ertegun said. "So Phil and I went to this big mansion, with a butler serving drinks around the pool and everything. We walked in, and I introduced Bobby to Phil."

"See, Bobby was a very prolific writer, and he would write 15 or 20 songs and play them all for me. And out of the 15 or 20, there would be three or four really good ones. So he started playing me songs like 'Jailer Bring Me Water' and I said, 'Well, that's great.' He played another and I said, 'That's great.' The songs weren't that good, but I knew the good ones would come up.

"Phil turns to me and says 'Just a second, man, are you crazy or am I? Those songs are horrible.' So Darin says 'Who the hell is this son of a bitch?' He was ready to throw Spector out, so we left.

"A year later, when Spector was hot, Darin says to me, 'Do you think you could get this kid to work with me?' I told him it was the same guy he threw out. He didn't remember."

Despite that inauspicious meeting, Darin and Spector did become acquaintances. In the 1989 Spector biography *He's A Rebel* by Mark Ribowski, Spector co-writer Terry Phillips related a story about he and Spector pitching songs to Darin and getting a favorable response.

Los Angeles Times pop music critic Robert Hilburn, while on a road trip with Spector in the early '70s, received first-hand evidence that Darin and Spector had a cordial relationship.

"In Vegas, Spector and I went to see Elvis at The International, then to The Desert Inn to see Darin," Hilburn recalled. "After the show, Spector and Darin sat around for four, five, six hours, reminiscing about the old days in New York."

Darin's final Atco single was "Things," a finely crafted country-pop effort which became his biggest hit since "Mack The Knife," reaching #3. Darin described "Things" as "sorta polite country and western. It was a gamble that paid off."

The lyric displayed Darin's ability to drop a relatively unusual phrase such as "heartaches are the friends I'm talking to" into a simple pop song. Though "Things" was not a country hit at the time, it has since become something of a country standard. Anne Murray, Buddy Alan, and Ronnie Dove each scored country hits with it in the 1970s. The song has also achieved notable covers by Dean Martin & Nancy Sinatra and Jerry Lee Lewis.

Atco hastily assembled a corresponding *Things And Other Things* album, which was filled out with various single A and B sides from '58-'61 which had not appeared on Darin LPs before. One of these was "Jailer Bring Me Water," the song Phil Spector hated. This Darin composition was subsequently covered by Johnny Rivers, Trini Lopez, The Bachelors, and Freddie and The Dreamers.

In July, Darin signed a new, lucrative contract with Capitol Records, ending his five-plus year association with Atco.

"That was a big shock to me," Ahmet Ertegun recalled. "Darin was the only really big pop artist we had at the time. He was being influenced by his managers. He was always told 'You're a big pop star, you shouldn't be on this funky little R&B label.'" Indeed, it was that exact pitch by Capitol which won Darin over.

"At that time, Capitol, RCA and Columbia were very prestigious labels," said Nik Venet, the first Capitol producer to work with Darin. "If you played nightclubs and wanted to do TV and film, Atlantic and those companies – which were really doing well – didn't have the prestige, or production offices in California. It was quite a thing to get on Capitol. The deal was so prestigious for Bobby."

Venet produced Darin's first Capitol single, the piano-driven, rock'n'roll-style theme from "If A Man Answers." It reached #32, but was hardly the smash the label was hoping for. In fact, there were hoping for a replacement for Frank Sinatra, who had left Capitol two years earlier to form his own Reprise label.

Darin tried to oblige with his first album, *Oh! Look At Me Now,* a collection of standards arranged big-band style by Billy May, who had worked extensively with Sinatra. (May had also previously handled arrangements for Darin's TV special and the *Two Of A Kind* LP.) Capitol staff producer Tom Morgan produced the album.

"Bobby wanted to do a Capitol type of album, with Billy May and the big studio orchestra," said Morgan. "I spent some time with Billy May and Bobby over at Bobby's house, where we picked the tunes and talked over what the charts were going to be. Bobby sang great, the music was great, and it was a very good album."

May, who had no appreciation for rock'n'roll, came to respect Darin's vocal ability. "I think Darin was a better singer than people in my generation classify him," May said. "I think he sang well in-tune. He phrased OK and all. He had the ability to develop a staying quality."

The Darin-May pairing sounded perfectly natural. Darin was not overwhelmed by the arrangements, and he didn't try to overexert himself. The album's few ballads, hampered by Ray Conniff-like background singers, tended to drag, but upbeat romps such as "A Nightingale Sang In Berkeley Square" was an absolutely classic Darin vocal (and the great brass arrangement was classic May).

Three Irving Berlin songs – "All By Myself," "Always" and "Blue Skies" – stood out as highlights. Darin's swingin' style also shone on "There's A Rainbow 'Round My Shoulder" and a jazzy reading of Duke Ellington's "I'm Beginning To See The Light."

Though the faux-Sinatra approach resulted in some excellent tracks, *Oh! Look At Me Now* stiffed commercially. But Darin was interested in pursuing his usual wide array of styles at Capitol.

"He didn't want to abandon the teenage audience," Nik Venet said. "He wanted to be able to do whatever he wanted, but he didn't want to offend anybody. He didn't want to offend teenagers by playing Vegas, and he didn't want to offend Vegas by making records that would appeal to young people. He didn't want to pander to anybody. He wanted to be a multiple talent. In those days, that was a problem. You were either a teenager singer or Frank Sinatra."

Of course, Darin had been both for Atco. His modus operandi was to consider all options – and occasionally the label's input – when it came time to choose which songs, and in which style, he would record.

"Bobby would let everybody at the table speak," Venet recalled. "If you had an idea, and you argued with him, he's go with you. You had to prove your conviction to him. You became his friend with your integrity. He made you put your money where your mouth was."

Darin and Nik Venet became close friends. The same age as Darin, Venet was by far the youngest producer at Capitol. In addition to Darin, he worked with The Beach Boys, The Lettermen, Ray Anthony, Jack Scott, and Tommy Sands. (He would later produce Linda Ronstadt and John Stewart.)

Venet produced three Darin albums and six singles. In the course of their work together, Venet also estimated that he would spend 10 to 15 weeks a year on the road with Darin. Those times gave Venet a unique perspective on, and understanding of, the Darin personality.

"Darin was a remarkable human being," Venet said. "I've worked with some heavy duty people, from Stan Kenton to Linda Ronstadt. But Darin was probably the most impressive person I've ever met in my life. Had he not been a musician, he would have been a senator or congressman."

Their close relationship gave Venet insight on Darin's generosity toward his friends. For example, Venet received an Jaguar XKE from Darin. Darin gifts would often be surprises.

"I once saw a wristwatch he was wearing and said, 'That's beautiful,'" Venet recalled. "The next day, there was a knock on my door. It was a messenger, with a $5,000 wristwatch. There was a little note attached to it – 'Thank God you didn't admire my wife.'

"The guy would give you the shirt off his back, and he did," Venet said. "He was the most generous man in the world."

Venet also learned how important loyalty was: Darin would never let one friend say something negative about another friend. Once Venet started to complain to Darin about Don Kirshner. The beef was nothing terribly nasty; Venet was just upset that some Kirshner-published songs he thought he had secured for The Lettermen were given to another act.

"Darin told me, 'Stop. Continue this conversation and I'm going to move to another table,'" Venet said. "I couldn't even begin a conversation about someone he knew – someone that was part of his 'family' – with one negative word. He wouldn't even entertain the thought of discussing it."

There were also many moments of humor. At times, Darin and Venet would astoundedly discuss their good fortune.

"I remember once, we were three sheets to the wind, laughing," Venet said. "He was married to Sandra Dee and I was dating Tuesday Weld. We were saying 'Jesus Christ, this is amazing, that this could happen to jerks like us from New York and Baltimore.' Talking like kids."

Darin could also be a practical joker. Once, after a long work session in which Darin and Venet had gone three nights without sleep, they stopped at a barbershop. When Venet fell asleep in the barber's chair, Darin paid off the barber to give him a crewcut.

"Touring with some other acts was a chore," Venet said. "Darin was great, because we were identical in our political beliefs, we had great conversations, and we met great people."

"Darin introduced me to Allen Ginsberg," said Venet. "He was a great fan of *On The Road* by Jack Kerouac – that was one of his favorite books. Darin was counter-culture before counter-culture had a title."

"Blowin' In The Wind"

The First Folk Phase

Though the Kingston Trio had been popular since 1958 (their breakthrough came only months after Darin's), folk music did not really become a stronghold in popular music until 1962. The upper echelons of the album charts, still the domain of soundtracks to movie musicals and Mitch Miller, were suddenly invaded by Peter, Paul & Mary, The Limeliters and Joan Baez.

Like many others, Bobby Darin liked what he heard. Previously, he had dabbled with a Vegas-y arrangement of the spiritual "Swing Low Sweet Chariot," and even taken a crack at writing a gospel-folk number in "Jailer Bring Me Water." But in early 1962, Darin decided to more deeply pursue folk music and to do some performing in that style, on stage and on record.

While it was easy to accuse Darin of jumping on a bandwagon (as some critics have done), his interest in and respect for folk music was genuine. "Back as far as 1954 or 1955, I have been a folk enthusiast," he explained in a 1960s interview. "The first three records I made were folk-oriented – commercial adaptations of old folk songs. The love of folk music has always been there."

Darin was not only into the newly popular folk of Peter, Paul & Mary and the Kingston Trio, but also some other respected artists – old and new – in the folk tradition.

"I remember packing tapes for when we would travel," recalled Nik Venet. "We used to play a lot of folk music: a lot of music from the Dust Bowl days, the '30s, the WPA albums. It was a favorite period of ours for digging up music."

"Cisco Houston (a compatriot and sometimes singing partner of Woody Guthrie) was a big favorite of ours," said Venet. "Darin was also a big Tom Paxton fan. He had all of Paxton's records."

Live, Darin's first forays in the folk area were a gentle reading of "Danny Boy" and the chain-gang-style blues "Work Song." He was working towards a folk segment of his concert act, during which the big band would rest, and Darin would take off his jacket and tie and sing with minimal instrumental accompaniment.

While Darin was mulling this over, he and Steve Blauner went to see Lenny Bruce perform at The Crescendo in Los Angeles. The opening act was another of the folk groups which had achieved a fair level of popularity, The Chad Mitchell Trio. During the show, Darin was impressed by the Trio's backup guitarist, who not only had great instrumental chops, but also would delight the audience with his clowning.

With his own folk segment in mind, Darin decided that the guitarist would be the perfect addition to his band. After the Mitchell Trio's set, Darin went backstage and offered the 19-year-old musician a job at double the weekly salary he was being paid by the Mitchell Trio.

The guitarist was Jim McGuinn, who after one-and-a-half years in Darin's band, would go on to found The Byrds, the seminal and hugely influential folk-rock band of "Mr. Tambourine Man" and "Turn Turn Turn" fame. (While with the Byrds, McGuinn changed his first name to Roger.)

(A&E publicity photo)

McGuinn, who had also previously backed The Limeliters, was making $150 a week. When Darin offered him a job, McGuinn hedged; he was bored with the Mitchell Trio, but was also considering an offer to join The New Christy Minstrels. Darin convinced McGuinn that he would get lost in the shuffle in that multi-member folk troupe.

McGuinn was leading something of a musical double life at the time. He was into the protest and topical forms of folk music, and hanging out in Greenwich Village with a hip crowd that included Bob Dylan. Those friends tended to look down on more "commercial" acts such as The Limeliters and The Chad Mitchell Trio (and it's hard to imagine that their view of Darin would have been any more charitable).

In some interviews over the years, McGuinn has been quoted as saying he was somewhat ashamed of his early commercial folk associations. However, in an interview about his work with Darin, he insisted that he is nothing but proud of that particular pre-Byrds association. McGuinn was adamant in his defense of Darin's musical integrity when questioned about whether Darin was sincere about folk music.

"Absolutely," he said. "There's no question in my mind. Bobby was more sincere than the other groups I had worked with.

"When he did something, he had an integrity about it that I didn't feel with The Chad Mitchell Trio," McGuinn said. "I felt they were more fluff than anything. Bobby was very interested in folk music and felt he wanted to be part of it."

McGuinn was brought into the fold to play twelve-string guitar and sing harmony during the folk segment of Darin's show. Rather than rehashing the Kingston Trio/Peter, Paul & Mary folk at the top of the charts, Darin concentrated on more "traditional" material during the segment, which was part of his shows throughout 1962 and 1963. Songs included Leadbelly's "Cottonfields" (for which Darin accompanied himself on guitar), "Long Time Man," "I'm On My Way Great God" (also known as "Canaan's Land"), "Boil That Cabbage Down" and, in one nod to pop-folk, The Rooftop Singers' hit "Walk Right In."

The segment went over well with both audiences and critics. "He sings his folk section with power and precision," said a *Variety* review, which noted that Darin seemed to put more effort into the folk segment than the rest of the show: "He has a tendency to casually throw away the numbers the audience is waiting and clamoring for, yet conversely, to work with great respect and discipline on less familiar material."

The interest in folk carried over into the recording studio, and Darin would take advantage of his Capitol contract to release two theme albums of folk material. To help out, Darin called on an old friend from his high-school band days, Walter Raim.

Raim had achieved some impressive credentials in the folk field, occasionally accompanying Harry Belafonte on stage (he played on the hit album *Belafonte Returns To Carnegie Hall*), and playing guitar and banjo on the landmark Judy Collins albums *Golden Apples Of The Sun* and *Judy Collins 3*. Darin phoned his old friend to ask for help with an album of folk songs.

"He saw in folk music a sophistication of some kind, a higher calling," recalled Raim. "He had in his mind that he was doing something more important than singing Las Vegas standards. He was attracted to the realness, the down-to-earth thing."

Although Capitol would hold its release for almost a year, Darin's first folk album, *Earthy*, was recorded shortly after the *Oh! Look At Me Now* sessions. Tom Morgan, who was not crazy about the project, oversaw the production. Raim helped Darin choose the songs, and wrote out the arrangements.

Earthy's theme was folk music from different cultures, which further differentiated Darin's project from the popular folk music of the day. The album was a varied collection of spirituals, blues, Latin American folk dance songs, and ballads.

Darin's vocal approach to the songs was markedly different from the way he sang rock'n'roll or popular standards. He substituted his voice's usual polish and strength with a restrained, softer, world-weary style. It seemed as if he was intentionally holding back, because that's how he felt the songs should be interpreted.

"I think he was trying to achieve another dimension as a singer," commented Raim, "just as a character actor would try to be someone else. Unlike someone like Sinatra, who always sounds like himself, I think Bobby was trying to be a different character when he sang those songs."

The project moved Darin to some of his all-time greatest performances. "Fay-O," a Haitian lament adapted and arranged by Raim, is one of Darin's most beautiful recordings. His absolutely moving vocal, sung partially in Haitian, is framed in a lovely minimalistic arrangement of acoustic guitar, bass, bongos and flute. The song was later recorded (as "Feuilles-O") by Simon & Garfunkel.

Likewise, Darin cut a top-notch version of Tom Paxton's mournful protest "Strange Rain," almost whispering his vocal over an acoustic guitar. Recorded less than a year after Dodd's birth, the song's line "What will become of my son?" may have made it particularly meaningful to Darin.

Paxton did not even know about Darin's recording until 2001, when he was asked to comment on it for a BBC radio documentary. He expressed surprise and admiration of Darin's choice of the song.

"That shows what an interesting guy he must have been," Paxton commented. "The song is about nuclear fallout. Why would a guy who had hits like 'Splish Splash' and 'Dream Lover' want to do a song like that?"

While somewhat outside the thematic framework of the album, "Work Song," written by jazz greats Nat Adderly and Oscar Brown, Jr., was another Darin *tour de force,* arranged in the bass-driven, dramatic jazz-blues manner of Peggy Lee's "Fever." Harry Belafonte received credit for the album's adaptation of "La Bamba" (radically different from the Ritchie Valens rock'n'roll hit). Darin was also strong on the gospel songs "I'm On My Way Great God," "When Their Mama Is Gone," and "The Sermon of Samson" (which Peter, Paul & Mary recorded as "If I Had My Way").

Throughout the album, the vocal and instrumental arrangements were solidly in the folk tradition.

"I don't think we thought much about being authentic, just about being true to the spirit of the song," said Raim. "We were not trying to be ethnic or pure. To do a folk song with anything but a guitar was considered commercial. We were trying to make a commercial album that would sell."

Earthy was not the swinging, cocky, in-control Bobby Darin the public had come to expect, but it showcased Darin as one of the great interpreters of his generation. Though it failed to chart, Darin did not give up on folk, recording a second album in that style called *Golden Folk Hits.*

Darin's folk sessions featured an impressive guest line-up. Glen Campbell played on both albums. Legendary guitarist James Burton can be heard on *Golden Folk Hits.* From the folk community, Bud Dashiel (of the duo Bud & Travis) played on some *Earthy* tracks. The folk group The Tarriers, who hit with "The Banana Boat Song" in 1957, were also employed. In 1962, The Tarriers also accompanied Darin on a tour and backed him during the folk segment.

Roger McGuinn played on some sessions, but believes his playing was largely lost in the mix: "I was just sort of along with the other guitarists in there. I don't know how much of my input got onto the records," he said.

Nik Venet also recalls that one of the giants of the '60s folk scene, Phil Ochs, was a frequent guest at the sessions.

"If someone tries to tell you that Darin didn't know his folk music," said Venet, "or that he was making folk music because it was hot, why would Phil Ochs come down to the session? Why would he hang out with us, if Darin was ripping that segment of music off?"

Venet produced *Golden Folk Hits,* released in November 1963. With accompaniment consisting of guitar, banjo, bass and background vocals, and with very faithful acoustic arrangements of the familiar folk of the early '60s, the album was more contemporary, but less ambitious than *Earthy.* If less thought went into this album on Darin's part, even less care was displayed by Capitol, which didn't even bother to put a picture of Darin on the front cover.

Still, it was interesting to hear Darin throw his hat into the ring of the top-of-the-charts folk familiarized by Peter, Paul & Mary ("Where Have All The Flowers Gone," "If I Had A Hammer"), The Kingston Trio ("Greenback Dollar," in which Darin chickens out of the "damn" that got the Trio censored), and the New Christy Minstrels ("Green, Green").

But the most noteworthy facet of the album was Darin's recording of two Bob Dylan songs. The first time McGuinn told Darin about a kid in Greenwich Village named Bob Dylan, Darin laughed and thought the kid was ripping off his name. But Darin was the first of the so-called "legitimate" singers to recognize Dylan and to incorporate Dylan songs into his recorded and live repertoire.

"Darin was impressed with the songs," recalled Venet. "He thought Dylan was important. We thought Dylan wasn't getting the shake he deserved. Some people weren't getting the message because of Dylan's singing style."

"I remember Darin in Vegas, sitting at the piano, playing Dylan's 'Don't Think Twice' with a big band," said Venet. "He was tearing up the house. The audiences at the ten o'clock and two o'clock shows were people in their 20s and 30s – it was the youth of Vegas. He was starting to get the message across."

The album's version of "Don't Think Twice" is marred by the inappropriate Jordanaires-style "Bop-bop-bop" of the background vocalists. (Darin would later record a superior version of the song for Motown.) However, Darin's reading of "Blowin' In The Wind," in his subdued voice, is a standout, and holds up very well against the myriad other recorded versions of the classic.

Darin's work in the folk idiom is largely overlooked, and often considered merely a sidetrack in his career. Even Walter Raim would comment, "Although he wanted to do this very much, it was not who he was." Still, precisely because it was such a left-field move at the time, Darin's 1962-63 foray into folk is fascinating. He would call upon his love of stripped-down, acoustic music to varying degrees throughout his career.

And there is a legacy left from this era, considering how effusive Roger McGuinn is in his praise of Darin, and how important a band The Byrds became.

Although the legend is that The Byrds were folkies who decided to plug in and play with a beat when they heard The Beatles, McGuinn suggested that at least some of the impetus toward rock came from his days with Darin.

"Bobby had a lot of influence on me," McGuinn said. "He convinced me that rock'n'roll was where it was at. He oriented me in that direction.

"It was a good training ground," McGuinn said of his days in Darin's band. "It gave me a lot of seasoning in the business. I knew things that the guys in The Byrds didn't know.

"It was almost like coming up in vaudeville or something. Bobby was like an old trouper. It was like he was from another era. He was a more professional performer than most people I know in the business today. He was punctual and he was precise and he hit the mark all the time. He was a brilliant guy, real bright, and he could do anything he wanted to do very well."

During this time, Darin got his first notions of how a performer might be able to do more than entertain an audience. Perhaps, through music, he could express his concerns about society, perhaps act as a catalyst for thought. Though it would be years before Darin would fully embrace this notion, the seed was planted. He also saw the potential volatility in the mix of the supper club circuit and progressive artistic vision.

"I remember him doing a show in the Catskills," recalled Nik Venet, "and I remember people saying, 'What happened to Bobby Darin? Did you hear those songs he was singing? He sounds like a communist.' Somebody else said, 'I came here to hear Frank Sinatra, not this rock'n'roll shit.'

"Some people were very disappointed in the show, because Darin was mixing it up. He used to say 'Just let 'em think about it.' He was so far ahead of his audience sometimes."

"Save The Country"

Though it has not been extensively publicized previously, Bobby Darin was very interested and active in the political and social causes of his time. Although much of the FBI's 96-page file on Darin (of which the agency released 43 pages to this author) concerns White House-requested name checks on entertainers or details on Darin's delinquency regarding induction into the military in 1958, the agency did not overlook his participation in marches and demonstrations.

In the early and mid-'60s, Darin's attention was captured by the cause of civil rights. He often spent long hours discussing his feelings with Nik Venet, who shared Darin's political views and accompanied him to the March on Washington.

"Darin thought the civil rights movement was the great revolution of the 20th century," Venet said. "The man was civil rights conscious long before it became radical chic. It was a passion of his."

Darin knew the Reverend Dr. Martin Luther King, Jr. and introduced the great civil rights leader to Venet. On another occasion, Darin introduced King to a less receptive audience – attendees of one of Darin's shows at The Copacabana.

That night, King came to the Copa during Darin's second show, arriving through the back entrance. Darin stopped the show to introduce King. The reaction from the older, white, decked-out Copa crowd was less than enthusiastic.

"It was silent," recalled Venet. "Then two guys in the back, and I think they were waiters, started applauding, and then slowly the applause rode from the back to the front.

"They finally applauded," Venet said, "but Darin felt that if he had introduced Sammy Davis, Jr., it would have been easier."

Indeed, Darin did not like the racial discrimination in the Las Vegas entertainment industry, which accepted Davis and Nat King Cole on stage, but seemed less receptive to African Americans anywhere else.

"He'd say, 'I can't believe it – you guys don't even have blacks as waiters here,'" said Venet. "They used to get mad at Darin. He'd threaten to bring in an all-black orchestra. He'd say, 'Next time I play here, you're not going to see a white face up here except mine.'"

While on marches, however, Darin tried to keep a low profile. Whenever a member of the press would recognize him, he would decline to make a comment, saying, "I'm here as a concerned citizen, not an entertainer."

The trips to Washington weren't without their lighter moments. Prior to the March on Washington, Darin had just wrapped up an engagement at the Copa. Neither he nor Venet had bothered to make travel arrangements. Hours before they intended to head to the nation's capital, they found that all flights out of New York, and all hotels in D.C., were booked solid.

Cover of a 1962–63 concert program

Their only option was to become true "limousine liberals" – they made the trip from New York to Washington in a limousine, hardly the mode of transportation favored by too many of the other civil rights demonstrators they would join the next day. "We felt terrible about having to take a limousine," Venet recalled.

For accommodations, they stayed at the home of Venet's brother, Ted Venetoulis, who was then working on the staff of Texas congressman Jim Wright. Venetoulis admired entertainers such as Darin and Sammy Davis, Jr. who participated in the civil rights marches without seeking publicity for it.

Darin was wearing a toupee by this time in his life, a piece that covered the front of his head to disguise his receding hairline. Just before turning in for the evening, he took off the toupee and hung it on a doorknob. During the night, it fell to the floor. Thinking it was a dead mouse, the maid who came early the next morning flushed it down the toilet.

Though Darin would later laugh heartily about the incident, when he awoke to find no toupee that morning, he was livid. The first order of business would be finding him a hat.

"He was always conscious of the hair, but in a good-natured way," said Venet. "He just didn't think the world was ready to see him without the front of his hair."

Naturally, with the city abuzz with tension and excitement, and the streets full of people, Darin was content to buy the first hat he could find. Unfortunately, it turned out to be a little straw hat, with a beer can on it, and the message "In case of accident, get me a beer." Thus, so properly attired, did Bobby Darin attend the March on Washington.

Darin made sure he personally practiced what he preached. "He wouldn't treat a porter secondarily, and then go march in a civil rights campaign," said Venet.

This was also true of Darin's attitude towards the musicians he worked with. "He was totally color-blind," guitarist Carol Kaye confirmed, adding that, as it pertained to her, "he was also totally gender-blind. He only cared about the musicianship."

Once, while driving through a Chicago ghetto in a limousine, Darin spotted a group of kids playing stickball with broomsticks and balls of rolled-up tape. Against even the advice of the limousine driver, Darin decided to get out and play with the kids, eventually sending off the driver to a hardware store to purchase better equipment.

"There we were in an all-black neighborhood, and Darin played stickball with a bunch of kids for an hour-and-a-half," recalled Venet. "Those kids still have no idea that the guy they played with was Bobby Darin."

Darin was a supporter and admirer of John F. Kennedy, and was devastated by Kennedy's assassination on November 22, 1963. "That was the beginning of a lot of changes in his feelings," recalled Venet.

Just days after the assassination, Darin began taping a guest appearance on "The Judy Garland Show." The atmosphere on the set, and within the studio audience, was naturally somber, but Garland, Darin and Bob Newhart, the other guest, put on their best "the show must go on" faces. (The show would air on December 29, 1963.)

Darin was every bit the assured show business professional, joining Garland for a long medley of songs with the loose theme of railroad travel, such as "Sentimental Journey," "Chattanooga Choo Choo" and "On The Atchison, Topeka And The Santa Fe."

For his solo segment, however, Darin came out without his suit and tie. In a darkly-lit setting, he sang two of the spiritual-style songs from his folk albums – "Michael Row The Boat Ashore" and "I'm On My Way Great God." It was an intense, superb performance, almost as if Darin was using this serious, religious music as a catharsis for his sorrow, for the nation's shock, in those troubled days.

Darin's commitment to issues such as civil rights would continue through his life. For instance, he joined the march from Selma to Montgomery, Alabama, to protest voting dis- crimination in March 1965. While FBI records note plans for "singing and entertainment" by Darin, Dick Gregory, Harry Belafonte and Peter, Paul & Mary at the conclusion of the march, it is not believed that Darin actually performed.

Darin's actions in the social arena may seem unremark- able, viewed from the context of 30 years later, especially when it later became commonplace for pop stars to lend a hand to numerous causes. But while some folk singers had gained activist reputations in the early 1960s, few in the pop field, especially among the younger generation of stars, had yet to become active in such causes.

"You didn't have your younger entertainers at that time going on campaigns about civil rights," said Nik Venet. "The mainstream entertainment industry was hands-off that sub- ject. Talking about it now seems mild, but at the time, Darin put his whole career, and the possibility of getting blacklisted, on the line."

Darin's passion for racial and social justice left a lasting impression on socialite and author Barbara Howar, who described Darin as "a young man with a conscience and the Elmer Gantry ability to convert those who did not share his convictions" in her book *Laughing All The Way*.

"I know it would make better reading to report that I began thinking of the world's problems through an exposure to John Kenneth Galbraith or at least Paul Newman," Howar wrote, "but it was Mr. Darin who...made me care."

"Settle Down"

1963

Musically, 1963 was another busy year for Bobby Darin. Four new albums were released (five, if Atco's from-the-vaults release of *It's You Or No One* is counted), and Darin scored back-to-back Top 10 hits for the first time in three years.

In addition to the two folk albums discussed earlier, two new Capitol LPs produced by Nik Venet were built around hit singles. The first was *You're The Reason I'm Living.*

The Darin-penned title-track single, which reached #3 in March, was a return to the country-pop style of "Things." In a 1969 overview of Darin's career, *Los Angeles Times* pop music critic Robert Hilburn called "You're The Reason I'm Living" "one of the best country-pop records ever made."

The song again found Darin emulating Ray Charles, whose *Modern Sounds In Country & Western Music* album was a huge hit a year earlier.

In fact, "You're The Reason" (which also achieved a surprising Top 10 placement on the R&B charts) seems patterned after Charles' "I Can't Stop Loving You" in its piano-based, relaxed tempo and use of a female backing chorus to sing the title line. However, while Nik Venet admitted that "You're The Reason" was borrowed, he said it was not from Ray Charles.

"It's influenced by two songs," Venet explained. "Bobby and I were talking about how Sam Cooke built 'You Send Me' from 'Blue Moon' and how Sharon Sheeley wrote 'Poor Little Fool' from a Diamonds record slowed down. The joke was to work on 'Happy Birthday.'

"The other song that's used is 'Red Sails In The Sunset,'" Venet said. "If you sing the chorus 'You're the reason I'm living/I'd be lost without you,' it's really 'Red sails in the sunset /Happy birthday to you.' That's an inside joke."

The song featured harmonica supplied by legendary blues musician Harmonica Fats, whom arranger Jimmy Haskell invited to the session. After recording the song in one take, Harmonica Fats told Nik Venet, "I don't know who this kid is, but goddamn, he's good." The session also featured Glen Campbell on guitar.

"Darin had the full orchestra and sang live to it," recalled Campbell. "He knew what he wanted and he would get it. I thought it was the sweetest, smooth-sounding thing."

Full of songs which overwhelmingly came from country backgrounds, the corresponding *You're The Reason I'm Living* LP is often considered Darin's "country" album. However, a listen to the arrangements, which often veer into big band territory, shows that Darin wasn't interested in making a run-of-the-mill country album.

"I always get pros and cons about whether Darin was chasing a trend," Nik Venet said. "He wasn't. He was always gathering contributions to music. He felt country music had contributions that could cross over to pop and jazz, and vice versa."

Thus, songs written by Harlan Howard, Don Gibson, Gene Autry, and Glen Campbell were turned into swing numbers

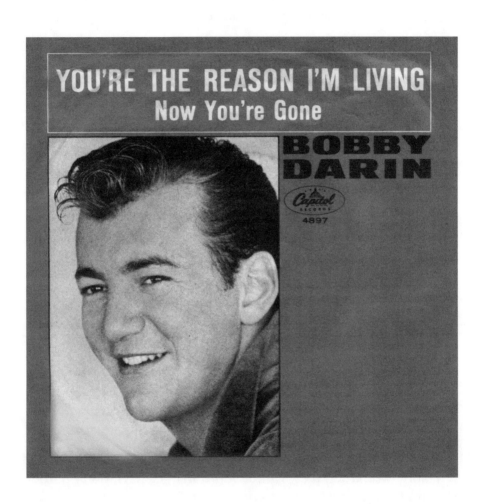

with heavy brass, courtesy of Shorty Rogers' arrangements. Highlights were renditions of Hank Williams' "(I Heard That) Lonesome Whistle" and Buck Owens' "Under Your Spell Again." The LP also included four songs arranged by Gerald Wilson, who had worked on Charles' *Modern Sounds* album.

"The horn players were all from Stan Kenton's band," Venet said of the *You're The Reason* sessions. "We were using dedicated jazz musicians, who played with Kenton and Miles Davis. We brought them on this session and they had the time of their lives. We worked charts there; they contributed a lot of the riffs.

"On every session with Darin, the musicians would all leave knowing they did something they felt good about," said Venet.

You're The Reason I'm Living also included Darin's first – and only – official recorded duet, with Mary Clayton on "Who Can I Count On." (After changing the spelling of her first name to "Merry," Clayton went on to enjoy some success in the '70s; in 1987 her song "Yes," from the *Dirty Dancing* soundtrack, became a hit.)

Darin's West Coast sessions featured some of the top-name studio musicians who later contributed to Phil Spector's famous Wall of Sound. But according to Nik Venet, Darin wasn't terribly picky about personnel, with one exception. He insisted that the drummer always be Earl Palmer, whose inventive beat had propelled the early rock'n'roll hits of Little Richard and Fats Domino.

"Bobby would tell me, "Nik, if you don't get Earl, don't bother building the band,'" Venet said. "Once, I called for Earl, and the contractor said he had him. We got to the studio and we had 40 or 50 musicians, but there was another drummer.

"It's the only time I ever saw Darin mad enough to punch somebody in the mouth," said Venet. "Darin got into it with the contractor. He cocked his fist. We had to grab Darin and pull him away."

In the studio, Darin was also very involved in working out arrangements. In fact, Venet goes so far as to say that Darin was co-arranger on nearly all of his Capitol tracks. Capitol producer Tom Morgan concurred that Darin was always there to chip in his two cents.

"Even with Billy May," Morgan remembered. "Bobby was trying to give Billy May total control, but he still had some influence." Morgan also recalled an instance in which Darin worked out an arrangement with Jimmy Haskell.

"We were in Studio A at Capitol, running down some tune," Morgan said. "We got to the ending and Jimmy Haskell, a brilliant guy without a big ego, asked Bobby 'What kind of ending do you want?'

"Bobby said, "If you're in the key of C, go to an A flat chord first,'" Morgan recalled. "I was impressed with that. I thought, goddamn, Bobby Darin doesn't have time in his life to fully study music. So as an arranger, he was not a thorough musician, but he would know, for instance, all the white notes on the keyboard."

Dick Behrke, who worked on Darin recording sessions and live appearances as both an arranger and musician, also confirmed Darin's hands-on work on arrangements.

"He had very strong and definite ideas of how he wanted it," Behrke said. "A lot of stuff evolved from rehearsal, stuff that had been in his mind for a while."

Guitarist/bassist Carol Kaye, one of the "Wrecking Crew" (the nickname later tagged to the small coterie of L.A. studio musicians who played on countless pop records of the 1960s, including Darin's) saw Darin's take-charge attitude from the musicians' perspective.

"He didn't just lie around and let other people do things for him," she recalled. "He wanted to make sure that it sounded good. He'd go in the booth and check the sound and check the arrangements. That's because he was a musician." Both his personality and his musicianship gave him a kinship with the musicians, she recalled.

"He was one of the guys, you know," she said. "He'd come in and hang out with the guys. I mean, he sat down and played some good drums. We'd jam on a little bit of jazz, or even a little bit of funk, because he was a pretty good all-around drummer. He had a good sense of timing. We'd all look at each other and say, 'Hey, this guy can play!'"

Meanwhile, Darin was on a hot streak as a songwriter. "18 Yellow Roses," his follow-up to "You're The Reason," also shot into the Top 10. Again featuring Glen Campbell on guitar, it was another country-style track (heavily influenced by Marty Robbins). Its too-corny lyric was saved by a surprise concluding twist.

The single was arranged by Jack Nitzsche, Spector's long-time arranger. The production's double-tracked lead vocal (in which Darin sang harmony with himself) was a relatively unusual feature on Darin's records. Venet recalled that Capitol Records was initially displeased with the results.

"They told me they weren't going to put it out," he said. "They didn't think it was a hit song. They thought they were getting Sinatra. They had no idea who Darin was."

The album *18 Yellow Roses and 11 Other Hits* was the first Darin LP to include cover versions of then-current Top 40 hits. Bobby Scott provided some interesting arrangements for Pomus & Shuman's "Can't Get Used To Losing You" (an Andy Williams hit) and a rockin'-with-horns take on Dion's "Ruby Baby." Most interesting was "Rhythm Of The Rain," in which Darin's relatively straightforward version was suddenly interrupted by Scott's jazz instrumental break. The album also featured four songs arranged by noted R&B arranger Bert Keyes, who had previously worked with Ruth Brown and LaVern Baker.

The album's best track was Darin's rendition of Skeeter Davis' "The End Of The World." He treated the classic weeper with the same restrained manner he used on *Earthy*'s folk tracks like "Strange Rain," and the performance was superb. Unfortunately, he coasted through the album's two genuine folk-based numbers, "Walk Right In" and "Reverend Mr. Black."

The sessions for the "18 Yellow Roses" single and album were grueling, recalled saxophonist Steve Douglas, who acted as contractor for the dates.

"I remember we did one of the longest sessions in the history of the union at the time," Douglas said. "We started a session at two in the afternoon. At 4:30 a.m., I'm on the phone calling musicians, because guys are falling out. I think that session went until ten in the morning, non-stop. A few of us got rich in one night."

Naturally, Capitol was not pleased with Darin's expensive approach to studio time. Douglas, who later produced some Darin tracks, recalled Darin's attitude about the label's rules.

"Bobby didn't give a damn," said Douglas. "He kind of ran roughshod over everybody. He ruffled a lot of feathers over there. Of course, Bobby was only a mild taste of what was to come with the rock bands."

For his next two 1963 singles, Darin abandoned country for the Brill Building teen-pop style associated with his old friend Don Kirshner's publishing empire. "Treat My Baby Good" (with a melody partially lifted from "Spanish Harlem") and "Be Mad Little Girl" (which echoed "Go Away Little Girl") almost sounded like genre exercises for Darin. While both were decent, neither stood out enough to make the Top 40.

Despite the plethora of releases, there were even more tracks recorded in 1963 which remained unreleased until the 1990s. Earlier that year, Darin recorded a number of standards (such as "Hello Young Lovers" and "Just In Time") with arranger Robert Florence, as well as additional songs with Gerald Wilson.

In the midst of all his recording activity, Darin was still knocking out audiences at spots like L.A.'s Cocoanut Grove, Harrah's Lake Tahoe, the Copa, and the Flamingo in Las Vegas. But in October 1963, he dropped a bomb. Darin announced that he was retiring from nightclub performances.

"Somehow [Flamingo chief] Morris Lansburgh got the idea that I wasn't going to work here anymore," Darin announced from the stage during his October 24th Flamingo opening. "Oh yes, I remember how he got the idea: I wrote him a letter and told him."

Variety wrote: "It will be a great loss to Las Vegas, because his act has hit a peak; he has definitely joined the few powerhouse performers who appear on the Strip."

Darin said his exit from the nightclub scene would allow him time to "widen his scope" in the entertainment business. No one could argue that he wasn't busy. But aside from the fact that he would have more time to devote to recording, films and television, there were three chief reasons for Darin's decision to give up the stage.

One was that he hoped it would save his marriage. In March 1963, Darin and Dee officially separated. Though they reconciled a few weeks later, Darin felt that giving up live performing was a sacrifice he could make to strengthen the marriage.

There was also a scare regarding Darin's health. He spent two days in the hospital after he collapsed following an outdoor concert at Freedomland in the Bronx in July 1963. Harriet Wasser recalled the scene backstage.

"He almost died," she said. "We thought it was going to be all over. They got the oxygen for him. The feeling was that he could not continue working the way he was working. That he would have to start thinking about other things."

The third reason was that Darin had found yet another area of the music industry to branch into. He had his own business to run.

Darin with Wayne Newton
(Las Vegas News Bureau)

15
"Green, Green"
The Music Publisher

Though Bobby Darin had always pronounced his respect and admiration for performers such as Ray Charles, Frank Sinatra and Donald O'Connor, there was another side of the entertainment business he was intrigued by. It was the side exemplified in many ways by his old friend Don Kirshner – the role of business mogul.

In the years since his initial work with Darin, Kirshner had built a pop empire of his publishing business. The company's stable of writers included Gerry Goffin and Carole King, Barry Mann and Cynthia Weil, and Jeff Barry and Ellie Greenwich. Without singing, playing or writing a note, Kirshner became a major force in the music industry.

Having seen the financial rewards it generated for Kirshner and others, and confident in his own ability to write and choose hit songs, Darin entered the publishing business with a bang in early 1963. He shelled out a half million dollars to purchase Trinity Music from his former managers Joe Csida and Ed Burton. As the Trinity umbrella included Adaris Music and Towne Music, Darin now gained publishing control over his own compositions.

Darin dubbed his new operation T.M. Music. In addition to its publishing activities, the firm would also act as a record production outlet for Darin. He would oversee a roster of songwriters and recording artists signed to the company.

While T.M. never built a staff to rival Kirshner's empire, Darin assembled some formidable talent. Writers Kenny Young and Artie Resnick teamed up to pen the Drifters' classic "Under The Boardwalk," and its hit follow-up "I've Got Sand In My Shoes." Another writer, Rudy Clark, delivered "The Shoop Shoop Song (It's In His Kiss)," a 1964 smash for Betty Everett. Clark and Resnick collaborated on "Good Lovin'," which The Young Rascals took to #1 in 1966.

Darin initially set up shop in New York's Brill Building. One of his first hiring decisions was to bring in his old friend and associate from the Atco days, Bobby Scott.

"I don't know what the hell you'd call me," Scott said of his approximately 18-month stint at T.M. "I was kind of director of personnel in the measure that Bobby had hired some young writers and was paying them a stipend every week and they were turning out material. And it was my job to kind of oversee what they were doing."

Scott felt Darin's branch into publishing was a wise move, based on Darin's own track record in the music industry: "He didn't pick losers very often. He knew how to write a hit song and he knew what good craftsmanship was. He was an excellent producer of records."

One artist brought into the T.M. fold by Scott was Jesse Colin Young, who would later go on to success with The Youngbloods (the band which recorded the '60s classic "Get Together"). Young's first album was produced by Scott under the T.M. aegis.

Scott enjoyed his T.M. experience, but he was somewhat taken aback by Darin's style when he put on the hat of publishing mogul.

"I saw that he naturally treated administrative people, of whom I was one, better than he treated the talent he had gathered together," Scott said. "He played the business-man well. I was surprised."

While Scott held great respect for Darin's songwriting ability, he felt that Darin expected other writers to share the same writing philosophy. As Ahmet Ertegun alluded to, Darin's method was "crank 'em out." Scott said Darin did not believe in the philosophy of a writer pouring himself into a pop composition at great length.

"The idea of 'great pains' totally escaped him," Scott said. "His understanding of the differing processes in differing talents was non-existent." Because of such philosophical differences, Scott eventually left T.M. on amicable terms.

Another past Darin associate, Jim McGuinn, also hitched up with T.M. McGuinn worked as a staff writer for the firm – at 35 dollars a week – for about a year. "The stuff I wrote wasn't commercially successful, but it was a good experience," he said.

McGuinn's most fondly-remembered T.M. composition was "Beach Ball," co-written with fellow staffer Frank Gari. After finishing the song, the duo played it for Darin, who liked it and immediately booked studio time. The demo for "Beach Ball" was recorded by a quartet consisting of Darin (on drums), McGuinn, Gari, and Kenny Young, with all four providing vocals.

After the session, Darin decided that the recording was too good to be a mere demo. He released it as a single under the name "The City Surfers," with the production credit "Produced by T.M. Music." Though not a hit, "Beach Ball" became a collectible among surf music fans and was so well-regarded that it was included in the compilation album *Summer Means Fun*, a volume of the "Pebbles" series of overlooked '60s gems.

"Somebody had fun making this one," wrote Nigel Strange in the album's liner notes. "The track itself is a remarkable transmutation of Spector's 'Da Do Run Run' into the beach idiom." A cover version of "Beach Ball" by Jimmy Hannan (with the then-unknown Bee Gees on background vocals) became a Top 5 hit in Australia in 1964.

Darin also opened up a T.M. office in the Capitol Tower in Los Angeles, and continued to show he had a keen eye for talented personnel. For a while, the office was headed by Steve Douglas, the ace session saxophonist who played on Darin's records, Phil Spector's productions, the records of The Beach Boys, and many others.

Another T.M. staff writer and producer in California was Terry Melcher. The son of Doris Day, Melcher had achieved some success as the youngest staff producer at Columbia Records. Along with his partner, future Beach Boy Bruce Johnston, Melcher had hits as lead singer of the Rip Chords ("Hey Little Cobra") and Bruce & Terry ("Summer Means Fun"). He would later go on to produce The Byrds and Paul Revere & The Raiders.

Shortly after opening the West Coast office, Darin called Melcher and lured him away from Columbia.

"There was a little celebrity enclave in Toluca Lake," Melcher recalled. "Bobby and Sandra were living in a house Sinatra used to have, by the Lakeside Golf Club, near Bob Hope's house. I used to go over on Sundays. Bobby was very personable. He was funny and he had a lot of magic and a tremendous amount of energy."

Darin and Melcher collaborated on a few songs, including "Hot Rod U.S.A.," an authentic, superb Beach Boys/ Jan & Dean-style rocker that Melcher recorded with The Rip Chords. It was proof that Darin could appreciate, and excel in, another genre of music. Another collaboration, "My Mom," was a minor hit for the Osmond Brothers. Also

138

for T.M., Melcher and Bruce Johnston composed "Beach Girl," a minor 1964 hit for Pat Boone.

In 1964, Darin produced an album by Los Angeles Rams football star Roosevelt Grier. *Soul City* included two Darin-penned songs, the title track and "Down So Long" (which was the B-side of Darin's "Treat My Baby Good" single). Darin also wrote the LP's liner notes, calling it "an album for everyone who has ever felt oppressed."

T.M.'s greatest success came with Wayne Newton, whom Darin signed personally. Because many of Newton's records bore only the "Produced by T.M. Music" credit, the extent of Darin's involvement in Newton's career was not widely known until years after Darin's death.

At the suggestion of Paul Anka and Dick Clark, Darin went to see an act called The Newton Brothers at The Copacabana in 1963. He was impressed by Wayne Newton, and signed the act to T.M. with the intent of spotlighting the young vocalist. The first couple of single releases were credited to "Wayne Newton with The Newton Brothers"; after that, Wayne Newton received solo credit.

Darin intended Newton to be a contemporary pop artist and many of Newton's initial releases produced under Darin's auspices bear little resemblance to the Vegas-style material Newton would become famous for.

For Newton's first single, Darin dipped not into his own T.M. bag, but into Don Kirshner's Screen Gems-Columbia Music for Barry Mann and Cynthia Weil's "Heart." With production supervised by Steve Douglas, the track had a solid, commercial sound, and reached #82 on the charts.

Newton's second single for T.M. would become his signature song, "Danke Schoen." The story of how "Danke Schoen" became a Wayne Newton record is legendary – and somewhat convoluted. But one fact all parties agree on is that the song was supposed to have been recorded by Bobby Darin.

Nik Venet first heard "Danke Schoen" while visiting Europe and searching for songs for a Ray Anthony album he was producing. It was a German instrumental hit, composed and performed by orchestra leader Bert Kaempfert (who had a huge American hit with "Wonderland By Night" in 1960). When Venet expressed interest in recording the song with Ray Anthony, the song's publisher, Hal Fein, informed him that an English lyric was being written, and that it would be ideal for a Bobby Darin vocal.

On the condition that Darin would agree to record the song, Fein offered Venet a United States exclusive – no other American artist or producer would even hear the song until Darin's record came out. After playing the demo for Darin (who agreed that the song was a smash), Venet, Capitol and Darin were granted the exclusive first crack at "Danke Schoen."

"In those days, when you got an exclusive on a song, that was a guarantee the song was being recorded," Venet said. "You never went back on your word."

According to Venet, Darin recorded "Danke Schoen" and then went into the studio with Newton. At that point, Newton recorded a vocal, using the instrumental track co-produced by and intended for Darin.

The session was then turned over to Steve Douglas to complete production. Production credit for "Danke Schoen," like "Heart," read "Produced by T.M. Music. Production Supervised by Steve Douglas."

The finished product sounded like a "Mack The Knife" sequel, and was one of the most vibrant non-rock records since "Mack." Jimmy Haskell's arrangement swung, and Newton's savvy vocal sold the song brilliantly. The record eventually reached #13 (and #3 on the Easy Listening charts).

When the record was released, everyone was pleased except "Danke Schoen" publisher Hal Fein, who wanted the song done by the proven hit-maker Darin, not the newcomer Newton.

"The publisher just shit," Steve Douglas recalled. "He was really furious, and I guess rightfully so. Bobby was very generous in giving that tune to Wayne. Bobby wanted Wayne to have a hit record."

Afraid that this sure-fire hit would be overlooked because Newton was still unknown, Fein called his initial contact, Nik Venet, on the carpet.

"I had to guarantee him," Venet recalled, "that if Newton's record didn't go to number one, Darin would do a 'Danke Schoen' single and album with five of Hal's songs on it. I had to guarantee him on my life. And while I was on the phone with Hal, Darin was in the other room, laughing his ass off, knowing that I was putting my life on the line with this publisher."

"Danke Schoen" didn't reach the top, although Fein was apparently pleased enough with the record's performance. Still, many at Capitol questioned Darin's decision to give the song away.

"I think if Darin would have done it, it would have sold five times as many records as Wayne Newton," Tom Morgan said. "It's really Bobby Darin's record, a 'Mack The Knife' feeling."

After "Danke Schoen," Darin continued to serve as a kind of "executive producer" of Newton's tracks, with most sessions being handled by Steve Douglas. While Newton's albums tended to veer toward middle-of-the-road standards, his singles retained a relatively contemporary pop sensibility.

Darin and T.M. staffer Rudy Clark co-wrote "Shirl Girl" as a follow-up to "Danke," but it reached only #58. A Darin-Artie Resnick collaboration for Newton, "Dream Baby," was a blatant re-write of "Dream Lover." Newton also recorded early compositions by Bruce Johnston ("Someone's Ahead Of You") and Barry Gibb ("They'll Never Know").

One of the strangest – and best – Newton records of that era was "Comin' On Too Strong," released in early 1965. Produced by Terry Melcher and Bruce Johnston, the track was styled after The Beach Boys' "Don't Worry Baby." Given instructions to produce a hit, Melcher and Johnston handled the bulk of the vocals themselves, with Newton only chiming in a few lines at the beginning of the verses.

"That was funny for Wayne, and I know it was a little awkward," Melcher recalled. "But my instructions were pretty much to go in and make it sound like a real 'West Coast' recording. We didn't think Wayne could handle the falsetto part."

The record reached #65 on the charts. In his autobiography *Once Before I Go,* Newton wrote that he asked Darin to "pull the record" after a couple of weeks because he did not want a hit he could not reproduce on stage, *sans* Bruce and Terry. According to Newton, Darin concurred, and promotion on the record stopped.

Darin's eye for recording and songwriting talent, combined with publishing royalties from his own compositions such as "You're The Reason I'm Living" and "18 Yellow Roses," made T.M. a success. The firm's gross business climbed from $321,000 in 1963 (Darin's first year) to $450,000 by the end of 1964. At that point, Darin predicted that the company would pay for itself by the end of 1966. Thirteen T.M. copyrights charted in 1964, and T.M. Music was ranked 18th in the Top 100 BMI affiliates for the year.

16

"The Good Life"

1964

The most acclaimed film role of Darin's career came in *Captain Newman, M.D.*, which opened in Los Angeles on Christmas Day, 1963.

Darin received "co-starring" credit amidst an impressive cast including Gregory Peck, Tony Curtis, Eddie Albert, Angie Dickinson and Robert Duvall.

Something of a precursor to *M*A*S*H*, the film is set in the psychiatric ward of an army hospital in 1944. Darin, Albert, and Duvall play patients under the care of Peck's Captain Newman. The script calls for all three actors to give over-the-edge performances in confronting their characters' problems.

Darin's performance gained the most attention. His character, Corporal Tompkins, carries around a load of guilt for deserting a friend in a burning aircraft. To get Tompkins to confront the problem, the doctor administers sodium pentothal.

The next ten minutes of the film are Darin's. In a long, tough, serious scene full of physical twisting, yelling and crying, Corporal Tompkins relives the experience of watching his comrade die in the crash.

Darin gave an intense, full-tilt performance which walked a fine line between remarkable dramatic characterization and scenery chewing. While *The New York Herald Tribune* wrote "Bobby Darin is a gem of miscasting...his contortions under sodium pentothal are at best embarrassing," *Variety* called his "high-powered histrionics...the film's most moving passage." Even *The New York Times* viewed the performance positively: "Believe it or not, Bobby Darin plays the kid touchingly."

Darin did the scene in one take, astounding director David Miller and the rest of the cast and crew. Nik Venet met Darin as he came off the set.

"I've made reservations for us to have lunch," Darin told Venet. "I knew that if I didn't get this scene done in one take that we couldn't have lunch, and I wanted to put myself up against the wall."

"I still don't know if he was pulling my leg," Venet said.

Co-star Gregory Peck praised Darin's acting ability in a 1966 interview. "It was certainly no surprise to me that Bobby could act and bring the same exciting qualities to his acting that he brought to his singing," Peck said. "Bobby conveys pathos. Bobby, in his work, is touching; he's moving. I hope to work with Bobby again. I like him very much."

Despite an ultimately pointless plot which continually drifts from one story to another only to kill time, *Captain Newman, M.D.* was a solid box office hit, the 21st biggest picture of 1964, according to *Variety.*

The film's success was helped by notice of Darin's performance. *Variety* remarked, "In addition to serving as a box-office stimulant via word-of-mouth, [it] may earn Darin a supporting nomination in the Oscar derby."

The prediction was accurate. The Academy Award nominations were announced on February 24, and Darin received a nomination for Best Supporting Actor.

The ceremony was held on April 13 in the Santa Monica Civic Auditorium. Though the Best Supporting Actor Oscar went to Melvyn Douglas for his performance in *Hud*, Darin called his brush with Oscar "the most exciting event of my life. The fact that I didn't win was totally unimportant."

Darin's performance also gained notice overseas. He received another Golden Globe nomination from the Hollywood Foreign Press Association, as well as the French Film Critics' Award for Best Foreign Actor. Feeling that his acting abilities were more appreciated abroad, Darin considered moving to Paris. In a 1972 interview with *The Los Angeles Times'* Estelle Changas, Darin expressed regret about not making that move.

"I didn't have the courage to do what I knew was right," he said. "I felt the French would have allowed me to have a career as both an actor and a performer. I didn't respond perhaps because it meant I would have to pull up stakes and forsake comforts. I'm not a man of regrets, but reflecting on this doesn't make me happy."

Darin was involved in another 1964 movie, though not as an actor. He wrote the music for the teen film *The Lively Set*, starring James Darren and Pamela Tiffin. Five Darin pop songs appear, including two numbers sung by Joanie Sommers and a Darin-Terry Melcher collaboration, "Boss Barracuda," sung by the Surfaris (of "Wipe Out" fame).

The most interesting writing credit was on "Look At Me," sung on the soundtrack by future game show host Wink Martindale. The song was written by Darin and Randy Newman, in their only collaboration.

Darin also appeared in two television dramas in 1964 – an episode of the series "Wagon Train" and an hour-long "Bob Hope Chrysler Theatre" drama called "Murder In The First."

Musically, 1964 was a low point for Darin. It was the first year he failed to land a Top 40 hit since 1957. Of course,

1964 was the year of the rock revolution ushered in by The Beatles and The British Invasion. Despite the fact that he was one of the American singers displaced by the Liverpudlians, Darin admired The Beatles.

"He loved them," recalled Nik Venet. "He had no negative reaction whatsoever. He just hoped there was enough time on the air for other people to be played. He felt The Beatles were a phenomenon like Presley.

"Bobby always thought Presley was a cosmic happening," Venet said. "He used to say, 'There have been two cosmic happenings in this century – Presley and Kennedy.' When The Beatles came, he said, 'I think I'm into my third cosmic happening.'"

Darin was also open to The Beatles' less-polished rivals, The Rolling Stones.

"He loved the way the Stones recorded," Venet said. "He liked that haphazard feeling. He liked Mick Jagger. He used to say 'If that guy ever hits Vegas, we're going to have to pack it up.' Of course, at that time, we thought everybody would eventually play Vegas. Bobby admired Mick Jagger for his recklessness with a song."

There was no chance that Darin's first single of 1964 could compete with the new sounds on the airwaves. Darin had recorded "I Wonder Who's Kissing Her Now," a song which dated back to 1909, at his first Capitol session in July 1962. Dusted off for single release in February, it charted at a lowly #93.

Its flip side was a leftover from the *Oh! Look At Me Now* session with Tom Morgan and Billy May. The snappy "As Long As I'm Singing" was perhaps Darin's greatest songwriting effort in the "standard" style. It crams a lot of energy into 1:35 and Darin used the number as the opener in his live show for years, as well as singing it on a memorable "Jack Benny Show" episode.

Darin tried the country style again on his next effort, "The Things In This House," but this time the country affectations seemed too forced. In fact, the song can be looked at as a bit of a parody, with lyrics such as "our dog won't eat." Still, it was a fine vocal, with solid production by Jim Economides.

The flip side, "Wait By The Water" was a rocking adaptation of the standard "Wade In The Water." With a big beat and electric guitar, it was Darin's most contemporary sounding single side since joining Capitol.

Ironically, Darin's highest chart placement of '64 came when Atco dug out his 1960 French-language recording of "Milord" (which had earlier been a hit for Edith Piaf). The record picked up a fair mount of airplay, hitting #45 on the pop charts, and #11 on *Billboard's* Easy Listening chart. Atco slapped "Milord" and its flip "Golden Earrings" on a "new" album called *Winners,* which otherwise consisted of the Bobby Scott-arranged jazz material recorded in 1960.

"Don't Rain On My Parade"

1965-66

For his first single of 1965, Darin joined the seemingly endless parade of singers who recorded "Hello, Dolly!" Re-doing a Louis Armstrong hit had worked for him once before with "Mack The Knife." To make the connection even clearer, arranger Richard Wess was brought back to the fold.

"Hello, Dolly!" opened with the "Mack" bass line, and its arrangement basically recreated the "Mack" swinging style. Fingers snapped in the background, and Darin even gave it a "Look out, old Dolly is back!" closing. But the song had already been beaten into the ground too much to duplicate the original's success. It reached only #79 on the *Billboard* pop chart, but became a respectable Easy Listening hit at #18.

The *From Hello Dolly To Goodbye Charlie* album contained some of the best standard-style recordings of Darin's career. Here, he tackled more recent compositions, rather than going back to songs of earlier eras. Highlights were Anthony Newley and Leslie Bricusse's "Once In A Lifetime (Only Once)" and Henry Mancini and Johnny Mercer's "Charade" (which Darin sped up significantly, much as he had done with "That's

All"). Both songs became regulars in Darin's nightclub act. The album also featured Darin's own version of the song he and Randy Newman co-wrote for *The Lively Set*, "Look At Me."

Darin's next single was an imported European ballad, "Venice Blue." For the single and corresponding album, Darin teamed up with Steve Douglas, then working as a staff producer at Capitol.

"By no means did I produce Bobby's records," Douglas explained. "I was the guy in the booth. He made his own records. You just kind of stood out of his way."

Douglas recalled Darin's enthusiasm about "Venice Blue": "I got a call from Bobby and he said, 'I found this fantastic song. We've got to get in the studio right away.' He was very enthused, very excited. A few days later, he played me the song, and I must say I wasn't too excited about 'Venice Blue.' I thought it was a fairly ordinary tune. I never did understand what he was excited about. He wanted the record rushed right out."

Despite a lush orchestral production and a fine Darin reading, "Venice Blue" could only "bubble under" to #133. Even Easy Listening stations stayed away from it.

Douglas' assessment of the song was much closer to the bone than Darin's. Its semi-appealing melody was sabotaged by its English lyric, which contained gems such as "To pigeons in the square I say my last goodbyes / Goodbye, oh vanished dreams, goodbye old bridge of sighs."

Despite the fact that MOR songs were having extreme difficulty cracking the pop chart, Darin inexplicably thought "Venice Blue" would succeed.

"I have a vivid memory of Bobby reading *Billboard* magazine," Douglas recalled. "I'm looking at him and he's real somber. He says, 'This is the first time a record of mine didn't get a Pick of the Week.' He was really quite upset by that. He genuinely believed that was going to be a hit record."

The *Venice Blue* album, like *Hello Dolly,* was a strictly MOR collection. Another Newley-Bricusse song, "Who Can I Turn To," stood out, as did Darin's version of the *West Side Story* song "Somewhere." The album featured a number of arrangements by Ernie Freeman (Sinatra's "Softly As I Leave You," Petula Clark's "This Is My Song"). The only stylistic variations came in two Darin compositions. "In A World Without You" (written with Rudy Clark) was perhaps Darin's best country-oriented song, with a fine lyric. "You Just Don't Know," loosely in the style of "You're The Reason I'm Living," was the most interesting pop-oriented song on the LP.

"I think the rest of the album was just done to get an album out," Douglas said. "It went by pretty quickly. I said, 'Gee, Bobby, how 'bout some more Bobby Darin songs?' I wish I could have worked with him on his stuff – the rock'n'roll stuff."

If Darin's recent efforts had seemed anachronistic in the pop world of 1965, his next single, released in June, would be surprisingly contemporary. "When I Get Home," co-written by Darin and Russell Alquist, opened with the loud bang of a drum, and progressed into a very contemporary folk-rock production. The record had "1965" written all over it and was Darin's best non-MOR single since "Multiplication." Though it stands as one of Darin's most appealing pop-rock singles, it was completely overlooked, becoming the first "regular" Darin single (not counting from-the-vaults reissues or seasonal songs) since the pre-"Splish Splash" days not to chart at all.

However, Liverpool's Searchers took notice and scored a British hit with the song later in 1965. It was the second time in '65 that a Liverpool beat group hit with a Darin song. Earlier, Gerry & The Pacemakers' cover of Darin's 1960 ballad "I'll Be There" became a Top 20 hit in both the U.S. and Britain. Perhaps Darin wasn't so anachronistic after all.

Darin's final Capitol single, released in August 1965, was "That Funny Feeling," the title song he composed for the third and final Darin-Dee movie. The song earned Darin a Golden Globe nomination for Best Original Song in a film. (Its flip side, "Gyp The Cat" was another "Mack The Knife" rip-off, this one written by Darin and Don Wolf.)

That Funny Feeling opened in Britain in June and in the U.S. in August. Though it was inoffensive fluff, it – combined with an 18-plus month absence from the screen – halted the momentum Darin's acting career gained with *Captain Newman, M.D.*

"Darin handles an undemanding role well," wrote *Variety*, while noting the "tortuous contrivance" of the film's screenplay. On the plus side, Darin had a chance to work with one of his idols, Donald O'Connor, who received third billing immediately after the Darin-Dee team.

During Darin's three-year span at Capitol, his status declined from one of pop's most dependable hit-makers to an artist who couldn't seem to buy a hit. Though he scored two Top 10 hits at the label ("You're The Reason I'm Living" and "18 Yellow Roses"), neither are considered "essential" Darin, and no Capitol recordings have survived as oldies radio staples the way a half-dozen of his Atco hits have.

When his Capitol contract expired in the summer of 1965, Darin decided it was time to move on. He moved to familiar waters – back to Ahmet Ertegun and Atlantic Records. Though Darin had left Atco more than three years earlier, the label hadn't given up. They continued to release old Darin records well into 1965, the last of which was a five-year-old recording of "Minnie The Moocher."

Darin's first single for the label found him squarely back into the contemporary rock scene. With a Searchers-like guitar, a big-beat, and an angry protest lyric, "We Didn't Ask To Be Brought Here" is literally the most electric record Darin ever made.

Though not an explicit anti-Vietnam protest, Darin's lyric exhibited the same kind of undefined anti-establishment disenchantment that characterized Sonny & Cher's "I Got You Babe." Like the earlier "When I Get Home," it should have been a hit, and perhaps only Darin's name held it back. The record "bubbled under" the charts at #117 in October.

A true rarity until its mid-'90s release on CD, "We Didn't Ask To Be Brought Here" is perhaps the greatest overlooked gem of Darin's career. It was another example of how easily – and how successfully – Darin could relate to another genre of music, one which no one of his show-business stature had embraced before.

The flip side, "Funny What Love Can Do" opened with Darin's wailing blues harmonica. Credited to Darin, the song lifts its melody from Jimmy Reed's "Baby What Do You Want Me To Do" and features a very heavy electric guitar. It was another effective, sharp break from the expected Bobby Darin style.

Nevertheless, Darin was still not about to throw his hat into the rock ring, and since The Beatles' arrival, no artist had successfully straddled the Vegas and rock sides of the music scene. The camps weren't warring; they merely had no relation to each other.

After "We Didn't Ask To Be Brought Here" bombed, Darin at least temporarily chose the familiarity of the Vegas world. The timing was right, anyway. Darin had grown restless during his retirement from the stage, and decided to return to live performances. He would open 1966 in the familiar confines of the Flamingo Hotel in Las Vegas.

It had been two-and-a-half years since Darin had performed on stage. Recording, writing, acting, and his T.M. business kept him busy but not satisfied. "I'm a singer of songs and anything I do other than that is an offshoot," Darin explained at the time.

Vegas welcomed Darin back with open arms. "Bobby Darin is back with an exciting act which is even better than the one he had here when he established the showroom's all-time attendance record," *Variety* wrote of his Flamingo return. "Darin is one of the few nitery performers who click with all age groups."

Groucho Marx attended Darin's opening night. Darin introduced him and briefly turned over the microphone to the legendary comedian. "When I first saw you, you were only a singer," Marx said to him. "Now you're a singer and an actor."

Darin's act included a 10-minute impression routine, in which he would impersonate James Cagney, Cary Grant, Marlon Brando, Walter Brennan, Dean Martin, Jerry Lewis, Clark Gable, Burt Lancaster, Jimmy Stewart, Robert Mitchum, and W. C. Fields. The routine was set in a Hollywood barroom and framed by the song "One For My Baby." Richard Wess conducted a 29-piece orchestra.

In March, Darin opened a celebrity-packed two-week stand at The Cocoanut Grove in Hollywood. Attendees included Andy Williams and Claudine Longet, Mia Farrow, George Burns, Jack Benny, Ben Gazzara, Henry Mancini, Anthony Newley, and Joanne Woodward.

Highlights included Darin's show-stopping performance of "Some Of These Days" and his more low-key version of Roger Miller's 1965 hit "King Of The Road."

"It's quite a thrill when a guy like that does your music," Miller said in a 1966 interview. "When I wrote 'King Of The Road,' I was trying to write something with a 'Mack The Knife'-type feel – that finger-snap thing."

That spring, Darin also set his sights on television, as he starred opposite Eve Arden in "Who's Watching The Fleshpot," a pilot for a projected comedy-drama series to be called "It's A Sweet Life." The pilot aired as an episode of the popular drama "Run For Your Life," with Darin playing a friend of Ben Gazzara's who operated a tour service at a fashionable resort on the French Riviera. "It's A Sweet Life" did not make NBC's fall schedule.

Darin returned to The Copacabana in April for the first time in almost three years. He performed The Beatles' "Yesterday" and accompanied himself on guitar for "I Got Plenty of Nothing" from *Porgy & Bess.*

His first Atlantic album also hit stores that month. Titled *Bobby Darin Sings The Shadow Of Your Smile,* the collection's first side featured all five songs nominated for the 1965 Academy Award Song of the Year.

Darin's lovely renditions of the title track (from *The Sand-pipers*), and "I Will Wait For You" (from *The Umbrellas of Cherbourg*) were top-notch. Side Two of the album was a hodge-podge of standards highlighted by fine versions of "Lover Come Back To Me" and "It's Only A Paper Moon."

The only Darin original on the album was "Rainin'," a Dixieland-folk hybrid. No producer was credited on the album, but an unreleased 1966 documentary about Darin, which shows scenes from the "Rainin'" recording session, provides incontrovertible evidence that Darin supervised these sessions, from both the studio floor and the booth.

On May 14, 1966, Bobby Darin reached a milestone it was once thought he would never achieve – his 30th birthday.

Some press members whom Darin had rubbed the wrong way noted the occasion. In a vicious article titled "Egotist Bobby Darin At 30 Hits Low Note As Legend." *New York Post* writer Bob Ellison concluded, "This Saturday is his birthday...It is not a national holiday."

For his next album, Darin shifted his sights from motion picture scores to the Broadway stage. The result was one of his most appealing albums and singles of the decade.

Darin at The Flamingo, 1966
(Las Vegas News Bureau)

Darin was back in his prime swinging mode for "Mame," the title song of the Jerry Herman musical which had yet to open. The track crackled with the show-stopper pizazz that had been absent from Darin's non-rock singles since the days of "Lazy River." While the single was too adult-oriented to crack the Top 40 (it peaked at #53), it climbed all the way to #3 on *Billboard's* Easy Listening chart, becoming Darin's all-time biggest hit in that format. (The chart did not exist at the time of "Mack The Knife.")

The corresponding *In A Broadway Bag* was classic Darin, arguably the best album of standard material he ever recorded. Darin's vocal performance was strong and stylistic on the uptempo songs, and tender and interpretive on the ballads.

Darin shone on yet another Newley-Bricusse composition, "Feeling Good" (from *The Roar Of The Greasepaint – The Smell Of The Crowd*), a rare show tune which incorporated some R&B overtones.

Two songs previously recorded by Frank Sinatra – "I Believe In You" and "Once Upon A Time" – also stood out, and Darin certainly gave Old Blue Eyes a run for his money with these two performances. The latter, an Andre Previn-Betty Comden ballad from *All American*, featured perhaps the most strikingly beautiful ballad performance of Darin's career.

Darin pulled out all stops for the *Funny Girl* tune "Don't Rain On My Parade." Shorty Rogers' arrangement swung furiously, and Darin took the opportunity to deliver one of his most dynamic vocals. The song suited Darin's swinging style so well that it appropriately became the opening number in his nightclub act shortly after the release of the album.

With a superb selection of songs, tasteful arrangements, and utterly brilliant singing, *In A Broadway Bag* was consummate Bobby Darin. Though some Darin fans favor his rock'n'roll, Top 40, or folk records more than his recordings of standards, this album is essential listening to grasp the essence of Darin's art. This is the style that many people remember Bobby Darin for, and he never did it better. Few have.

On August 1, 1966, Darin recorded 13 tracks in Los Angeles including "Danke Schoen," "On A Clear Day," "What Now My Love" and "Mountain Greenery." No tracks were ever released, and it is believed that these tracks (as well as three dozen additional unreleased Darin cuts spanning 1958-1967) were destroyed in a fire in Atlantic's warehouse.

August also saw the public acknowledgement of the end of the Darin-Dee marriage. On August 12, Dee filed for divorce in Los Angeles Superior Court, charging extreme cruelty and mental suffering, and asking for custody of five-year-old Dodd.

According to the UPI news report, Dee testified that Darin "woke up one morning and didn't want to be married anymore," then packed his belongings and left the family home.

A report surfaced that Dee's mother had moved into their home, much to Darin's displeasure, but when asked why the marriage ended, Darin only replied, "I don't know. Sandra doesn't know. Nobody knows."

The divorce was finalized on March 7, 1967, with Darin paying a monthly child support of $1,200.

Atlantic Records publicity photo

"If I Were-A Carpenter"

On August 15, 1966, three days after Sandra filed for divorce, Bobby Darin recorded two songs in Los Angeles. Both were written by Tim Hardin, a singer-songwriter attracting attention on the post-Dylan folk circuit. Hardin's debut album had gained critical notice, but few sales.

His songs were gentle and poetic in a somewhat mysterious way. They did not adhere to the traditional pop song structure, yet they were in neither the protest nor stream-of-consciousness veins that marked the work of many of Dylan's disciples. As a lyricist, Hardin eschewed clever wordplay; his rhymes were often obvious, sometimes even awkward. Yet there was a beauty in the subtle way they conveyed a feeling rather than a message. You could always empathize with Hardin, even when you couldn't completely understand his songs.

The first Tim Hardin song Darin recorded was "If I Were A Carpenter." It would change the course of Darin's career.

Obviously, Hardin's material was a departure for Darin, especially coming off his *Shadow Of Your Smile / In A Broadway Bag* recordings. A few years earlier, Darin and Nik Venet had gone to see Hardin perform at The Tin Angel in

Greenwich Village. Venet recalled that Darin and Hardin hit it off well, but Darin apparently never seriously considered recording any of Hardin's songs until he was approached by the men who owned the company that published them: Charles Koppelman and Don Rubin.

Koppelman and Rubin, appropriately enough, started in the business under Don Kirshner. They began as songwriters at Aldon Music in 1962, then learned the ropes of publishing and production. By 1966, they operated Koppelman-Rubin Associates, a record production company which handled the recordings of Tim Hardin, The Lovin' Spoonful, and The Turtles, among others. Faithful Virtue Music, their publishing arm, had a goldmine with the songs of Hardin and the Spoonful's John Sebastian.

The story of how Koppelman and Rubin pitched songs to Darin became something of a legend over the years. A 1966 article in the British music publication *Melody Maker* quoted Darin as saying that the pair unsuccessfully pitched John Sebastian's "Do You Believe In Magic," "Younger Girl" and "Daydream" to Darin before they got him to record "Carpenter."

Darin himself incorporated a comic take on the story into his nightclub act of the 1970s, adding "Summer In The City" (another Spoonful smash) into the tale. Darin joked about how he continually turned down these eventual million sellers, and how the publishers' approach to him would change every time they returned with new material. They first addressed him as "Mr. Darin"; then, as they became cockier, they greeted him as "Bob," then "B.D."

While these stories made for good copy (and comedy), they exaggerate the truth. "Do You Believe In Magic" was the Spoonful's first hit, and Koppelman and Rubin were not about to give it away while they were trying to break the band.

When asked about Darin's story that "Magic" was part of their original pitch to him, Don Rubin said, "That does stretch it a bit. That was the Spoonful's first hit, and it was only after that success that we could pitch John Sebastian songs to other singers."

Rubin confirmed that "Daydream" was offered to – and turned down by – Darin: "He kind of looked at us crossed-eyed and shook his head and said, 'That's not for me.'"

Though neither Koppelman nor Rubin remember for sure, it's likely that the "Younger Girl" part of the story is also true. If so, Darin's rejection of the song is much more understandable. Its lyric would not have been credible coming from Darin, and it never became a Top 40 hit despite attempts by The Spoonful, The Critters and The Hondells.

Still, Koppelman & Rubin's increasingly successful track record was enough to convince Darin to accept their next offer. "I'll record anything you tell me to record," he told them the next time they visited his office. When they played him "If I Were A Carpenter," he said, "This is the song. I'm not letting this one get away."

In a *Melody Maker* article titled "Darin Bounces Back – Thanks To The Younger Guys," Darin gave credit to Koppelman and Rubin for pointing him in the new musical direction.

"I was still hipped on big bands and strings and all that," Darin told the publication. "I'd gotten to think that was my bag."

"Bobby was kind of going through his own metamorphosis at the time," recalled Don Rubin. "He kind of changed his mind-set. He wanted to shed his cabaret image and get with the music of the '60s."

Darin insisted that Koppelman and Rubin produce his record themselves, though they usually relied on producers Erik Jacobsen (The Spoonful, Hardin) and Joe Wissert (Turtles). Perhaps because he was trying a different direction, Darin agreed to be less involved in the production than usual. Still, despite the fact that he decided to leave the producing and arranging to others, Darin's musical instincts wound up as a significant factor in the success of "If I Were A Carpenter."

While working on the song, Koppelman, Rubin, and arranger Don Peake were having problems coming up with the right bass arrangement.

"Darin walked over to the bass player," said Rubin, "and within a few minutes, Darin sang what he thought the bass line should be. It turned out to be the bass line we used, and the main lick in that record is the great bass line."

After the session, Koppelman, Rubin and Darin felt they had a special combination of top-notch song and inspired vocal performance. Rubin flew to New York to play the track for Atlantic's Ahmet Ertegun and Jerry Wexler. Both Koppelman and Rubin recall that the Atlantic brass was taken aback.

"Ahmet and Jerry were very set on Bobby's cabaret style, and very locked into that," said Rubin. "They couldn't see this change. They kind of rejected this weird notion that Bobby was now going to be a folk-rock singer."

Undaunted, Koppelman and Rubin decided to take their case to radio directly. Their promotion man took the tape to KHJ, then the top radio station in Los Angeles. KHJ played the tape, which put pressure on Atlantic to release the track as a single. Once that decision was reached, the label put its full promotional muscle behind the record.

Another Hardin song, "Misty Roses," was recorded the same day as "Carpenter," but temporarily held from release. Atlantic issued "If I Were A Carpenter" backed with the Darin-composed "Rainin'" (the lone track from *The Shadow Of Your Smile* which could pass for contemporary pop).

Despite the initial KHJ acceptance, "If I Were A Carpenter" was initially a tough sell to radio. It had been three years since Darin's last Top 40 hit and in the interim, the pop revolution ushered in by The Beatles virtually swept away all performers who had roots in the 1950s. The fact that the overwhelming majority of Darin's previous mid-'60s singles were aimed at the adult market didn't help either.

Ironically, those same "good music" stations which had spun Darin's "Hello, Dolly!" and "Mame" emphatically rejected "If I Were A Carpenter." Though the song now seems a perfect example of a record which could be appreciated by both the Sinatra and Donovan crowds, it was then considered too left-field, and the release never dented *Billboard's* Easy Listening chart.

But more importantly, Top 40 radio soon came around, and "Carpenter" entered the charts on October 8, 1966. It eventually climbed all the way to #8. (The song also reached #9 in Britain.)

Considering the obstacles, the success of "If I Were A Carpenter" stands as one of the greatest triumphs of Darin's career as a recording artist, testament to both a great song and a brilliant interpretation. Though it has since been recorded by literally scores of other artists, from The Four Tops to Johnny Cash & June Carter to Bob Seger, Darin's version still stands as the first, and the definitive, cover.

Darin himself had such regard for the song that it remained in his repertoire for the rest of his life. That is no small indication of how important this particular song was to him. "Splish Splash" drifted in and out of Darin's concerts over the years. He even became briefly disenchanted with "Mack The Knife" and dropped it from his set for a short period. But "If I Were A Carpenter" was performed at every full-length concert Darin gave from late 1966 until his death.

"If I Were A Carpenter" earned Darin a Grammy nomination in the "Best Contemporary (Rock and Roll) Solo Vocal Performance" category, but the award was won by Paul McCartney for "Eleanor Rigby."

The success of "If I Were A Carpenter" again prompted some criticism of Darin for "bandwagon jumping" in order to resuscitate his career. But, as Charles Koppelman pointed out, "There really wasn't a bandwagon. It wasn't as if Tim Hardin were a household name."

Folk-rock was certainly "in," but its most popular forms were the electrified guitar jangle of The Byrds or the psychedelia-enhanced style of Donovan. The Lovin' Spoonful had delved into some softer material, but they were still better known for their "good time" pop sound.

While "Carpenter" now seems to go hand-in-hand stylistically with other 1966 hits such as "Monday Monday" or "Elusive Butterfly," at the time of its release, it was far from a sure-fire hit. While the fact that Darin had nothing to lose made it an easy gamble, it nevertheless was a gamble, and not a bandwagon-hop. When so many performers of Darin's generation were criticized, often justifiably, for not keeping up with the times, it seems ironic that Darin was criticized for the very opposite – the sin of keeping up with the times, and succeeding at it.

With the single riding high, an entire album in the loosely-defined "new folk" style was planned. Darin had no intention of framing "Carpenter" in an MOR album, and not just because of commercial considerations.

"He was very committed to the new style," said Don Rubin, "and not from the standpoint of 'this is a new gimmick I'm going to cash in on.' He felt it. He started wearing jeans and boots. I think he went through a change in his whole being that made him want to feel part of that time period, and the music that was becoming symbolic of that time."

Twelve more songs were recorded on October 31 and November 1. Not surprisingly, considering Koppelman and Rubin's involvement, the selections included a fair number of Tim Hardin and John Sebastian copyrights. But business

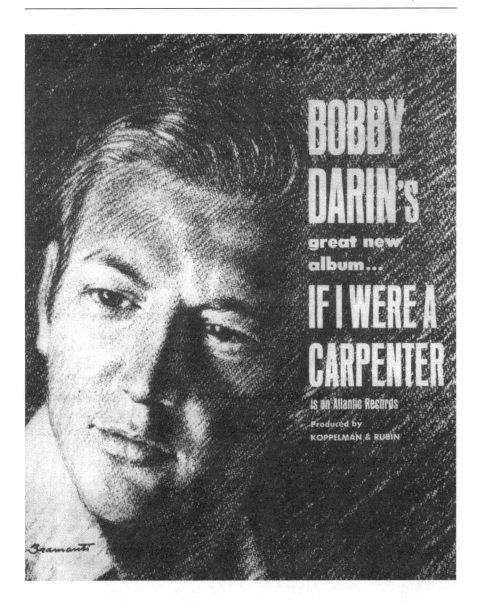

aside, it's hard to argue that the choices weren't correct, given Darin's superb readings.

Much as he had done on *Earthy* back in 1962, Darin took the "show" out of his voice and sang in a soft, subdued, even pained manner which suited the material perfectly. In addition to the hit title track, the *If I Were A Carpenter* album also included "Misty Roses" and three additional Tim Hardin songs: "Reason To Believe," "Red Balloon," and "Don't Make Promises."

With the exception of a few very hip music critics, Darin was the first person to call attention to Hardin's considerable songwriting talent, showcasing it to both the industry and the general public. His interpretations showed that he had an artistic understanding of Hardin's songs.

"He related to the lyrics," said Charles Koppelman. "Bobby was a very honest, compassionate person, and I think those lyrics and that genre of music struck a chord."

Don Rubin concurred: "Timmy's very poetic way of expressing himself just got to Bobby. The lyrical approach that Tim took was kind of the opposite of the show material Bobby had done previously. He adapted to Timmy's material incredibly."

Darin's renditions of these songs never veered far from Hardin's own recorded versions (which were produced by Erik Jacobsen). Don Rubin acknowledged that Hardin's originals were used as blueprints for Darin's covers.

"Bobby heard these songs originally via Timmy's versions," he said. "It was common of the way records were made then. You had very talented songwriters who made great demos. When you recorded one of their songs, it was almost impossible to get away from their interpretation. It's part of what sold you on the song in the first place."

For example, Darin's version of "If I Were A Carpenter" was sweetened only slightly. In addition to the Darin-arranged enhancement of the bass part, Darin's hit features strings and a string-led instrumental break not featured in Hardin's version. Likewise, the difference in the versions of "Misty Roses" is only a string arrangement, which is absent from Hardin's record, but comes in during the second verse of Darin's.

While Hardin's "Red Balloon" was accompanied only by acoustic guitar, Darin's features a bass and drums from the start, and strings shortly thereafter. Conversely, Hardin's "Don't Make Promises" is a full upbeat electric production from the start, while Darin's opens acoustically, then gradually incorporates a bigger beat.

Though not exactly carbon copies, the similarities of the versions, combined with the fact that Darin was a Vegas star who appeared to be appropriating the style of this hip Village folkie, led some to level the charge that Darin "ripped off" Tim Hardin. Darin himself would joke that he heard of people telling Hardin "Bobby Darin stole your song."

Nik Venet, who knew both men and had accompanied Darin to The Tin Angel to see Hardin years earlier, said such comments came from members of a self-appointed "in crowd" who couldn't accept that Darin beat them to the punch.

"I think that so few people knew of Tim Hardin," Venet said, "that in order to prove you knew Hardin, you had to say that Darin ripped him off. That way, you'd show you knew who Tim Hardin was before Darin did his songs."

Unfortunately, when it came to choosing the follow-up singles to "If I Were A Carpenter," the other Hardin songs were passed over. The beautiful "Reason To Believe" would have been a most likely candidate for the Top 40. Other than Hardin himself, Darin was the first to record this gem, later given famous renditions by Rod Stewart, The Carpenters, Wilson Phillips, and others.

Instead, "The Girl That Stood Beside Me" was selected as the second single. The song came from British songwriter Geoff Stephens, who had produced some of Donovan's early hits. In late '66, Stephens was the writer/producer behind the novelty studio group The New Vaudeville Band, who scored the #1 hit "Winchester Cathedral."

Although a solid contemporary song with a perhaps too-ambitious production (featuring a backward-tape effect similar to the sound on The Beatles' "Rain"), "The Girl That Stood Beside Me" stalled at a disappointing #66.

Darin got back into the Top 40 with a third single, John Sebastian's "Lovin' You," which climbed to #32. (It would be Darin's last Top 40 hit.) Darin treated Sebastian's songs a little less reverentially than he treated Hardin's, and he put a little more show-business into his reading of "Lovin' You." Ironically, considering the cold shoulder adult radio stations gave to "Carpenter," "Lovin' You" became an Easy Listening hit, reaching #18.

The album also included Darin's cover of the song he turned down earlier that year, the Spoonful's "Daydream." Sebastian's "Younger Girl" was also recorded for the LP (as was a cover of The Beatles' "Good Day Sunshine"), but neither was released. The album was rounded out by John Denver's early "For Baby," Buffy St. Marie's "Until It's Time For You To Go," and Darin's own "Amy," a ballad (from his forthcoming film *Gunfight In Abilene*) which, though not folk, was "sensitive" enough to fit in with the rest of the album.

Start to finish, *If I Were A Carpenter* is one of the most consistently enjoyable albums Darin ever recorded. The arrangements and song choices are entirely tasteful, and Darin's performance was more than merely credible, it was inspired. In 2000, the album was recognized in the book *The Mojo Collection: The Greatest Albums Of All Time*, which detailed *Mojo* magazine's selections of pop's greatest albums released in the second half of the 20th century.

Atlantic was pleased. The album finally hit the chart in early 1967, a feat which eluded both *Broadway Bag* and *Shadow Of Your Smile*. It eventually reached #142 and was Darin's last album to dent the *Billboard* LP chart.

As all parties appeared satisfied with *Carpenter*, a follow-up album was recorded in March 1967 and released that spring as *Inside Out*. Hoping to repeat the hit magic, Tim Hardin's "Lady Came From Baltimore" was chosen as the first single. It is one of Hardin's most fascinating and moving compositions, an entire short story told within two-and-a-half minutes. But from a commercial standpoint, it lacked even the mysterious pop appeal of "Carpenter," and the single stiffed at #62.

Darin gave a terrific reading of John Sebastian's most beautiful love song, "Darling Be Home Soon," but given that the Spoonful took it into the Top 20 only a few months earlier, it was doomed as the second single, making only a token chart appearance at #92. The only logical reason for its choice as a single may have been hope that it would reach the Easy Listening audience the Spoonful hit had eluded, but it wasn't to be.

The album was fine, but it lacked the spark of the *Carpenter* collection. There were far fewer up- or mid-tempo selections, and you could almost hear the concept grow increasingly tired as the album progressed. It seemed as if Darin had taken the laid back approach a step too far.

While little on the album could be called exciting, there was plenty that was interesting. The two Hardin songs ("Baltimore" and "Black Sheep Boy") were almost note-for-note copies of Hardin's originals. Darin also tackled three songs by a new pair of writers in the Koppelman-Rubin stable, Gary Bonner and Alan Gordon. Earlier in '67, the pair struck paydirt with The Turtles' "Happy Together." Of their contributions to *Inside Out,* the most interesting was "About You," which both the Turtles and Spoonful would later record as "Me About You" with completely different arrangements.

Darin was one of the first of many singers to cover "I Think It's Gonna Rain Today," by his old "Look At Me" collaborator Randy Newman. And, in perhaps the most daring cover choice of his career, Darin closed the album with a rendition of The Rolling Stones' "Back Street Girl." Considering that both albums passed on the by-then obligatory Beatles and Dylan covers, the choice of a Jagger-Richards number is indicative of how Darin was open to new material which ran counter to expectations. Darin pulled off the pretty-but-not-tender Stones ballad quite effectively.

Inside Out also included Darin's most autobiographical composition to date, "I Am," a well-written navel-gazing rumination which pre-dated Neil Diamond's "I Am I Said" by four years.

As neither the album nor its singles succeeded commercially, this direction would not be pursued any further. The next, and final, Darin-Koppelman-Rubin collaboration would be a single of Bonner and Gordon's "She Knows," recorded in July 1967. The production was patterned after "Happy Together," and though it was a fine pop effort, the song lacked the glorious hook which made the Turtles' record a classic. "She Knows" got a smattering of airplay and sales, but only "bubbled under" the charts at #106.

"I remember 'She Knows' as being a turn to the right at the time," said Don Rubin. "It could have been the beginning of the next album, but I don't think anyone involved, either ourselves or Bobby, was that pleased with the outcome."

With that, Darin's second "folk phase" came to an end. "It only lasted for two albums, as far as encapsulating that particular mood and that style of music," said Rubin. "But it was great. He was a joy to work with. Every time he walked into the studio, he was prepared and right on, and gave you a great performance."

Like Darin's 1962-63 folk phase, the "If I Were A Carpenter" era was a surprise to many. By the time Darin would get to the third phase, he would not just surprise, but shock.

"At The Crossroads"

1967-1968

Despite his new musical direction on record, Bobby Darin retained his swinging, Vegas image on stage and on television throughout 1967. While "If I Were A Carpenter" and "Lovin' You" were added to his club act, the show was still stacked with big band-accompanied standards such as "Don't Rain On My Parade," "Charade" and "The Shadow Of Your Smile." Darin explained the rationale behind his set list in a 1966 interview.

"'Mack The Knife,' 'Beyond The Sea,' things like that, done with whatever was 'my treatment' was the bag that the country had clearly and simply defined for me," Darin said. "As long as I wear the mantle 'performer,' I must do that. If I decide one day to 'private island' it, so to speak, and want to entertain me and a handful of people I know, then I'll make that decision and not have to answer to public demand."

For his 1967 concerts, the Cole Porter standard "I've Got You Under My Skin" was livened up with a Motown-ish arrangement, and Darin returned "18 Yellow Roses" (for which he played guitar) and "What'd I Say" (for which he played piano) into the set list.

Calling Darin "one of the youngest senior statesmen in the entertainment business," *Billboard's* Aaron Sternfield lauded Darin's March 1967 stand at the Copa: "As a singer, mimic and purveyor of light banter, Darin goes to the head of the class. He's all showman."

While Darin's admiration of Tim Hardin proved that he appreciated contemporary songwriting, he made it known that he was not abandoning the standards of the pre-rock decades. To emphasize the point, Darin joined The Supremes, The Mamas & The Papas, Petula Clark and Count Basie in an amazing television musical special called "Rodgers & Hart Today," which aired on March 2, 1967.

Under the musical direction of Quincy Jones, the show opened with Darin performing "The Lady Is A Tramp." Over the course of the hour, there was some terrific musical teamwork. Darin and Clark sang a long medley of Rodgers & Hart classics. Darin and Diana Ross and The Supremes, backed by the Count Basie Band, performed "Falling In Love With Love." Later, the Basie band swung behind Darin on "I Wish I Were In Love Again."

Darin also starred in a British television special, "Bobby Darin In London," which aired on the BBC that May. It showcased a swingin' and very assured Darin in a concert performance setting. His demeanor had a bit more intensity and a bit less playfulness than before, evidenced by a very dramatic performance of "Once Upon A Time."

The show became more relaxed and musical after Darin's celebrity impressions comedy routine. He acknowledged Tim Hardin before performing "If I Were A Carpenter" and the straightforward pop-folk arrangement of "The Girl That Stood Beside Me" was far superior without the gimmicks which marred the studio version. He concluded the special by showing off his musicianship – playing blues guitar on "Funny What Love Can Do" and a great rocking piano on "What'd I Say."

Darin at The Flamingo, 1967
(Las Vegas News Bureau)

Also in May, *Gunfight In Abilene*, the last film in which Darin would have a starring role, opened. It was a Western, with Darin playing an ex-Confederate officer who was appointed sheriff. No surprisingly, it bombed, both critically and commercially.

Even before the film opened, Darin suggested that he was unhappy with the way his once-promising movie career was progressing. He told *Variety* that of all his films, he was only proud of *Captain Newman* and *Pressure Point* and vowed, after *Abilene*, to take on roles with "extreme caution."

His next film, *Stranger In The House*, opened in Great Britain in July 1967. In his smallest role since *Hell Is For Heroes*, Darin received third billing after James Mason and Geraldine Chaplin. The film was not released in the U.S. until January 1968, under the name *Cop-Out*.

Darin continued to write music during this time, copyrighting eight songs on April 14, 1967. Although the fate of titles such as "Face To Face," "Ballet Dance" and "The Greatest Lover In The World" is not known, it is possible that some of them are instrumental pieces used in the score of *Gunfight In Abeline*.

On July 4, Darin performed at the Melodyland Amphitheater in Anaheim, with the British duo Chad & Jeremy as opening act. "Born Free" and "I've Got The World On A String" were added to the Darin repertoire.

Darin was soon back in the studio for a project which still puzzles those who were enamored with his "Carpenter" direction. Released in August 1967, *Bobby Darin Sings Dr. Dolittle* found Darin singing ten Leslie Bricusse songs from the movie musical.

Though a few of the score's softer, contemporary ballads such as "After Today" wouldn't have sounded out of place on the earlier albums, for the most part, the entire first side of the album featured slow melodies which tended to

Darin in Gunfight In Abilene
(Universal Pictures publicity photo)

run together. Side Two, which featured uptempo melodies and more inspired lyrics, was better.

Songs like "Beautiful Things" and "Talk To The Animals" provided Darin with material he could sink his teeth into, albeit in the old style. As ridiculous as it seemed as a follow-up to Tim Hardin and John Sebastian songs, "Talk To The Animals" is a classic Bobby Darin show-stopper.

Contrary to what might be believed, the album was indeed Darin's idea, and not encouraged by Atlantic Records. Twenty years later, Ahmet Ertegun still referred to the collection as "those animal songs," and said that he tried to talk Darin out of the commercially unsuccessful project. Even Easy Listening stations declined to play "Talk To The Animals."

"It wasn't a very good idea," Ertegun said of the *Dolittle* album. "Bobby would get an idea, and it was hard to get him off it."

In the studio later that year, Darin recorded more interesting and contemporary material, including Jerry Reed's "Tupelo Mississippi Flash" and the Motown/Stax-influenced soul efforts "Prison Of Your Love" and "My Baby Needs Me" (only the latter of which has ever been released, surfacing as a bonus track on a 1998 British reissue of the *If I Were A Carpenter* and *Inside Out* albums).

He also recorded three excellent original compositions – the contemplative and relaxed "I'm Going To Love You," the bluesy "Everywhere I Go," and the country-ish "Long Time Movin'." The latter, which Darin sang with Bobbie Gentry on an early 1968 "Kraft Music Hall" TV episode, is another prime example of Darin's often surprising lyrical depth, as he casually drops the words "manifesto" and "paranoia" into a simple melody. These three tracks were finally released on the 1995 *As Long As I'm Singing* box set.

Darin became hot news that August, but not because of his record, film or stage efforts. He was linked in press

reports to Diane Hartford, the 25-year-old wife of A&P heir Huntington Hartford. The millionaire accused Darin of "monopolizing his wife." Darin, who claimed the relationship was platonic, quipped "I don't play monopoly. Hartford does. He has enough money for that."

The press, notably the *New York Post* and *New York Daily News*, treated the situation as a juicy scandal, trailing Darin and reporting on his every move in and out of New York for weeks.

On one of those trips, Darin went to Monaco at the invitation of Princess Grace to headline at her annual Red Cross gala. "She was an excellent dancer, in addition to being a charming princess," Darin graciously said of the monarch.

That October, Darin returned to network TV to host the "Kraft Music Hall" special "Give My Regards To Broadway." Set in 1917, the show was a tribute to vaudeville, with Darin portraying the legendary George M. Cohan.

Never having seen Cohan work, Darin went to George Burns for advice on his portrayal. "Cohan worked like you work," Burns told Darin. "He was sure of himself, creative, wrote all his own material. He was a down front performer."

Rather than imitating Cohan, Darin tried to capture the spirit of his songs (including "Yankee Doodle Dandy"). The performance didn't satisfy everyone. "A competent performer in his own right, Darin lacked any authenticity or warmth in aping the famed songwriter and vaudevillian," said *Variety*.

Darin opened 1968 by hosting yet another "Kraft Music Hall" program, "A Grand Night For Swinging," singing "Mack The Knife" and "Talk To The Animals" and performing a vaudeville routine with Bobby Van.

In his stage act, Darin used "Talk To The Animals" as a springboard for his impressions routine, which now included Rex Harrison, James Cagney, Cary Grant, Clark Gable,

*Bobby Van and Darin on "The Kraft Music Hall: A Grand Night
For Swinging," 1968
(NBC publicity photo)*

Jimmy Stewart, Tony Bennett, Robert Mitchum, Dean Martin, W.C. Fields and Al Jolson. In a concert review, *Variety* noted that "Mack The Knife" was "unfortunately parodied and tossed around like a bit of fluff," but called Darin "a completely authoritative saloon star."

But, speaking to columnist Earl Wilson that March, Darin hinted at restlessness with his supper-club success. "To be called the greatest entertainer may mean being paid more than anybody, or having four limousines," he said. "These are not essential to me anymore. Being accepted as an entertainer and human being are."

Darin was looking for – and finding – a new outlet for his energy: politics. In early 1968, he joined Jimmy Durante in Indiana to entertain at a rally for U.S. Senator Birch E. Bayh. By May, he would place his support behind the man he believed would be the next President of the United States – Robert F. Kennedy.

"Reason To Believe"

20 RFK

"He was someone I could believe in," Bobby Darin said about Robert F. Kennedy.

Armed with the belief that RFK could help heal a racially-divided and war-torn America, Darin threw his support behind Kennedy's presidential bid and joined the campaign in the spring of 1968. "I stepped out for a man I thought could help re-direct the system," Darin explained.

Darin was a believer, not a show-biz friend of Kennedy. He had only met RFK a few times, and their most lengthy meeting was during the campaign, on a plane along with 50 other people. "In that short time, everything I felt about the man was confirmed," Darin said.

Darin was part of the official traveling campaign for only a brief time, probably about ten days. He kept a low profile, so low that Frank Mankiewicz, Kennedy's press manager, would say 20 years later that Darin had "no role of any significance in the campaign."

Although aware that Darin was on the campaign "briefly," singer-songwriter John Stewart, who had just left The Kingston Trio to act as "resident campaign singer" at RFK rallies, also never crossed paths with Darin. Still, Stewart said that at the time, he was not surprised to learn that Darin was helping their cause.

"He went through so many surprises that he ceased surprising me." Stewart said of Darin. "I wasn't surprised; it seemed very Darin-like."

Nik Venet believes that Darin contributed to RFK's campaign in a behind-the-scenes capacity. "Darin was talking to very big businessmen about big bucks for the campaign," Venet said. "He was hitting a lot of TV producers, movie producers. He was raising money personally, meeting people one on one."

When publicly visible on the campaign, Darin would warm up crowds with a few words and a song before Kennedy would speak. "RFK was a great fan of his," recalled Fred Dutton, who was in charge of the campaign's "road show."

Accompanying himself on guitar, Darin would sing the campaign's theme song, Woody Guthrie's "This Land Is Your Land" (reworked as "This Man Is Your Man"), and then exchange a small amount of banter with RFK before leaving the microphone to the candidate.

Music was an integral part of the Kennedy campaign, for tension relief if nothing else. On one occasion, Darin had the opportunity to sit down next to RFK on a plane and sing for him.

"There was a party atmosphere on the plane," recalled John Stewart. "Kennedy loved to hear people sing. Requests would come from RFK, the press, or campaign workers. Having someone with Darin's talent on the plane, it was inevitable that someone would request him to pull out his guitar."

During that performance, Darin was at least partially responsible for opening RFK's eyes to the musical poetry of Bob Dylan. Journalist Jack Newfield, who chronicled the RFK campaign in the 1969 book *Robert Kennedy: A Memoir*, had tried, but failed to turn Kennedy on to Dylan earlier.

"I had this running attempt with Kennedy to try to get him to appreciate Dylan, because he hated his voice," said Newfield, who was a Darin fan and fellow alumnus of Hunter College. "Darin was the perfect transition."

The following day on the plane, Kennedy made a point of stopping Newfield and telling him that after hearing Darin sing "Blowin' In The Wind," he was impressed with Dylan's lyrics.

"Now [Kennedy] had heard a more traditional singer sing Dylan's words," wrote Newfield, "and it had registered on Kennedy's contemporary sensibility."

On May 30, Darin began a week's run as the first performer at a new San Francisco nightclub called Mr. D's. While there, he learned of the events of June 4, 1968. After winning the California primary election, Kennedy was shot at the Ambassador Hotel in Los Angeles, and died a day later.

Darin attended the RFK memorial service in New York, and the funeral at Arlington National Cemetery on June 9. Stunned, he stood at the gravesite for almost seven hours. Still there when the guards lowered the coffin and filled the grave, Darin was the last person to leave.

"With him in the ground, part of me went, too," Darin said. Later, he would explain that he had a "spiritual revelation" that night.

"It was as though all my hostilities, anxieties and conflicts were in one ball that had been flying away into space, farther and farther from me all the time, leaving me finally content with myself," he told columnist Earl Wilson.

Watching a television report about Kennedy's funeral, John Stewart noticed that the cameras caught Darin leaning on a fence in a crowd shot.

"I thought it was a very poignant picture of how committed Darin was," said Stewart. "He didn't ask for VIP treatment;

he went down with the crowd. He was up against the fence with the populace, looking at the funeral."

Though Darin said the gravesite vigil left him with a "peace and calm I've never had before," the pain stayed with him for years. As late as 1972, he was still talking about Kennedy's death in interviews.

"In some way, I felt I contributed to his death," he told Estelle Changas of *The Los Angeles Times*. "I was one of those who said 'I'm going to work for him,' and through this encouragement to his candidacy, helped make him publicly vulnerable to tragedy."

"Most people took four days to get over his death," he told *TV Guide* later that year. "It took me almost four years." Indeed, Geoff Edwards, who worked with Darin in 1972-73, recalled that Darin was distraught about RFK even then. "It was on Darin's mind until he died," Edwards said.

"I Guess I'll Have To Change My Plan"

The Direction Years

June 1968: In the previous two months, both Martin Luther King, Jr. and Robert F. Kennedy had been assassinated. And the United States was still knee-deep in Vietnam.

Suddenly, Bobby Darin felt that merely entertaining people in hotel showrooms and supper clubs had lost its relevance. Making an audience smile with a song, a dance or a joke was not enough for him anymore. He had to say something about the world, try in some small way to make things better. He set about to do it the only way he knew how – through his music.

Many previous reports and articles about Darin have suggested that he stopped performing and dropped out of sight after RFK's death. In truth, he was back at The Frontier in Las Vegas about a month after the assassination, and initially, little changed in his show. One number that he hadn't performed in a while was back in his set list: Alone on stage, sitting on a stool with guitar in hand, Darin sang the spiritual "I'm On My Way Great God," the same song he performed on "The Judy Garland Show" days after President Kennedy's death in 1963.

By early October, Darin added Otis Redding's classics "Try A Little Tenderness" and "Dock Of The Bay" to his live repertoire, plus Bob Dylan's "I'll Be Your Baby Tonight." But Darin saved the biggest surprise for his October 30 opening at L.A.'s Cocoanut Grove in the Ambassador Hotel – the hotel where Bobby Kennedy had been gunned down.

The show opened traditionally. Backed with a 21-piece orchestra, Darin started with "Let The Good Times Roll," "Mack The Knife," "Try A Little Tenderness" and "Talk To The Animals," still replete with his celebrity impersonation routine.

Then the orchestra left the stage, as did Darin, who changed out of his tuxedo and into a blue denim jacket. Upon his return, backed by only his four-piece combo, Darin debuted a new original song called "Long Line Rider." It was a hard-hitting rock number with lyrics referring to an incident at an Arkansas prison where a number of skeletons were uncovered in the ground, and the incident's subsequent cover-up by officials.

"All the records show so clear / Not a single man was here / Anyway, Anyway / That's the tale the warden tells / As he counts his empty shells / By the day," Darin sang. It was hardly "Mack The Knife" and the audience was a bit taken aback.

Darin continued, accompanying himself on guitar for "If I Were A Carpenter" and "I'll Be Your Baby Tonight." Darin then pulled out his harmonica and the band tore into some electric blues for "Got My Mojo Working." Finally, he sat down at the piano for a long, wild rendition of "What'd I Say," during which Darin also threw in bits of the Aretha Franklin/ Otis Redding R&B classic "Respect." Darin's new act went over well with the entertainment critics in attendance.

"If the mitts were not exactly torrid, it is because the new Darin comes as something of a surprise," said *Variety*. "There is now a far more appealing, grown-up image. He definitely is headed in the proper direction."

Bob Darin, 1969
(Group W publicity photo)

"Bobby Darin is developing into a social commentator in his nightclub act," proclaimed *Billboard's* Elliot Tiegel, while *The Los Angeles Times'* Leonard Feather wrote, "Leaning on his own special and highly-charged R&B rhythm section, he is first and foremost a rhythm singer of exceptional power and conviction."

The changes in Darin were not confined to the stage. In fact, his change in direction in the recording studio would be even more radical. In late July, Darin announced the formation of his own label, Direction Records.

The label would release Darin's own recordings, which would now, he announced at a press conference, reflect his thoughts and concerns about a troubled society. In addition to his own music, Darin intended to cultivate a roster of "statement makers," other artists he believed in.

In late September, Darin released his first Direction album, *Bobby Darin Born Walden Robert Cassotto*. "Bobby Darin has something to say about changing times," said the Direction trade advertisement trumpeting the album's release. "It is the first time the artist has used the recording medium to express himself with his own thoughts through his own music."

The album was not only unlike anything Darin had done previously, it was unlike any record ever made by a major mainstream entertainment figure.

The Bobby Darin who wrote and performed these songs essentially had no ties to the Bobby Darin who had been a pop star for ten years. It was as if Darin had wiped the slate completely clean – starting with the "Bobby Darin" persona, as the album's title and cover art made clear.

The cover featured a blurred photo of a tuxedoed Darin to the left, with a grainy boyhood photo of young Walden Robert Cassotto superimposed to the right. As *The Los Angeles Times'* Estelle Changas noted, "The feeling is of the artist searching for his origins, attempting to return to the most essential part of himself, an identity obscured and distorted by the slick superficiality of his celebrity image."

For the first time on a Darin LP, lyrics were printed on the album's gatefold. Stream-of-consciousness poetry graced the album's back cover, and the credit read "This album was Written, Arranged, Produced, Designed and Photographed by BOBBY DARIN." But the most shocking element of the package was the music inside, a surprise to both those who adored Darin and those who dismissed him as irrelevant in the post-*Sgt. Pepper* pop world.

The album showcased the songwriter rather than the singer. The songs demanded little vocal effort and Darin's trademark vocal personality never encroached on them. Instrumentally, the arrangements were sparse, with guitar, bass and drums dominating.

Thematically, the album was certainly "heavy." "Long Line Rider" was included and released as a single, reaching #79, a far better showing than "safer" efforts such as "Talk To The Animals." Darin tackled environmental pollution in "Questions" and questioned the validity of organized religion in "Sunday."

On a more personal note, "Change," a musical cousin of Dylan's "Don't Think Twice," explored Darin's personal and musical evolution ("Music that used to seem hollow now seems to fit in your range...Damned if what you're feeling isn't change").

The album was more interesting lyrically than musically. Many of the melodies were basic and most songs contained no outright chorus or bridge. But the lyrics never failed to be intriguing, as Darin displayed a previously undeveloped knack for rhyme and wordplay.

He also displayed a biting wit. "The Proper Gander" was an allegory about the cold war, told via the story of a community of mice whose leader convinces them to fear a mythical three-eyed Siamese cat ("They sang this land is mice land/ Mice country tis of thee").

The album peaked with its final song, as Darin put his feelings about Robert F. Kennedy's life and death into music. "In Memoriam" featured only Darin's whispered vocal and his acoustic guitar in a quiet, mournful performance which seems to be mixed at a lower volume than the rest of the album. Although the melody is only rudimentary, the song's painful honesty makes it one of Darin's most compelling compositions and performances.

"In Memoriam" opens with the words of Bobby Kennedy's enemies – "He's a ruthless opportunist" – and proceeds through Darin's observations of his own Arlington cemetery vigil. At the end, Darin comes to terms with his belief in Kennedy – "Now no man has the answers and he was just a man / And yet I can't help feelin' that he knew a better plan." Darin's conclusion about the RFK tragedy, repeated at the end of the song's six verses was, "They never understood him, so they put him in the ground."

Born Walden Robert Cassotto was an absolute artistic triumph for Bobby Darin. It would have been a commendable effort from any artist, but the fact that it was the product of a man so ensconced in the traditional show business world made it that much more compelling. No Las Vegas artist, before or since, has spoken out so eloquently in protest of mainstream corporate and political America.

Unfortunately, but not surprisingly, the album was largely overlooked. Though it seemed to be an obvious effort to reach the *Rolling Stone* audience, that publication did not acknowledge its existence. *The Los Angeles Times*' Robert Hilburn, who would come to be regarded as one of the most respected pop music critics, was the first of the new generation of pop journalists to recognize Darin as a serious artist, but even he would wait almost nine months to chime in with praise of the album.

Later, in a profile of Darin, *Times'* writer Estelle Changas would say of the LP, "The songs convey an urgent sense of someone beginning absolutely fresh. They offer what is unusual in recorded music, an opportunity to glimpse the artist at a key transitional stage in his life. These compositions are a striking contrast to what many would identify as the public image of Darin the nightclub performer."

During the album's production, Darin hooked up with a new, younger group of musical mates. The album's basic tracks were originally recorded in Los Angeles, then mixed in Las Vegas by engineer Brent Maher, who in the 1980s would become one of the hottest and most respected producers of country music (for The Judds, among others). Maher recalled that Darin's reputation preceded him in Vegas studios.

"I was with another engineer in the studio," Maher said, "and when he heard I was going to work with Bobby, he said 'Oh, you poor soul. The guy's known to be a terror. You can't please him.' So I wasn't really looking forward to this, and when Bobby brought in the tape, I was kind of dubious about what I was going to be in for.

"What I found out about Bobby," Maher continued, "was that he just wanted people to work as hard as he worked. He didn't have much patience with people who didn't give 100%. If you gave more than 100%, he was more than appreciative, and was really a great guy."

When Darin gave Maher the tape, the engineer felt that a couple of the tracks weren't quite right, and asked Darin if he could re-cut the songs using a Nashville group he was working with. Darin agreed and liked what he heard of Maher and the group's work. So much so, in fact, that he hired the Nashville band – pianist Bill Aikens, bassist Quitman Dennis, drummer Tommy Amato, and guitarist Bubba Poythress – as his own group.

Darin grew quite close to Amato (who would remain as the band's drummer until Darin's death) and Dennis (at whose wedding Darin stood as best man). Dennis recalled that in the summer of 1968, the young band members, all into rock'n'roll, had no preconceived notions about Bobby Darin, Vegas superstar. Darin appreciated that fact.

"He was just being a guy like the rest of us, and we just started clowning around and doing stuff in the studio," Dennis recalled. "I really didn't know this 'other' Bobby Darin, and neither did the rest of us, so he loved that. We weren't afraid of him; that's what he liked. Everybody else was intimidated by him, or wanted something from him. All we wanted to do was play music, and we liked the guy. He was just trying to be one of the guys, and play rock'n'roll."

In hooking up with the new band, and in concentrating on new music, Darin was breaking ties with his former manner of doing business.

"I'm bailing out of what I'm doing at The Frontier," Darin told Dennis at the time. "I work and I make 40 grand a week, and I've got a manager, an agent, this person, that person, and by the time it's all said and done, I got zip. So I told them all to go away."

In August 1968, Darin sold T.M. Music to Commonwealth United Corporation. Earlier that year, Commonwealth had purchased Koppelman-Rubin Associates, and Darin's former producers were now running the corporation's expanding music publishing and production subsidiary. Darin received his reported $1 million take in Commonwealth United stock. (Eventually, the corporation collapsed, and Darin lost his million, in addition to his copyrights.)

Darin began 1969 with a January 2 opening night gig at The Copacabana. His stage show had changed little from the one he presented at The Cocoanut Grove a few months earlier. He played his opening four songs, including "Mack

The Knife," with a big band, then introduced "Long Line Rider" as a song "that has a little something to say which I'm proud of." He concentrated on the folk-rock material from that point.

But there were some obvious changes in Darin's appearance. He now sported a mustache. He did not wear his toupee. He wore denim from the beginning of the show. And dispensing with the traditional big introduction, he simply walked on stage and began to sing.

"Introductions are part of the phony," he told columnist Earl Wilson. "I figure they must all know who they came here to see."

Open-minded critics were digging the new Darin: "Bobby Darin is a study in the musical evolution of an artist," wrote *Billboard's* Claude Hall in a glowing review of the Copa performance. "He exhibited an attitude of involvement with today's serious music – progressive rock."

Even *Variety,* often less concerned with the artistic merits of a show than its ability to draw customers, gave Darin a good review and did not mention any audience dissatisfaction. But some of the Copa clientele was not receptive to the new Darin. Some walked out, and some others that stayed voiced their dissatisfaction to the Copa brass.

Darin's new act was not the kind of entertainment the conservative Copa crowd wanted to see, and after this engagement, Darin became *persona non grata* at the club where he established himself as a top nightclub star.

It wasn't just nightclub management or patrons that did not appreciate the new Darin. Some other musicians were mystified. Darin's old friend and arranger Bobby Scott, never a fan of rock music, saw the Copa show and did not understand what Darin was trying to accomplish.

"The fans who came out and paid a hell of a lot of money did not come for that guy," he said. "They might have taken that guy if he had also done some of the other things. But he was already making fun of some of the hits he had. He had kind of passed it by, but the audience hadn't."

While Scott thought the 1969 Darin was "a vestige of his former self," he could tell that Darin was content when they met backstage. "I did detect that he was at peace, exuding a non-characteristic relaxation, miles away from the Darin of '59," Scott said.

Another former Darin arranger, Dick Behrke, concurred that Darin's latest stylistic shift wasn't effective. "He was too much of a chameleon," Behrke said. "People thought he was changing wherever the wind blew. I don't think he was just making commercial changes to make commercial changes. He was really looking to do something that meant something to him at the time."

Indeed, Darin did not appear terribly concerned about anyone's dissatisfaction with his new act. During his Copa engagement, he told Earl Wilson he wanted to give up night-clubs. "I want to get into college concerts," Darin said. "I don't want business or politics. You can't tell the truth."

Later that month, a nationwide television audience would get a taste of what The Copacabana's patrons experienced. Without his toupee, and sporting a mustache, long sideburns, and a denim jacket (and flashing a peace sign), Darin hosted the special "Kraft Music Hall: The Sound of the Sixties."

The program featured some of the most amazing moments of Darin's career. He played acoustic guitar while dueting with Judy Collins on Dylan's "I'll Be Your Baby Tonight." He engaged in a soulful, call-and-response duet with Stevie Wonder on "If I Were A Carpenter," displaying outright joy throughout what was likely the most rousing version of the song ever performed.

Later, Darin sat down at the piano to play – for the first time on stage in over five years – "Splish Splash." In another completely left-field song choice, Darin flirted with the music of the drug culture, playing guitar and harmonica on "Take A Whiff On Me." Though it was decades old (both Woody Guthrie and Leadbelly had performed it), the folk song, also known as "Cocaine Blues," had been re-popularized via the repertoires of '60s folkies such as Tom Rush, Dave Van Ronk, and Hoyt Axton.

Finally, Darin and his four-piece band attacked "Long Line Rider" in an arrangement which rocked much harder than the record. The entire "Kraft Music Hall" repertoire and performance was not likely what anyone (establishment or counterculture) expected out of a program hosted by Bobby Darin, but it perfectly captured the fascinating musical phase he was going through.

Darin butted heads with the entertainment establishment again in late January, when he was scheduled to appear on "The Jackie Gleason Show." For his solo number, he chose "Long Line Rider." On the night of the taping, CBS' Programming Practices Department ordered him to cut the lines "This kind of thing can't happen here / 'Specially not in an election year." Rather than censor himself, Darin walked off the set.

While absolving Gleason of any responsibility for the decision, Darin told the press he would sue CBS. "I don't care if I never do another TV show in my life, they are not going to interfere with my right to express myself," he said.

Darin didn't have to wait long before experiencing the crowning moment of this stage of his career. In May, he opened a six-night stand at Los Angeles' Troubadour. The club generally showcased the hippest folk and rock acts, and would never have booked the old Bobby Darin.

Darin was accompanied solely by the four-piece band of Dennis, Amato, Aikens and Poythress. Additionally, Darin played acoustic guitar for much of the set and chimed in on harmonica often. "Mack The Knife" was not performed. Darin debuted a number of new original songs, and besides the Hardin and Dylan holdovers, he added new songs to his set: The Beatles' "Lady Madonna," Joe South's "Gabriel," Hank Williams' "(I Heard That) Lonesome Whistle" and Leadbelly's "Midnight Special."

A few new originals such as "Distractions" and "Me And Mr. Hohner" were previews of Darin's next Direction album. But the Troubadour gig's set list was most noteworthy for the debut of a new Darin composition, "Simple Song of Freedom." It was the zenith of Darin's move into composing topical, meaningful songs, validation of the entire move into folk-rock.

The song neatly summed up Darin's newfound belief that music – the simple act of singing – could be the forum in which people could stand up and demand peace. In the lyric, Darin reached out his hand not only to black Americans, but also to Alexander Solzhenitsyn in the Soviet Union ("Tell me if the man who is plowing up your land / has got the war machine upon his mind").

He lashed out at governmental lies and war-mongering leaders, singing "Let's all build them shelves and let them fight it out among themselves / And leave the people be who love to sing."

The last line of the chorus summed up Darin's most pressing concern, one shared by millions of Americans at the time – "We the people here don't want a war."

Just as "Simple Song Of Freedom" was the new Darin's high water mark as a songwriter, the Troubadour concerts were his high point as performer. He was completely accepted on his own terms – simply on the quality and integrity of his new music.

Reviewing Darin's opening night at The Troubadour, Pete Johnson of *The Los Angeles Times* wrote, "This latest transition is remarkable and seems to have left Darin nearly as

surprised and delighted as it left his opening night capacity audience. The overflow crowd loved him and his newly-assembled combo."

That summer, Darin and the band embarked on a series of dates at outdoor fairs. It succeeded at getting Darin off the supper club circuit, but it failed at finding audiences even remotely as accepting as The Troubadour's. For these dates, there was one more, major change: Darin's name.

To completely connote the break from his previous persona, he now wished to be known as "Bob" Darin: more adult, more serious, and distanced from the show-biz swinger. But Darin found that audiences couldn't wipe the slate clean nearly as easily as he could himself.

"People were eminently dissatisfied with what happened on stage," Quitman Dennis said of those fair dates. "It was the four-piece band, with Bobby playing acoustic guitar. He was still a good entertainer, but the material was going over their heads. He would not do the things they wanted him to do. Zero."

Ironically, Bob Darin received a much warmer reception in Las Vegas, when he stopped there for a one-night stand at The Bonanza on July 16. "Bob Darin has Vegas buzzing and favorably so," wrote *Variety*. "Obviously deeply committed to his new songbag, he makes believers out of cynics here."

Also in July, Darin released *Commitment*, his first and only LP released under the name "Bob Darin." While a hatted Darin's back was turned on the album's cover, the inside sleeves showed a non-toupeed Darin replete with mustache and denim jacket.

Like *Born Walden Robert Cassotto*, the second album showed no trace of the dynamic Darin voice, and its songs, again minus choruses and bridges, were not crafted for the pop market. Unlike the first record, where at least every lyric was interesting, there were a couple of songs on *Commitment* which lacked even curiosity appeal.

But the highlights of *Commitment* rose above even the best tracks from the previous album. "Me And Mr. Hohner" stood out, with Darin delivering some clever rhyme schemes in a manner similar to the fast-talking style John Sebastian used on some Lovin' Spoonful records such as "Jug Band Music" and "Pow." The track was released as a single, but only reached #123 nationally. It received significantly greater airplay in select markets such as New England, which caused it to "bubble under" the *Billboard* Top 100 chart for five weeks, an unusually long time for a non-hit.

Though Darin associates have no recollection of him using drugs, on *Commitment* he at least philosophically aligned himself with the drug-accepting counterculture. Not only are "pot" and "hash" referred to in "Mr. Hohner" (a large reason for radio's resistance to the song), but in "Water Color Canvas," Darin sings of "frying pans of coffee 'cause the only pot we had would not oblige." In "Jive," (the LP's second single) he sings of being "stoned."

Darin's knack for wordplay and personal insight came to the forefront on "Song For A Dollar," an autobiographical tune in which he confronted his own motivation for making music. A superb bass line propelled the song, and Darin found fresh ways to combine rhyming words such as "moral quarrel."

Another noteworthy song was "Sausalito (The Governors Song)," significant in that Darin was at least a dozen years ahead of most in coming out with an anti-Ronald Reagan song. "Sounds from Sacramento shouldn't be heard," he sang of the then-governor of California. Alluding to The Mamas & The Papas' 1966 classic "California Dreamin'," Darin sang, "To paraphrase Papa John, we're living in a California nightmare."

Again ignored by record buyers, *Commitment* did receive notice from critics. In fact, Darin's whole musical evolution was the subject of an insightful article by Robert Hilburn.

Noting that some cynical listeners might now consider Darin a trend-follower, Hilburn wrote, "Maybe the real Bobby Darin is beginning to stand up. I hope so...Darin seems to be involved in a painful search for identity. It is a search that holds promise of rich rewards."

Cashbox magazine covered *Born Walden Robert Cassotto* and *Commitment* in the same glowing review: "Both belong among the dominant social documents of our time...They are shattering songs of social consciousness that belong in the mainstream of our new American revolution."

Darin also wanted to make sure his new messages were recognized in the music industry. To this end, Direction Records took out full-page ads in trade publications. With small white lettering against a black background, the message simply read "Peace...Bob Darin." Direction and Commonwealth United also took out a two-page *Cashbox* spread reprinting the lyrics of "Me And Mr. Hohner" in full.

However, even the people Darin was working with were not necessarily tuned into his lyrics.

"I really didn't agree with a lot of his politics," said Brent Maher, who had contributed significantly to the production of *Commitment.* "I was a lot more conservative, after putting in four years in the Air Force. Of course, as history proves, he was right. Bobby was dead on about some of these issues."

"At the time, a lot of it went over my head," said bass player Quitman Dennis. "He was coding things into those songs, and if you didn't have the insight into the politics of the time, you might miss part of it. I was in my 20s and I didn't have the awareness to be on the same train as him."

During his work with Darin in the studio and on stage, Dennis observed Darin's *modus operandi* as a songwriter and musician.

"He understood the craft of songwriting," Dennis said. "He'd keep crankin' them out, and every now and then, he got hold of something. He understood the process – that some of them will be good, some of them will be not so good, and every now and then, you get one that really flies.

"He was a very good musician, a natural musician in his own way," Dennis said. "He didn't have the patience or the discipline to develop any considerable skills on an instrument, but he could tackle an instrument and learn to do a tune or two with what appeared to be authority. That's a very unique gift. He could do that with drums, vibes, and piano, but his repertoire in each of those was limited. I appreciate his musicianship in that regard."

Although record buyers and radio stations shied away from Bob Darin's records, he did hit the chart as a songwriter. In August 1969, none other than Tim Hardin, the writer of "If I Were A Carpenter," charted with a version of "Simple Song Of Freedom."

Hardin was still under contract with Koppelman-Rubin Associates, and was recording his first album for Columbia Records. Though generally pleased with the album, the label wanted a single it could push to radio. Darin told Koppelman and Rubin that "Simple Song Of Freedom" might work for Hardin. Because Hardin did not usually record other songwriters' material, it was a tough sell, recalled Don Rubin.

"Timmy didn't really want to do it," said Rubin. "We played it for him and used the angle that it's Bobby's payback and it could be a big hit. He finally relented and agreed to do it. It was a little more to the pop side, not something Timmy was noted for. I think he agreed to do it because of the lyric. It didn't compromise his own feeling."

Hardin's record reached #50 nationally, although it was a larger hit in many regional markets. Ironically, considering Hardin's own gift as a writer, it was his only hit single.

The recording probably did more for Darin than Hardin. It gave Darin a bit of hip credibility, and he was very proud that a songwriter of Hardin's reputation recorded the song. For years, before performing the song himself, Darin would always mention that Hardin had the hit with it.

"Bob" Darin made his prime-time network TV debut that October with a guest appearance on "This Is Tom Jones," singing "Distractions" (a *Commitment* track) and joining Jones for a medley of "Aquarius" and "Let The Sunshine In."

Darin's final single of 1969 was an impressive one. "Baby May" expanded his sound to include a Memphis soul feel, with Steve Cropper-like guitar licks and a horn section. The song called for – and Darin delivered – some of the vocal dynamism he suppressed on the two previous albums.

The song was inspired by the suicide death of Art Linkletter's daughter. In the record's publicity material, Darin said he felt Linkletter could have assumed more responsibility, and the lyric included the line "Baby May had to pass away to hear her daddy say I was wrong." Although the song is quite good and Darin's intention was to promote inter-generational communication, calling attention to the Linkletter tragedy may have been a mistake, as it made Darin come across as somewhat judgmental.

The single's flip side was another gem – a quiet acoustic ballad called "Sweet Reasons." It was the first song in which Darin lyrically addressed his own mortality, with lines such as "Oh, Sweet Reason, please be kind / I haven't much time / And I just want to be."

Darin had begun the composition back in 1963, after a conversation with Nik Venet in which Darin confided his concern about his health.

"That was the first time we really discussed the possibility of his passing away," Venet said. "That song was very special to him, because he wrote it in that mood. A lot of people didn't realize that he had so little time. And that was the first time he discussed it at length with me."

Musically, this melancholy, beautiful song proved that Darin had been listening to Simon & Garfunkel, and it's a shame that neither it nor "Baby May" was ever included on a Darin LP.

The single's label revealed a few changes. First, Bell Records, which had distributed previous Direction product, was no longer in the picture. The record was distributed by Commonwealth United Records, Koppelman & Rubin's label. Secondly, the production credit had changed; both sides were produced by "Maher, Dennis and Amato for ABQ Productions."

"What he wanted to do there was give us a little to run with and see what we could do," Dennis said of Darin's decision to remove himself from the producer's chair. "I think he felt that when he was trying to control everything, he was limiting himself. He wanted to see if we could make some records that would wind up on the charts, but still have his message coded into the lyrics."

As 1969 wound down, Darin wanted to make sure that even the motion picture industry knew that he had changed. For a small role in *The Happy Ending*, released late that year, he was billed as Robert Darin.

Even after all these changes, Darin still had one surprise up his sleeve. He would do the one thing he had never done before: stop working.

Bob Darin, late 1969
(Las Vegas News Bureau)

22

"Nature Boy"

Big Sur

Although there was intermittent, interesting work, Bob Darin took a sabbatical from the fall of 1969 through the spring of 1970. For about nine months, work took a back seat to Darin's desire to sort things out, relax, and get in touch with himself.

He chose Big Sur, California. Darin bought a trailer and parked it in the back of a friend's 70-acre farm.

So that he would be completely unencumbered by any previous ties, before the move, Darin divested himself of vast quantities of his belongings, including his cars, homes and wardrobe. To Big Sur, he took only a few denim jackets, jeans, books, and tapes of music.

"I just decided I didn't want to be owned by anybody," he told *Melody Maker*'s Bernard Barry. "I felt myself losing touch with a great many things: life, the earth, everything."

Darin spent his days reading, listening to music, chopping wood and even working on the farm to pay for his trailer space. "I know it sounds mundane," he explained, "but I just felt things closing in on me."

"He wasn't secluding himself," said Nik Venet. "He was just trying not to be 'Bobby Darin, Entertainer.' I think Bobby thought he was going to die. He couldn't deny the fact that he was not going to live to be 70 or 60 or even 50. I think that weighed heavily on him. He just didn't know what he wanted to do for the last couple of go-rounds."

Darin re-emerged temporarily in December 1969 for another confrontational Bob Darin gig, this time for two weeks at The Sahara in Las Vegas. Many Vegas showrooms simply went dark for the pre-Christmas season, but The Sahara took a chance on Darin – at $40,000 a week.

It was Darin's first Vegas showroom date in 14 months (the Bonanza was a one-night stand), and he wanted to make sure the audience knew what to expect. He had a full-size cut-out picture of himself (with mustache, Levi jacket and jeans, and a cowboy hat) placed in the showroom's entrance.

The warning didn't stop people from walking out. During the engagement, Darin heard boos, catcalls and heckling, especially when he turned down requests for "Mack The Knife."

Darin's show was essentially the same one he had performed at The Troubadour and Bonanza. Between songs, he would comment on topics such as the Santa Barbara oil spill, or knock the Nixon-Agnew administration, referring to "Slicky Dick and Zero Agnew."

Again, critics were kinder to Bob Darin than audiences were. While noting that Darin was "certain to lift the young establishment enemies into ecstasy," the *Variety* review noted, "He makes his point in a profound, interesting, musical manner."

The *New York Post*'s Alfred G. Aronowitz, long a Darin fan, noted the absurdity of the shocked reactions to Darin's protest songs: "Is there a more revealing commentary on

Las Vegas than the fact that it considers Bobby Darin's appearance here its first major confrontation with the youth underground?"

The reaction to Bob Darin in Vegas wasn't always negative, recalled Brent Maher, who recorded the Sahara dates for a potential live album which never materialized.

"It would depend on the crowd," Maher said. "Sometimes the people went there and expected to hear Bobby Darin and what that represented in their minds. Those people weren't willing to listen. Especially on weekends, the demographics of the people were age 35 to 40 or older. They were probably on the conservative side.

"Some other nights, you'd have people standing up and yelling 'Right on,'" he said. "People were really in his corner, respecting where he was at and digging the music."

Darin appreciated The Sahara's decision to book him: "It took a lot of guts on the Hotel Sahara's part to try me out doing what I'm doing now," he said from the stage on his final night. "They pay me a lot of money for something I would have done for nothing."

But The Sahara's motives weren't purely altruistic. Darin could still draw a crowd of big-spenders, and Aronowitz reported that during Darin's engagement, the Sahara casino "reported some of the briskest handles on The Strip."

Darin spent a fair amount of his $80,000 paycheck by bringing in a film crew to tape a couple of shows for a potential TV special.

"None of it worked technically," recalled Quitman Dennis, who said Darin refused to alter the stage lighting to accommodate the cameras. "He had a couple of rolls processed and it was all too black to print."

Darin would also periodically return to Los Angeles from Big Sur to work on a movie he had written, and would produce and direct, called *The Vendors*. The plot centered on the relationship between a heroin addict and a prostitute, and the cast reportedly included Mariette Hartley, Gary Wood, and Dick Lord. (Dick Bakalyan has also previously been reported to be in the cast, but he was not.)

Darin had been tinkering with *The Vendors* since 1966, going as far as to set up a shoot that year, with his old guitarist, Jim McGuinn (then flying high with The Byrds) cast in the lead role. Back in the early '60s, McGuinn had told Darin that he wanted to get into movies and Darin gave him this advice: "Become a rock'n'roll star and then you can do anything you want."

McGuinn initially agreed to play the *Vendors* role, but backed out. "I read the script and liked it," he said. "Then I showed it to a friend who said, 'Jim, you're going to get typecast in this junkie role and it's not a good way to start out.'"

"I was doing drugs at the time, and I got a little paranoid," said McGuinn. "So, the day of the shooting, Bobby was there with the camera crew all set up, and I called him and said 'I don't want to do it.' I told Bobby I'd pay for the crew, and he sent me a bill for the shoot."

Darin was more successful at getting the movie filmed in 1969-70, but not in getting it in condition to be released. As late as 1972, he still intended to put the film out, and *The Los Angeles Times* reported that *The Vendors* would be released in late 1972. However, the film never surfaced.

In early 1970, while Darin was editing *The Vendors*, Terry Melcher, his old T.M. Music associate, approached him with a song he thought would be great for Darin, Jackson Browne's "Federal Review." Melcher offered to produce it, and thought the song's anti-war message would fit in nicely with Darin's new image. Darin liked the song, and Melcher went ahead and cut an instrumental track, but the record was never completed.

Darin's next single, "Maybe We Can Get It Together," would be his last for his own Direction label. It was a gospel-oriented song, which featured background vocals by three young African American girls Darin and Brent Maher recruited from a Las Vegas choir.

Darin enjoyed his occasionally-interrupted Big Sur sabbatical, telling reporters it was "absolutely necessary for my spiritual survival." But by May 1970, he was ready to go back to work. And, as much as he believed in his new music, he was bothered when people walked out of his shows. Alienating audiences ran counter to everything he had ever strived for.

For his return, Darin decided to compromise. He would go back to being "Bobby Darin." Not the Bobby Darin who was king of Vegas supper-club standards. But not the Bob Darin of hard-core protest either.

He tried to find a happy medium. He would still play "Long Line Rider," "Simple Song Of Freedom," and of course, the Hardin and Dylan set staples. But he would also re-insert "Mack The Knife" into his show, and throw in some contemporary pop hits such as "Everybody's Talkin'," and "Spinning Wheel."

In 1972 interviews, Darin reflected on his reasons for making the compromise. "I thought I could present myself differently," he told the *Los Angeles Times*, "and that by this change in appearance, I could be closer to my own personal statement. But I turned off so many people, they didn't hear me, and those whom I've known for years swore to me that I had tried to be a hippie."

The bottom line was that Darin genuinely missed the thrill of turning on an audience. "As much as I needed to divest myself of all these games and toys and possessions," he told *Melody Maker's* Loraine Alterman, "I accumulated all that by doing something I really enjoyed. I did not have to divest myself of performing. I said I'd like to work in places where they'll accept the compromise that I'm willing to make."

"I'm doing what you have to do as an entertainer for the people who want to be entertained," he told *The Los Angeles Herald Examiner*. "But I'll do the other thing at The Troubadour as well."

Although he agreed to veer away from protest songs, Darin didn't want to soften his sound musically. Before his "comeback" at the Landmark Hotel in May 1970, Darin appointed bassist Quitman Dennis as his "musical director" and instructed him on the sound that he wanted.

Darin would still perform with his four-piece band, but he augmented them with a seven-piece horn section. He told Dennis he wanted four saxophones and three trumpets, and arrangements to make them sound like a Little Richard/rock'n'roll horn section. "He wanted a rock'n'roll band," Dennis attested.

"It was still not what people expected," Dennis recalled. "But it was strong musically and it was entertaining. I didn't notice any dissatisfaction from the public."

Indeed, upon his return, Darin found Vegas waiting with open arms: "Bobby Darin is back, and he brought 'Mack The Knife' with him," proclaimed *Variety*. "This time around, Darin compromises – but not enough to sacrifice his integrity. The slight surrender results in a strong, excellent turn."

It wasn't just the Vegas establishment that was glad "Bobby" was back in town. Many of Darin's friends and musical comrades believed that he sacrificed too much of his unique performing charm during his protest phase.

"No one was happier when he went back to being Bobby Darin," said Darin's Capitol Records co-hort, saxophonist Steve Douglas, who had seen Darin's protest act. "Bobby wasn't a folkie. He seemed to be a guy pretty lost, searching for something. He didn't seem comfortable. Bobby was at home on a stage in Vegas, entertaining the folks. That's what he was – a great entertainer."

All in all, Darin's retreat to Big Sur and subsequent return to Vegas has been greatly exaggerated. For example, in his autobiography *Once Before I Go,* Wayne Newton writes of Darin becoming a recluse immediately after Robert Kennedy's death, and of a Darin "comeback" performance in Reno, saying, "This was the first time in three years Darin had stood in the spotlight of a nightclub stage."

Even if the Bonanza gig is not counted because it was a one-shot, the longest Darin was away from Vegas was slightly more than a year. And even if the two-week "experiment" at The Sahara is not counted, the span between Darin's regular Vegas engagements – The Frontier in late 1968 and The Landmark in mid-1970 – was only 18 or 19 months.

Darin and Mike Douglas on "The Mike Douglas Show", July 1970
(Group W publicity photo)

"The Breaking Point"

Just because Bobby Darin was back in Las Vegas, it did not mean that he was keeping his political opinions to himself. In May 1970, Darin took out newspaper ads denouncing President Nixon's decision to invade Cambodia.

On May 12, in the wake of the U.S. military action, Darin participated in an anti-war demonstration at Los Angeles City Hall. A number of speakers, including future L.A. mayor Thomas Bradley, addressed a crowd of about 600, consisting mostly of USC students.

When Darin took the microphone, he announced a project called "Phone For Peace" and urged the crowd to telephone the White House and leave a peace message for Nixon. He said he hoped a tie-up of the White House switchboard would cause the president to take notice. Darin's comments and participation in the protest were duly noted by the FBI.

Back in Las Vegas, Darin continued to refine his new stage show at The Landmark. He added a Beatles medley and Neil Diamond's "Sweet Caroline" to the act. With the exceptions of "Mack The Knife," "If I Were A Carpenter" and "Splish Splash" (part of a closing rock'n'soul medley), he eschewed performing songs that he popularized.

"He didn't want to do his previous hits," explained Quitman Dennis. "He wanted to keep moving forward, and experience the buzz of doing new, exciting material, rather than reiterating the past."

Sometimes that new material would be a classic associated with another artist. Television actor Alan Thicke, who would later work with Darin, recalled being impressed by Darin's early '70s rendition of Jackie Wilson's "Higher and Higher."

"I think Bobby did the definitive version of 'Higher And Higher,'" Thicke said. "It had real rock'n'roll credibility, even in his Vegas presentation. It was as authentic rock'n'roll as Vegas had seen at the time."

Darin also decided to get back to mainstream audiences via television. Shortly after leaving Big Sur, and only months after denouncing Nixon, Darin went about as middle-America as you can get when he co-hosted the daily "Mike Douglas Show" the week of July 27.

Darin, still without his toupee and sporting his mustache, chatted, sang and danced with Douglas, whose show was broadcast during the day in most markets. The guest list for the week reflected no counterculture, but both Little Richard and Wilson Pickett appeared, giving the show an unusual R&B flavor.

That fall, Darin also became something of a semi-regular guest on "The Flip Wilson Show," appearing on four programs between September and January. Wilson, who four years earlier was opening for Darin in Vegas, was now one of television's hottest stars. His NBC variety show was among the highest-rated and hippest programs on the air. Darin appreciated the opportunity to return to prime-time television via Wilson's high-profile vehicle.

"You do not know when that kind of relationship is going to turn around, and the other party is going to do something for you," he said of Wilson. "I could not help his ratings particularly at all. It was a true gesture of a real genuine friendship. I love him very much."

On the program, Darin sang songs from his act such as "Gabriel," "Higher And Higher" and "If I Were A Carpenter" and even revisited, for the first time in years, "Lazy River." A song that he performed in September, "Melodie," would be his new single for a new record label – Motown.

Motown seemed an unusual home for Bobby Darin, but in 1971, the label had also signed other white '60s pop stars such as The Four Seasons and Lesley Gore. Although Motown planned to make Darin's first LP a live recording (with the tentative title of *Finally*), "Melodie," which was not released until April 1971, was not a live track. Quitman Dennis does not recall the song ever being performed live.

The record's sound was definitely more Motown than Darin. Darin was a fine R&B singer, but he was no soul shouter, and the production of "Melodie" was tailored for a singer more along the lines of the Four Tops' Levi Stubbs. "Melodie" was far from sensational, but it certainly deserved more attention than the total indifference with which it was greeted by radio.

Its flip side, a cover of The Supremes' swan song hit "Someday We'll Be Together," ranks as perhaps the worst track Darin ever recorded. From background vocalists warbling "Sing It Bobby" to Darin's strained vocal which never stays on the melody, this Motown debut was a disappointment after the always-interesting original material Darin waxed for Direction.

In further evidence of the confusing state of his recording career, Darin initiated recording sessions which featured him covering four standards popularized by Nat King Cole. For the first time in over seven years, Darin reunited with former arranger and bandmate Richard Behrke.

"I flew out and did four tunes at a session," Behrke recalled. "Bobby produced them. It was an odd project, because there was a big band, but the songs were not supposed to be done in the big band style. I don't know if the vocals were ever done. Bobby wasn't feeling well that week, so he was going to overdub vocals the next week."

In October 1970, Darin went to Toronto to tape a Canadian TV special called "The Darin Invasion." The hour-long program was syndicated in the U.S. a year later. The show was a curious, yet effective mix of old and new Darin.

The musical guests were The Poppy Family and Linda Ronstadt (and Darin accompanied Ronstadt on guitar during her performance of "Long Long Time"). George Burns also guested, and he and Darin reprised their old Vegas "I Ain't Got Nobody" soft-shoe routine.

Darin also presented himself as an actor. He and Pat Carroll performed a sketch about a working class couple in a kind of updated "Honeymooners" style. And Darin, in full costume and makeup, performed "Reviewing The Situation" from *Oliver*.

But the highlights were Darin's own musical numbers – "Higher And Higher," "Hi-De-Ho" and "If I Were A Carpenter." To close the show in grand fashion, Darin picked up his guitar and began "Simple Song Of Freedom." As the song progressed and the arrangement built, Darin's performance grew more intense and joyous. His face exhibited a look of complete musical satisfaction, and he reveled in the audience's warm reaction.

In January 1971, Darin began an engagement at The Desert Inn in Las Vegas. By this point, Darin dropped "Long Line Rider" and all his original protest songs from the act, save for "Simple Song Of Freedom." "Gabriel" was replaced as the set opener by Laura Nyro's "Save The Country," an attractive composition to Darin because of its references to

Darin at The Desert Inn, 1971
(Las Vegas News Bureau)

"We Shall Overcome" and "the dream of the two young brothers." (His politics were also advertised when "Mr. Agnew" took the place of the devil in "Hi-De-Ho.") A superb acoustic version of James Taylor's "Fire And Rain" was also added.

During his run at The Desert Inn, Darin struck up a friendship with the Inn's maitre d', Georges LaForge. Darin spoke fluent French and often conversed with LaForge between shows or over dinner.

"He was a very down to earth person, no pretensions whatsoever," LaForge recalled. In one of their conversations, Darin told LaForge he had always dreamed of opening a French restaurant and proposed that LaForge join him in this business venture.

Darin offered to finance the restaurant, which LaForge would run, on two conditions: that it be located in Beverly Hills, and that it be named "Pamplemousse" (the French word for grapefruit). LaForge inquired about Darin's insistence on that name.

"All my life, I have thought it was the most beautiful word in French," Darin told him. "I love the sound of it. With a name like Pamplemousse, it can do nothing but succeed."

The two never got their restaurant open, but years later, LaForge himself opened a restaurant in Las Vegas. In tribute to Bobby Darin, he named it Pamplemousse.

Also during Darin's Desert Inn engagement, Motown brought in an eight-track mobile unit to record the shows for a scheduled live album release (one which did not reach the public until more than a dozen years after Darin's death).

The live recording showed Darin in fine form. The presentation was unmistakably Vegas, and surprises in the song selections were few and far between. However, Darin's version of "Simple Song Of Freedom" was both stronger and more commercial than Tim Hardin's. Motown released it on a promotion-only single to radio, but strangely, not to the public. And Darin's closing rock-and-soul medley of "Chain Of Fools," "Respect," "Splish Splash" and "Johnny B. Goode" proved that he and his band could cook with the best rock ensembles.

Darin's Desert Inn performance was top-notch. Usually, that was a given, but it was absolutely remarkable in light of the fact that Darin entered the hospital the day after his closing night – for major heart surgery.

In 1970, Darin's damaged heart finally caught up with him. His old friend Harriet Wasser saw the evidence first-hand when she visited the set of the "Darin Invasion" special.

"That was a horrible scene," she said. "After that show, he was so sick that he sat in front of his dressing room door. He could not get up. They put him in bed. He said to me, "I feel like I'm running a hundred miles an hour around this room.'"

Oxygen masks and avoidance of stairs was no longer sufficient to keep Darin going. Six times, he went into intensive care for electroconversion. His heart would beat 140 to 160 times a minute, instead of the normal 72 to 80.

Open-heart surgery was the only option he had. "My valves had deteriorated to the point where if [surgery] was not now, then it would have to be the next year, and in the meantime, I'd have to curtail my activities," he explained.

Doctors had advised him to undergo surgery earlier, but Darin was committed to his Desert Inn gig for the first six weeks of 1971. "You give me these six weeks to work," he told his doctors. "Somehow, you keep me alive by remote control, and the moment I close, I'll go home, check myself into the hospital and give myself to you."

During a nine-hour open-heart surgery procedure at Cedars of Lebanon Hospital, two plastic valves were inserted into Darin's heart. He came precariously close to death. He was in intensive care for five days, and (he later told writer Alfred Aronowitz) he remembered nearly dying three times. He spent six weeks in the hospital.

Darin was advised, and agreed, to take it slow upon his release and allow enough time for adequate recuperation. Even accepting summer work would be rushing it.

Darin tried to reassure worried friends and associates by throwing a party that summer to celebrate the success of the surgery. On his property, he imported a carnival, and set up tents and carnival games. He introduced everyone to his surgeon, Dr. Josh Fields. "He was that happy to be alive," recalled Darin's old friend from *Pressure Point*, actor Dick Bakalyan.

"I had expected to kick off by the time I was 30," Darin told reporters upon his re-emergence. "So I bought a few extra years."

"Everything's Okay"
Post-Surgery

Although Darin considered it to be a long recuperation period, it was only seven months after open-heart surgery that he resumed performing activities. He opened at Harrahs in Reno on September 1, 1971.

Post-surgery Bobby Darin would be very similar to pre-RFK Bobby Darin. The denim was gone, replaced by the standard nightclub tuxedo. The toupee went back on. More comedy, and even the celebrity impersonations, returned to the act. Darin seemed resigned to the fact that he was at his best as a Las Vegas-style entertainer. He seemed to no longer care if he appeared unhip, even irrelevant, to the under-30 crowd.

He thought all this out completely during his recovery, he told *The New York Post*'s Alfred Aronowitz. "I had tried to put my street self on stage," he said of his denim phase. "But then I began to think...What they want is an actor on the stage.

"I'm an actor," he continued. "An actor wears a costume and makeup. There's nothing wrong with that. You go out and you entertain them. If what they hear is what they see, then indeed, let me put on my tux. I'm comfortable in it. I don't have any inner arguments anymore."

Darin also took a renewed interest in acting upon his return, guesting on a number of television series. Within a four month span, he appeared in dramatic roles in episodes of "Night Gallery," "Ironside," and "Cade's County." And, back on "The Flip Wilson Show," he displayed the best of his old-new act by performing "Mack The Knife" and "Simple Song Of Freedom."

As 1972 dawned, Darin was back on the nightclub scene with a vengeance. Critics again greeted him warmly. "Making a triumphant return to the Strip after open-heart surgery, Bobby Darin was relaxed, happy and great," wrote *Billboard's* Laura Deni in a review of his February show at The Desert Inn.

Variety concurred: "The 'new' Bobby Darin is the 'old' Bobby Darin; he's dumped the jeans and is back in a tux singing tux-type songs." To prove this point, Darin returned "That's All" and "Beyond The Sea" to his act. However, he didn't completely abandon folk – the triumvirate of "If I Were A Carpenter," "I'll Be Your Baby Tonight" and "Simple Song Of Freedom" still closed the show.

While Darin had little doubt that he would succeed at The Desert Inn, he was challenged by a return to The Copacabana. Neither he nor the Copa brass had forgotten his disastrous 1969 gig there. Darin asked for another chance, and offered an olive branch. He had an intermediary call Jules Podell.

"Tell Julie I want to play [the club] and settle the situation" were his instructions. "I did a bad thing last time. One thing I know now is that I'm a saloon singer." He opened at the Copa on February 24, slightly more than three years after the '69 debacle.

Darin at The Hilton, September 1972
(Las Vegas News Bureau)

This time, he completely satisfied both the audience and Podell. Darin was asked to come back to the club again eight months later.

New York Times writer Don Heckman tried to be as hard on Darin as possible in his review of the February Copa show. Heckman accurately reported Darin's step back to show-biz traditions, noting that he "is clearly more comfortable with the Frank Sinatra-Dean Martin style." Along the same line, the writer called Darin's act of whipping off his tie "a routine that now looks as humorously antiquated as Al Jolson getting down on one knee to sing 'Mammy.'" While Darin might have been upset with that interpretation three years earlier, he probably regarded it as a compliment in 1972.

Despite his reservations, Heckman found that Darin was a hard act to dislike: "Elusive though his style may be – folky-humble at some points, Vegas-flashy at others – Darin is still a first class performer."

Darin found himself back in the New York media spotlight during his Copa engagement, although he grew tired of questions about his heart surgery.

"I don't want to talk about that," he testily told *New York Daily News* reporter Patricia O'Haire. "Yes, I did have such an operation one year ago, and that's all I wish to say about it. We can talk about the future, we can talk about the past, we can talk about my work, or we can talk about the weather, but I don't want to talk about the surgery."

Darin also took his act to the West Coast, returning to The Grove for the first time since shortly after RFK's death. Longtime Darin admirer Robert Hilburn, the *Los Angeles Times* critic, liked what he saw: "He's better than ever, a consummate nightclub performer," Hilburn wrote. "As with the best entertainers, he makes it look effortless. Darin moves with the grace and confidence of a superbly trained athlete, one who knows he is in control of the situation."

Darin won over more fans that summer with a concert in New York City's Central Park. "A lot of kids there hadn't come out to see Bobby Darin so much as they just wanted to come out to the park," wrote Alfred Aronowitz, "but when the show was over, the crowd was screaming for more. He can still sing, but more than that, he can make you have a good time."

Indeed, Darin's act now featured so much comedy that many considered it the highlight of his show. "There is a tremendous amount of comedy and talk in his turn," wrote *Variety,* reviewing his October Copa show. "In all, Darin impresses as a performer who has gone beyond the singing medium."

Moving the act into the multi-media arena, old silent-film clips of car crashes and chases were projected during Darin's drum solo. He impersonated W.C. Fields, Marlon Brando and Dean Martin. And his humor could be very self-effacing; Darin wasn't afraid now to joke about his height and toupee.

"If I can laugh about it," he told columnist Earl Wilson, "that shows it doesn't bug me anymore." Darin reveled in a line Steve Lawrence was using in his act – "Did you hear about Bobby Darin's accident at the Copa? He fell off his shoes."

In Vegas, Darin moved from The Desert Inn to The Hilton that September, with Shirley Bassey as his opening act. The extensive live work didn't keep him from other activities. He was a presenter at the 1972 Grammy Awards. He told *The Los Angeles Times* he would begin work on his first novel. And in August, his first album in three years was released.

Bobby Darin, on Motown, was in many respects a typical early '70s MOR album, which was a bit of a disappointment after Darin's previous progressive efforts. The songs were contemporary and relatively modern in their lyrical themes, but they never approached rock, not even the "soft rock" style then in vogue via Carole King and James Taylor.

Strings and horns were added to nearly every track, and background vocals, often an intrusion on Darin records, were again overblown here. The motivation behind some of Joe Porter's production decisions was also mysterious: "I've Already Stayed Too Long," a fairly interesting country-influenced song, was faded out before even reaching its second chorus.

The album did get off to a great start, with Darin's cover of Randy Newman's "Sail Away," a choice which proved that Darin still hadn't lost his great taste in material. With a relatively unobtrusive arrangement which featured a Darin harmonica break, the track seemed to be the culmination of everything Darin tried to accomplish at Direction. Unfortunately, when released as a single, the record stiffed.

Throughout the album, Darin's voice sounded a bit weaker and more vulnerable than it was in the pre-operation days. He appeared to be straining at times, although the effect did not detract from the album.

The chief reason for the album's commercial failure was its lack of a standout, sure-fire hit. Besides "Sail Away," the most interesting track was the only one Darin had a hand in writing. "Something In Her Love," written with drummer Tommy Amato, was the most old-fashioned, middle-of-the-road song on the LP, but it was a finely crafted ballad. Vocally, Darin never sounded more like Sinatra than he did on this track.

The fact that Darin co-wrote only one of the ten songs was a disappointing indication of his abdication of any artistic responsibility, save for his singing. He offered an explanation on his lack of writing to *Melody Maker*, saying his sunken publishing deal with Commonwealth United, in which he lost control of his copyrights, would not end until 1973, and he didn't feel like writing much until then.

Despite his recording, performing and acting activities, Darin still took time to get away and relax. He had a new companion, Andrea Yaeger, a former Beverly Hills legal secretary. In interviews at the time, Darin casually referred to her as "my wife" or "Mrs. Darin," although they were not then legally married. "We've just dispensed with the bureaucratic involvement," he explained.

Darin still found his favorite method of unwinding to be camping. He and Andrea would drive to the California countryside, pull out sleeping bags, sleep in the open air, and cook their own food. They would bring only a few canned goods, some fishing gear, and some cooking equipment on sojourns which would usually last one-to-three days. According to Terry Melcher, Darin would also drive his motor home to Big Sur on occasion, and spend some time parked on the ranch owned by Beach Boy Al Jardine.

However, there would be less time for relaxation with the advent of Darin's next project, one which would build his popularity, but wreck his health.

Carl Reiner (left) and Darin (as Groucho Marx) on "The Bobby Darin Amusement Company," August 1972
(NBC publicity photo)

Freda Payne and Darin on "The Bobby Darin Show," 1973
(NBC publicity photo)

"They All Laughed"

The TV Show

Despite the fact that Bobby Darin was further from "hot" than he'd been at any time since 1958, prime-time network TV came calling in the summer of 1972. The "Dean Martin Show" was going on its usual summer hiatus, and Darin was chosen to star in a short-run summer-replacement variety series on NBC.

Some impressive talent was associated with his show. Producers Saul Ilson and Ernest Chambers, both TV veterans, had produced Frank Sinatra's 1968 TV special, and The Smothers Brothers' controversial comedy series, which had been yanked by CBS a few years earlier. The producers saw potential in a Darin-hosted show with an unusual twist.

"Bobby was certainly a great singer, but that's not an important consideration in a television hit," Ernest Chambers said. "But we felt he had a range and personality, and that properly handled, he could be a success. What we had to do was create some pieces for Bobby to do, and create a supporting cast."

In the same way that CBS' "Sonny & Cher Comedy Hour" was titled to emphasize the program's emphasis on comedy, not music, Darin's program was christened "The Bobby Darin

Amusement Company." (Technically, it was called "Dean Martin Presents The Bobby Darin Amusement Company"; the introductory credit didn't sit well with Darin from the ego point of view, said Ilson.)

"We called it 'The Bobby Darin Amusement Company' specifically to tell the audience that it would not just be an hour of a guy singing," said Chambers. Though Darin had done numerous variety shows and some light comedy in films, the weight of carrying a broad comedy show was a new challenge to him. Darin relished the opportunity to show people outside the Vegas circuit that he was more than a singer.

"He was not a great comedian," recalled Chambers, "but he was a good actor. If you gave him a character to play, and some lines, he could do that."

"He did it very well," said Ilson. "I thought he had natural abilities. He could do jokes, sketches, and he was very instrumental in the show. He added a lot."

Some regular characters and bits were set up. One featured comedian Steve Landesberg (later of "Barney Miller") as a Freud-like psychiatrist who analyzed Darin.

"We knew Darin had a reputation for being volatile and arrogant, so we addressed that issue head-on by having Landesberg play his psychiatrist and come on stage and talk to him," recalled Chambers. "It was very effective because the fact that Bobby could laugh at that quality in himself helped take the sting out."

One of Darin's best impersonations, his Groucho Marx, was incorporated into many shows. (A picture of Darin and Tom and Dick Smothers as Groucho, Chico and Harpo still hangs in Ernest Chambers' office.) Comedian Rip Taylor appeared as "Skyway Silverman," a goofy helicopter traffic reporter.

Another recurring and silly bit showcased Darin in drag as "The Godmother," an old Italian woman. His sparring partner in these sketches was often Geoff Edwards, an L.A.-area disc jockey who would go on to success as a game show host on programs such as "Jackpot" and "Treasure Hunt." Edwards called his experience on the Darin show a joy.

"Everybody was having a great time and all of us loved him," Edwards recalled. "Working on that show was the happiest six months of my life."

Edwards' "interviews" with The Godmother were loosely scripted, but the segments highlighted Darin's ability to humorously improvise, sometimes to the point of breaking up Edwards on camera. In one sketch, when Edwards, looking at cue cards, stumbled through the question "Are there any telltale signs to indicate that a marriage is in trouble?" Darin shot back "Yes, and there are also tell-tale signs to indicate that you can't read."

"Bobby always surprised me," Edwards said. "He had an incredible instinct for comedy."

Perhaps the most fondly-remembered, and certainly the most consistently good, sketch on the show was "Carmine and Angie" (also called "The Neighborhood"), a weekly segment revolving around the conversations of two friends sitting on the front porch stoop in an old Italian neighborhood. This segment was conceived and developed by Darin himself, who played Angie. For the part of Carmine, Darin called in his old friend from *Pressure Point*, Dick Bakalyan. The producers initially balked at Darin's choice.

"They called me in and we had a meeting," recalled Bakalyan. "The producers told me, 'Your hair's too white.' Bobby said, 'Put a rinse in it.' They said, 'We need a comic to do this part.' Bobby said, 'Dickie's an actor; he'll play a comic playing the part.' Bobby afforded me the opportunity to do a lot of things that I wouldn't have had the opportunity to do."

Darin's casting instincts were correct, as the chemistry between he and Bakalyan worked very effectively. Darin, dressed in a Mets cap and jacket, played the married, know-it-all cynic with submerged hope and heart. Bakalyan played the less-worldly innocent who still lived with his mother and was easily swayed by the whims of the numerous "chicks" he was chasing. Both spoke with a New York-by-way-of-Italy accent, and the bits were laced with ethnic references to the "old country."

"Carmine and Angie really came out of a conversation we had with Bobby," remembered Saul Ilson. "He used to talk about sitting on a stoop with his friend, and talking about how they were going to solve the world's problems."

"That stoop was Bobby's neighborhood," said Bakalyan. "That was the front of his place in the Bronx where he grew up."

Like the Godmother sketches, "Carmine and Angie" was scripted, but Darin and Bakalyan used their own instincts often. (In fact, Bakalyan received writing credit for one week's segment.) The sketches were never out-and-out hilarious, but they were not intended to be. They succeeded as heartwarming, humorous characterizations and situations based on real immigrant neighborhoods.

"The thing was, there are real people out there like Carmine and Angie," Bakalyan said. "I still get mail from people from Italy who remember that. We got mail from all over the country, even from people who weren't in cities, because they understood about a pal leaving the neighborhood."

Through the two Italian paesanos, Darin occasionally snuck in some of his social opinions or ironic humor. In one bit, Darin's Angie scoffed at actors who change their names. In another, Carmine, egged on by a girl, pushed the Sierra Club to a cynical Angie.

"Bobby had a great sense of humor and put-on," said Bakalyan. "I remember being at a screening at his house once. He went into the bathroom for a long time, and we kept waiting for him to come out. We finally went in, and there was nobody in there. He had crawled through this very small window, climbed along the ledge, came in through the kitchen, and was watching everybody look for him in the bathroom. It was hilarious."

Another long-time Darin friend and associate, Dick Lord, acted as "comedy consultant" for the show. But some new talent also joined the Darin circle. The youngest member of the writing staff was Alan Thicke, who would go on to great television success as the star of the late '80s sitcom "Growing Pains."

"I was a genuine fan of Darin," said Thicke, who had made several television appearances in his native Canada before heading for the U.S. "For my audition piece at the CBC, I did 'If I Were A Carpenter,' ripping off his sound as closely as I could manage. On my very first show, my first professional broadcast number was 'If I Were A Carpenter.'"

Being an avowed Darin fan helped Thicke (who later produced and wrote for the cult TV classic "Fernwood Tonight") land a slot writing special musical-comedy numbers for the "Amusement Company."

"I think what got me the job was when I relayed an anecdote to the producers," he recalled. "In 1967, in my last year of college, a buddy and I, after striking out with these two girls at our fraternity prom, jumped in my little Volkswagen at about two in the morning, and in our tuxedos, drove from London, Ontario to Miami Beach.

"I took 40 dollars and spent it on one of those 'blue-haired lady' bus tours, where you got two hotels and a beverage," he said. "Bobby Darin was at the Deauville Hotel. While my buddy went to pick up girls, I went with a bunch of old ladies, sat in the back of the room, and watched Bobby."

Thicke came up with some special musical material that Darin liked, such as a mock-rock version of "Macbeth," which told the Shakespeare story with parodies of '50s and '60s rock'n'roll songs. Darin took a liking to the "kid" of the writing staff.

"I think we had a pretty warm relationship for a staff writer-star kind of situation," recalled Thicke. "He was very kind to me, and generally kind to the staff. I was quite honored that he came to my house for dinner one night. We spent the night shooting pool and shooting the breeze. I don't think he saw me as just another writer doing just another job. I think he enjoyed teaching me, and being my mentor in some ways."

All participants were very optimistic about the show, and by all accounts, Darin was very involved in the creative planning for the summer replacement run. In fact, *TV Guide* writer Leslie Raddatz, in a behind-the-scenes preview article, wrote, "Darin seems to be the man in charge, an effect he accomplishes with an air of quiet authority, rather than the brashness that might be expected."

In planning the show's music, Darin decided to play it safe and, for the most part, stay in the middle of the road. He went back into his own standards songbag for material such as "Beyond The Sea," "That's All," and "Artificial Flowers." He also utilized songs from his current club act such as "Can't Take My Eyes Off You" and "Spinning Wheel." Darin's only folk-flavored selections were also straight out of his regular act: "Carpenter" and "I'll Be Your Baby Tonight."

Each show also featured Darin singing a duet with a different female guest star, ranging from respected contemporary songstresses (Dionne Warwick, Dusty Springfield) to actresses (Debbie Reynolds, Florence Henderson) to an old friend (Joanie Sommers). One duet per show was performed in what Ilson came to call the "mouth-to-mouth resuscitation" format. Darin and his partner started the song while facing each other in extremely close proximity, and gradually moved their mouths even closer until, at song's end, they kissed.

The only part of the show in which Darin seemed uncomfortable was, ironically, his signature number, "Mack The Knife," which he performed each week as the closing credits rolled. His discomfort was understandable. First, as Darin had to share screen space with the credits, the number lost much of its impact. Also the rote week-after-week reading seemed to bore Darin, who at mid-song would turn his back to the camera and shuffle down a long corridor off-stage.

"He didn't want to do that," Ilson acknowledged. "I had to talk him into it. He said, 'I'm not a dancer, I don't do those things.'"

The show was slated for a seven-week run, but the producers had bigger things in mind. "We don't do summer shows," Ilson told *TV Guide.* "We expect to be back in January."

Despite the smaller summer show budget, the program's sets and production numbers were elaborate, and guest start were of high quality. George Burns, Burt Reynolds, Donald O'Connor, Joan Rivers, Carl Reiner, The Smothers Brothers, Pat Paulsen, and Debbie Reynolds all appeared.

"The Bobby Darin Amusement Company" premiered on Thursday, July 27, 1972 at 10:00 p.m. on NBC. George Burns, Burt Reynolds (whose booking was quite a coup, coming shortly after his highly-publicized nude pose in *Cosmopolitan*) and Bobbie Gentry were Darin's guests.

Variety gave the program a generally favorable review, noting that "the musical portions were generally standout, with the comedic endeavors a trifle spotty, but still promising. Pacing and overall concept were knowingly deft."

The seventh and final episode of the summer series aired September 7, 1972. NBC was pleased enough with the show – and its ratings – to renew it for a regular run beginning in January 1973.

It would come back with a new concept and a new look.

On Friday, January 19, 1973, "The Bobby Darin Show" premiered. It didn't take a genius to figure out that the change in the title indicated more emphasis on Bobby Darin, less on the former "Amusement Company."

Rip Taylor, whose segments never really hit the mark, was gone. So was Steve Landesberg's psychiatrist bit. Echoing what the *Variety* review pointed out, Darin felt that music was the show's strongest element, and he decided to give it greater prominence.

"Bobby put his foot down and said he didn't want any of those people; he wanted to do a straight music show," said Chambers. "He got rid of the psychiatrist because he didn't like being insulted every week. As a result, the show lost a lot of its comic energy. It became a softer show, more music. I think that hurt the show's power to hold an audience. It became too narrow."

Looking back, Ilson agreed with Chambers' assessment of the change, but was more understanding of Darin's position.

"It's not uncommon," he said. 'If you look at any show, the minute the stars start feeling their oats, they usually take over and try to dictate, and that's where it becomes a conflict.

"He wanted to do certain things on the show," Ilson continued. "Some of it, we disagreed with; some of it, the network disagreed with. But to be honest about it, Bobby contributed a lot to the show. He had a lot of ideas, a lot of good things to say, and he was worth listening to."

In Alan Thicke's opinion, the change in the show's direction was a positive step.

"It shifted away from the variety format and got closer to the roots of Bobby Darin, who he really was, and what his music was all about," Thicke said. "I think that when the network got more comfortable with how strong Bobby's music was, they figured they could go with more of that, and less fancy footwork."

Truth be told, Chambers' opinion that the show lost its comic energy is justified. The second series did not match the quality of the summer run, though certainly not entirely because of the Darin-directed changes.

The Godmother remained, and "Carmine and Angie" continued to be high-quality, heart-warming comedy. But too many of the other sketches were unimaginative. While Darin's musical numbers continued to be superb, the show offered little to those who felt indifferent to yet another hour of a singer, no matter how talented, on TV every week. The show also failed to attract as many A-list guests. As opposed to the summer debut with Burt Reynolds and George Burns, the winter premier could only offer Burl Ives and Dyan Cannon.

Variety's review of the January premier was not positive: "There is more to being a variety show host than telling a few jokes and singing a couple of songs. Bobby Darin still has not entirely made the transition." The review also noted that the comedy sketches were not "developed fully enough to get off the ground."

"The Bobby Darin Show" was, unfortunately, very formulaic TV variety for the most part. With the exception of Darin's singing, the program presented little that a viewer couldn't get from a dozen other shows of the day. In particular, the show offered no enticement to the younger, hipper, audience. Too many of the guest stars were the usual TV faces who had almost already worn out their welcome: Joey Heatherton, Charles Nelson Reilly, Cloris Leachman, Tim Conway, Andy Griffith, Phillis Diller, Artie Johnson.

The musical guest list fared slightly better, as the program featured some acts with then-current chart hits – Bread, Seals & Crofts, Bill Withers. But few musical bookings were surprising, with the exceptions of blues singer Taj Mahal and guitarist David Bromberg. In retrospect, one wonders whether Darin ever considered former associates such as Tim Hardin, John Sebastian, or Randy Newman, all of whom would have been palatable (at least for a couple of numbers) in middle America's living rooms in 1973.

With more emphasis on music, Darin's own song list expanded, though it stayed decidedly middle-of-the-road. His *That's All, This Is Darin, Oh! Look At Me Now, From Hello Dolly To Goodbye Charlie*, and *In A Broadway Bag* albums were mined. However, some contemporary songs were also part of the mix. He performed very tasteful versions of Bread's "If," Don McLean's "Dreidel," and Kris Kristofferson's "Help Me Make It Through The Night" as well as an interesting jazzy arrangement of Gilbert O'Sullivan's hit "Alone Again (Naturally)." Darin also seemed to take a particular shine to the compositions of Neil Diamond, performing "Brooklyn Roads" and "Shilo" in effective semi-acoustic settings, "Song Sung Blue" in a swingin' pre-rock arrangement, and a dynamic "Sweet Caroline."

Strangely, considering his relatively unimaginative song choices, Darin never performed many of his own hits. "Dream Lover," "Queen Of The Hop," "Things," "18 Yellow Roses" and many other Darin classics were all conspicuous by their absence. He also passed over the more contemporary choices from his albums. While one could not have reasonably expected "Long Line Rider" and its ilk, none of the '66-'67 Atlantic material (save "If I Were A Carpenter") was performed. Similarly, songs from the August 1972 *Bobby Darin* Motown LP were completely ignored.

Not that the shows were devoid of musical highlights or surprises. Darin and Helen Reddy sang a wonderful duet version of Dylan's "If Not For You." Darin and Nancy Sinatra heated up the screen in a "mouth-to-mouth" duet on "Light My Fire." And Petula Clark and Dusty Springfield made welcome appearances.

Nine shows had aired when NBC announced cancellation of "The Bobby Darin Show" in April 1973. Four more shows would air in April, and then the plug would be pulled. Ratings were unspectacular, though certainly not bottom-barrel.

"Today a network would kill for those kind of numbers," said Ilson. Thicke added, "It was a marginal hit; by today's standards it would certainly be on."

Even before the announcement, people on the set realized things weren't working, and there was some tension when new ideas were brought up. Dick Bakalyan recalls that he and Darin favored scrapping the show's format entirely and making it one half music, one half "Carmine and Angie."

"Bobby was anxious to do 'The Neighborhood' for a half-hour," said Bakalyan, who had no doubt the sketch could have successfully been expanded. "We had great ideas the producers didn't want to do."

One bizarre idea that Darin did get past Ilson and Chambers' objections was a chess segment, in which he would make chess moves against a computer. It was hardly the stuff of riveting television.

"NBC was violently against it," Ilson recalled. "They thought it was boring. They thought it was kind of an esoteric thing that never belonged, but he wanted to do it. I guess he felt that it would give him a little more dignity, class him up a little bit. We did it until one day the network said 'No more; that's it.'"

A more serious problem reoccurred as the weeks went by: Darin's health declined dramatically. His heart fibrillations increased, the oxygen mask was ever-present, and Darin's energy level was precarious. Looking back 16 years after the show ended, those working with Darin at the time had differing recollections as to how obvious – and how much a point of controversy – Darin's health problem was.

Alan Thicke: "It was only during the end that we became aware of it. He didn't like to talk about it. He intimated to me a couple of times that he didn't quite have the energy and he was going to have some tests."

Geoff Edwards: "I'd go into his dressing room to rehearse and he'd be breathing oxygen. He'd have to take the mask off to laugh, and then he'd put it right back on. Bobby was really sick, but the producers didn't believe that. They thought it was his temperament. They didn't treat him well."

Dick Bakalyan: "He was fighting with the producers. They thought he was faking it. I went into their office and told them 'This is for real. The man is really sick, guys. Lighten up.'"

Ernest Chambers: "As I recall, it [Darin's health] wasn't a big factor. He was a hard worker, volatile, and all that. I don't recall that it was factor."

Saul Ilson: "He was quite ill toward the end. I didn't know how serious it was. None of us did at the time. I remember the last couple of shows, it was very sad. He could hardly get through them."

Quitman Dennis recalled paying a visit to Darin on the set: "He just sat there slumped. It was terribly uncomfortable. I couldn't even get a conversation going with an old friend."

Nevertheless, the show-business trouper made it through the shows, though Darin appeared in fewer comedy sketches as the series wound down. Whatever was happening in

Darin's dressing room, the public saw the usual finger-snapping, hard-working entertainer.

"I spent an awful lot of time with him on the last three or four shows," Saul Ilson said. "Sometimes, I thought he would never, ever get up to do those shows.

"I remember the second-to-last show, he was in his dressing room and he was quite ill," said Ilson. "I didn't know what to do, we just blocked around him. The time came for him to go out, and usually he would warm up the audiences; he would talk to them. And in this case, I told him, 'You don't have to do that.' But he went out anyway. They started to applaud and the man just grew and came to life. I don't know how he did it."

"He found it somewhere," recalled Bakalyan. "He reached way inside and came up with the smile on his face and the whole deal. No matter how bad he felt, he never laid it on other people."

At one point, an exhausted Darin told Saul Ilson, "It's getting tougher and tougher to get up every morning and look in the mirror and become Bobby Darin."

Darin was not about to let the series go down without a bang. The final episode would be a spectacular, in-concert show featuring Darin and special guest Peggy Lee.

"He knew the series was over," said Chambers, "and his attitude was 'screw the world, I want to do one show just the way I want to do it.' If he had his druthers, he would have done nothing but 60 minutes of music every week."

Even though there were no production numbers to be staged, the taping was difficult. Because of his health, Darin was unable to come out to the set for rehearsal, so the music was piped into his dressing room. When he eventually got to the set, he was displeased with the sound, and irritable with the crew, in one of the few times he lashed

out at the people he worked with. (Darin's anger was usually reserved for those in "authority" positions, such as the
producers and the network.)

"The crew was very upset with him," Ilson recalled. "We
were running long and we got into a situation where we
had to take a mandatory break. All we had to do was one
more number. One song to go and Bobby could have gone
home.

"The only way we could waive the break was to poll every
member of the crew, and they all had to agree to it. Somebody in the crew said no, so we had to take the break and
he had to hang around. It was sad."

As usual, the public saw none of the problems, health or
otherwise. What they saw, on April 27, 1973, was the episode
generally regarded as the high point of the Darin series.

"The final show of the series was the best," Alan Thicke
said. "In hindsight, you wonder if you would have been
better had you started at that point."

Peggy Lee performed two songs solo, and joined Darin for
five duets. The remainder of the show was prime Darin in
the setting he loved – the concert stage. The unedited tape
of the entire final performance (later released on video as
"Bobby Darin Live!") shows that Darin treated it not as a
television show, but as a nightclub appearance at which
cameras just happened to be present.

Throughout, he made no remarks about the series and no
reference to a 'final show." When, in the middle of "Bridge
Over Troubled Water," Darin picked up the wrong harmonica
– and did not realize it until a few sour notes had been blown
– there was no yelling "cut" and no re-doing the number.
Darin simply joked his way out of it after the song was over.

This attitude was most evident in Darin's patented introduction to "If I Were A Carpenter." As he did in his concert

act, he relayed the comically twisted Koppelman and Rubin pitch to him. Explaining his turn-down of "Younger Girl," Darin cracked, "I can't do a song about a younger girl; they'll throw my ass in jail." Then, acknowledging the fact that you couldn't say "ass" on television in 1973, he remarked "Get out the scissors!"

The set list for the final taping was typical of late Darin. Though he abandoned any pretense of sympathizing with the hip rock crowd, and also gave up trying to present himself as a songwriter, it's still hard to find critical fault with a set that included songs by Paul Simon, Leadbelly, Tim Hardin, Hank Williams and Bo Diddley.

Among the show's many highlights was Darin's performance of "Bridge Over Troubled Water" in his restrained folk voice. It made one wish that he'd have taken one more crack at the interpretive contemporary style he embraced in 1966-67. With this song, the Neil Diamond material performed on earlier shows, and a few others, another strong album could have resulted.

Darin took off his suit and tie for "Midnight Special," then strapped on a guitar for Hank Williams' "(I Heard That) Lonesome Whistle." Darin could still joke about his hairpiece; patting his head, he told the audience to notice how carefully he put on the guitar.

The encore/finale, while no surprise to anyone who had caught Darin's at-the-piano R&B encores in concert since 1968, was still a delight for those who might have justifiably thought that Darin had repudiated his rock'n'roll roots.

It began with a bit of "You Are My Sunshine," sung Ray Charles-style. Darin then sat down at the piano for "Bo Diddley." Finally, after a long instrumental passage during which the band was introduced and Darin played harmonica, he tore into "Splish Splash," playing rock'n'roll piano, Jerry Lee Lewis-style. It was a driving, intense rendition, and

Darin was obviously enjoying the release. He showed a look of complete musical contentment, the same look he had when performing "Simple Song Of Freedom" on the Canadian TV special three years earlier.

Fittingly, the last line Bobby Darin ever sang on his prime-time network TV variety show was "Roll over Beethoven, dig these rhythm and blues." It is impossible to view this number and still contend that Darin did not like rock'n'roll.

Darin went out his way and he went out spectacularly. But that could not obscure the fact that the series failed.

"I think Bobby was a real competitive guy," observed Thicke, "and I think he took any form of failure personally."

"I'm positive he was hurt by it," Ilson said.

Despite the fact that the short-lived series never really got off the ground, those who worked on the show retain fond memories of that time, and of Darin. Darin would often join the staff for softball games, or invite them to his home's screening room to watch a movie. During the show's run, he also held a picnic for the crew and their families.

"Remember the character The Godmother?" said Ilson. "Well, Bobby liked to think of himself as The Godfather. After every show, he would choose a restaurant and the staff would join him, so he could hold court. He'd sit at the head of the table. So there was a part of him that loved that role of being in control, of being that Godfather figure."

As opposed to Thicke and Edwards, who looked up to Darin, or Bakalyan, an old friend, producers Saul Ilson and Ernest Chambers have personal recollections about Darin forged only from those 20 weeks of hard, occasionally trying work. The team made television shows with stars such as Frank Sinatra, The Smothers Brothers, Carol Channing, Doris Day, Tony Orlando, Pearl Bailey, Leslie Uggams and Danny Kaye. But even after more than a dozen years, both producers retained vivid recollections of Darin's talent and personality.

Ernest Chambers: "I found him a fascinating character. He was a very contradictory character. He was a very tough kid who came up really rough. And he loved great music, drama and literature, and had tremendous respect for the finer things in life. So he was this kind of schizoid character. On the one hand, he was a real back-alley street fighter, a survivor. On the other hand, a guy of tremendous dignity, great aspiration and artistic gifts. On the set, he was extremely courteous with people. He'd lose his temper with us, the bosses. But he would never pick on the little guy. I liked him very much and felt a lot of affection and respect toward him."

Saul Ilson: "If you didn't know him, he came across as a very cocky individual. I got to know him, and there was that side to him. But I got to really like him a lot. We didn't always see eye-to-eye. My philosophy was, when I felt he was wrong, I would tell him. I think he respected me. He wasn't the easiest, but none of them are. We've done a lot of entertainers, a lot of shows. As an entertainer, he was right up there."

"The Curtain Falls"
The Final Days

In addition to being back on television, Bobby Darin was also back on the charts – for the first time in four years – as 1973 opened. In late 1972, Darin recorded "Happy," a song written by Michel LeGrand and Smokey Robinson for the film *Lady Sings The Blues*.

To work with Darin on this track, Motown brought in producer Bob Crewe, who had produced The Four Seasons' classics of the 1960s, as well as hits by Mitch Ryder and others. Darin and Crewe had known each other since the early '60s, so the paring seemed ideal.

"He was terrific, very easy to work with, the consummate professional," Crewe said of Darin. "A lot of people thought he was temperamental. I never did. He wanted things right."

"Happy" was an orchestrated MOR ballad. It was cut in New York with a 46-piece orchestra, and, at Darin's insistence, it was recorded live, with no overdubbing. Though Darin had to sing over a powerful arrangement, he came through with his best showstopper voice. Like the earlier Motown album, this single was aimed at an older audience. But Crewe said that Darin did not explicitly set out to pursue the MOR path at Motown.

"I don't think he thought in those terms at that time in his life," Crewe said, recalling that Darin was still "very interested in what was going on in the world; very socially involved."

Darin and Crewe believed they had a potential hit with "Happy," but Motown had little experience with a white MOR record.

"Motown had not had this kind of record ever – mainstream, white, big orchestration," Crewe said. "The promotion department didn't quite know what to do with it. I personally went out on the old proverbial road to help break the record."

"Happy" stalled on the pop charts at #67 after eight weeks. It fared better, though still not spectacularly, on the Easy Listening chart, reaching #32. "We all thought it was going to be bigger," Crewe said. "I think it could have done a lot more if there had been a concentrated effort behind it." Both Michael Jackson and Smokey Robinson recorded the song shortly thereafter.

In January 1973, Darin extended his reach into another area he loved – chess. As other entertainers sponsored golf tournaments, Darin saw no reason why he shouldn't be the first celebrity to have his name attached to a chess tournament. The Bobby Darin International Chess Classic was planned for October and described as the "richest tournament ever," with $25,000 at stake.

While Darin was presenting himself as the slick, old-fashioned show-biz pro on his weekly television series, he showed another side during an appearance on "The Midnight Special" in March.

Appearing in a casual jacket and no tie, and accompanied only by his four-piece band (which still included Quitman Dennis and Tommy Amato, along with pianist Bob Rozario and guitarist Terry Kellman), Darin opened his segment with "If I Were A Carpenter."

He then sat down at the piano and began a song curiously absent from his nightclub act for years – "Dream Lover." After a couple of verses, Darin shifted into an uninhibited rendition of "Splish Splash."

The band rocked with abandon, while Darin tore into piano breaks and wailing harmonica solos. Terry Kellman took an absolutely blistering electric guitar solo. The studio audience loved Bobby Darin, rock'n'roll bandleader, and Darin appeared much more into this performance than anything he'd done on his TV show. Again, any conception that Darin could not rock, or did not like rock'n'roll, was emphatically, undeniably refuted by this performance.

In one way, it was a simple matter of Darin knowing his audience: rock'n'roll was what the younger, hipper "Midnight Special" viewers wanted. Darin was aware that there was a revival of interest in '50s rock, and he correctly believed that his contributions should not be forgotten.

"I think it's a kick to have somebody include me in a revival of the oldies and talk about one of the grand old men," he told *Melody Maker.* "It's much nicer to be included as time goes by than to be excluded."

With the TV show canceled, Darin had some time for personal matters in the spring of 1973. On June 25, Darin and Andrea Yaeger made their marriage official, with a ceremony held in Walnut Grove, California. The union didn't last, however, as the couple was divorced by November.

Also in the legal arena, Darin tried to recoup some money from his failed sale of T.M. Music to Commonwealth United, and to get out of his songwriting contract with that firm. In June, Darin filed a breach of contract suit against Commonwealth United, five related firms, and Charles Koppelman, asking for the 1968 contract to be rescinded, and for all T.M. assets to be returned to him.

Darin was also back on the big screen that summer in his first movie in almost four years. He received third billing in the film *Happy Mother's Day...Love, George*, also featuring Patricia Neal, Cloris Leachman, and a young Ron Howard. While *Variety* called it Darin's "first good role since *Captain Newman, M.D.*," his scenes were edited heavily (as was the film itself).

By the time Darin opened his Hilton engagement on July 18, it was apparent to many of his friends and associates that time was running out. Journalist Al Aronowitz, who had written a number of insightful *New York Post* articles on Darin over the years, and who had bonded with him in the 1960s because of their shared political and social views, received a phone call from Darin earlier in 1973.

"He called me up and said, 'It's memoir-writing time.' He knew he was going to die," Aronowitz recalled.

Before his wedding, Darin spent six weeks in the hospital with blood poisoning. The ailment was reported to have resulted from Darin not receiving proper antibiotics prior to having dental work done, an essential precaution against infection for patients who have had heart surgery or rheumatic fever.

Darin's heart was again beating out of rhythm, he was having difficulty breathing, and he began losing weight. He told his band members that he thought he would die before the end of the year, and word spread among Darin's friends that the end seemed near.

"I got a phone call from a friend who said that Bobby was really ill and probably didn't have long to go," recalled Darin's high school bandmate and Capitol arranger Walter Raim. "I went out to his house in Las Vegas and spent a couple of days with him. He was so thin and weak that he spent his days lying on a raft in his swimming pool all day long."

Darin at The Hilton, July 1973
(Las Vegas News Bureau)

But at The Hilton, it was a different Darin. "We saw him do an hour-and-a-half of the most fevered, energetic, unbelievable performance," Raim said. "You couldn't believe that he could do it. He was a demon."

Darin inserted a few extra "fake encores" into his show, which allowed him to take a bow, run off stage, take oxygen, and then return. Vegas audiences never knew how ill he was. Reviews noted his usual energetic showmanship. But it was killing him.

"I know why he was doing it," Raim observed. "That's what he loved. One of his great fantasies as a kid was that he was going to die on stage."

Darin played three weeks at The Hilton, took a break for Elvis Presley's engagement there, then returned for ten days in late August. His last performance was on August 26.

Darin was experiencing heart fibrillations again, and in early October, he was treated for congestive heart failure. Though he was in bad shape, he tried to keep reasonably active. Geoff Edwards visited him in the hospital and remembered that Darin had an appointment each day to play chess with a 70-year-old woman.

Again on December 10, Darin reentered Cedars of Lebanon Hospital. The two artificial valves he received in the 1971 operation were malfunctioning. A second open-heart surgery was the only option, and on December 19, Darin underwent an eight-hour surgery. Finally, his heart gave way. The four-surgeon team said he was "just too weak to recover."

Bobby Darin died in the early morning of December 20, 1973, at Cedars of Lebanon, at the age of 37.

"Something To Remember You By"

27

Post-Mortem

There was no funeral or memorial service for Bobby Darin. His will directed that his body be donated to medical science, and it was taken to the UCLA medical school for use in research.

Because Darin's death occurred so close to Christmas, combined with the fact that his career was in a down cycle, news and reaction to his passing were somewhat buried.

His death was front-page news in *The Los Angeles Times*, where celebrity passings at Cedars are treated as a local story, and in *The New York Post*, which had always regarded his comings and goings as big news.

In an uncharacteristically vengeful move, *Time* magazine felt it had to get in one last shot at Darin while noting his death. A one-paragraph item citing the passing of "Walden Robert Cassotto, the crooner known as Bobby Darin" brought up Darin's old comment about wanting to be a legend by 25. "He never made it" was the *Time* obit's last line.

Surprisingly, the publication which noted Darin's death with the most dignity and accuracy was *Rolling Stone*, which ignored Darin while he was alive. In 1969, the publication failed to even notice *Born Walden Robert Cassotto* and *Commitment* – albums aimed straight at the magazine's constituency. But the *Rolling Stone* obituary treated Darin's career with the respect and importance it deserved.

Referring to Darin as "the brash and ambitious pop singer," the article was accompanied by a series of photos tracing different phases of Darin's career. Steve Blauner and Dave Gershenson (who acted as Darin's publicist and was once Sandra Dee's manager) were quoted, with Gershenson going public with the story of the dentistry foul-up for the first time. Blauner also dropped the news that Darin had received release from his Motown contract and was planning to record an album with hot producer Richard Perry.

Another fine tribute to Darin came in *Down Beat*, the respected jazz-oriented magazine which had put Darin on its cover in 1960. Writer Michael Cuscuna unabashedly stood up for Darin in retort to "cynics of his talent," specifically in the jazz community.

"Darin was an unusually talented singer and a consistent songwriter," Cuscuna wrote. "He phrased beautifully, singing lyrics with the freedom, understanding and sincerity of the best jazz singers. Each record was professionally and tastefully arranged, using top jazz studio musicians and continually illustrating Darin's talent as a sensitive and interpretive singer."

Darin's pop culture presence has ebbed and flowed in the years since his death. At various times, particularly throughout much of the 1980s, it seemed that he was often overlooked or underestimated in many historical pop music or entertainment overviews. There have also been some events which have generated revivals of interest in Darin, and positive reassessments of his abilities and career.

Darin's name was brought up in a couple of noteworthy records. He is among the dead rock stars mentioned in

The Righteous Brothers' morbid 1974 hit "Rock And Roll Heaven." And when Frank Sinatra recorded "Mack The Knife" for his 1984 album *L.A. Is My Lady*, he added a lyric verse acknowledging previous "Mack" hitmakers Louis Armstrong, Bobby Darin, and Ella Fitzgerald. This action led to further doubts about any rumored feud between Darin and Sinatra. As late as 1991, Sinatra still included "Mack The Knife" in his concert repertoire.

In 1982, Darin took his place alongside numerous other show-biz greats, with the dedication of his star on the Hollywood Walk Of Fame. The ceremony occurred on May 26, 1982, and Darin's star was placed at 1735 North Vine Street, in front of the Palace Theatre, and across the street from Capitol Records.

Darin's star, the 1,749th placed on the Walk Of Fame, was sponsored by Dick Clark, who spoke at the ceremony, and Dave Gershenson. Darin's star lies between those honoring Jim Backus and Roy Rogers.

Nina Cassotto, by then publicly acknowledged as Darin's mother, and Dodd Darin attended the ceremony.

In May 1988, Atlantic Records celebrated its 40th anniversary with a concert and party held at Madison Square Garden (and telecast live nationally by HBO). A segment of the concert honored two of Atlantic's most important stars who had passed away – Otis Redding and Bobby Darin.

The tribute to Darin – a performance of "Mack The Knife" by a 1980s Atlantic artist – was originally supposed to have been handled by Bette Midler. When Midler pulled out at the last minute, singers Tim Hauser and Alan Paul – the male half of the Grammy-winning jazz-pop vocal group The Manhattan Transfer – were asked to step in. As Darin fans, they gladly accepted.

"Alan and I were influenced by Darin," Tim Hauser said. "When 'Mack The Knife' came out, I was completely floored by that record. I thought it was one of the best things I had ever heard in my life. I was into 'legit' singers as a kid. I was into Darin's phrasing. I identified with any white cat who could really sing in the groove, because there were a lot of white singers who did not."

Also in the late 1980s, Darin's cache in rock circles was boosted by praise from a seemingly unlikely source – the respected rock artist Neil Young, who became the first major, critically-acclaimed rock figure to publicly champion Darin in the press.

In a 1989 *Los Angeles Times* interview, Young (who consistently jumped between the hard rock, soft rock, folk, and country genres) surprised writer Robert Hilburn by naming Darin as the early rocker he most identified with.

"That guy went through more changes than anybody," Young told Hilburn. "Think of the swing from 'Queen Of The Hop' to 'Mack The Knife.' That was off the wall completely, but he managed to make two classics."

Darin's place among rock immortals again came up in deliberations about the Rock and Roll Hall of Fame. During the Hall's fifth annual ballot, in 1989, Darin gained entrance along with The Who, The Four Seasons, Simon & Garfunkel, The Kinks, The Four Tops, The Platters, and Hank Ballard.

Darin's nomination was greeted with some of the same cynicism about his "rock credentials" that he met during his career. As usual, Dick Clark stood up for Darin in a *Rolling Stone* interview, bluntly saying that those who criticized Darin's induction made him want to throw up. "The man was one of the most multi-talented individuals I ever met," Clark said.

Complaints aside, Darin had the backing of a sizable number of voters, including long-time fan Robert Hilburn, who had no trouble placing Darin among rock'n'roll greats.

(Las Vegas News Bureau)

"He started off in rock," Hilburn said. "I liked all the components – folk, country, R&B. As long as he could make interesting records in each of those styles, it didn't bother me which way he was going. He had that kind of questioning attitude and defiance. There was individuality in what he said. To me, that added up to rock'n'roll."

"I called the Rock and Roll Hall of Fame and recommended that they get Neil Young to induct Darin," Hilburn said. "That would have been a good statement to show that Darin was admired by really critically-acclaimed people."

It ended up being Darin's old friend Paul Anka who gave the induction speech for Darin during the ceremony held on January 17, 1990 at the Waldorf Astoria Hotel in New York. Dodd Darin accepted the Hall of Fame Award and thanked "everyone who voted on my dad's induction. I'm very proud; this is something I'll never forget," he said.

Dion DiMucci, an inductee two years earlier, was chosen by *Rolling Stone* to provide the tribute to Darin in the magazine's Hall of Fame section. He eloquently summed up Darin's genius: "Bobby's act at the Copa was just unreal...He was up there doing jazz and folk and rock and anything else he wanted...Singles like 'Splish Splash' were great, because Bobby knew how to rock, but he also knew how to have fun with it."

Darin's greatness as a songwriter was formally recognized later in the 1990s when he was inducted into the National Academy of Popular Music's Songwriters Hall of Fame (alongside Bruce Springsteen, Peggy Lee, and Tim Rice). Ahmet Ertegun gave a moving speech inducting Darin at the ceremony held on June 9, 1999.

Darin's "swingin'" persona got hipper with the 1990s revival of lounge music and Vegas-style retro-chic. The Darin influence was obvious and intentional in a number of popular recordings by Brian Setzer. The former member of the neo-rockabilly Stray Cats recreated Billy May's exact charts (and therefore Darin's records) for his renditions of "A Nightingale Sang In Berkeley Square" and "There's A Rainbow 'Round My Shoulder" on his *Brian Setzer Orchestra* CD in 1994. In 1998, Setzer recorded Darin's own "As Long As I'm Singing" on his *The Dirty Boogie* CD, and his 2000 release *Va Voom* included a winning, nearly note-for-note cover of "Mack The Knife."

Darin's songs and recordings have periodically popped up in some high profile settings. In the movies, "Mack The Knife" was heard in director Robert Redford's *Quiz Show*, and "Beyond The Sea" has been used in the films *Diner*, *GoodFellas*, and *Apollo 13*. A number of national television commercials have featured Darin recordings, exposing even non-hits such as "The More I See You," "More," "Two Of A Kind," "Beautiful Things," and "Call Me Irresponsible" to temporarily massive audiences.

Darin's career and life have been given the documentary treatment in two noteworthy television settings. In 1998, PBS affiliates nationwide aired "Bobby Darin: Beyond The Song," an "American Masters" series program which included comments from Darin friends and associates and a generous selection of clips from Darin's television appearances. The program was later released on home video. Likewise, in 2001, Darin was the subject of an episode of the popular series "A&E Biography."

A motion picture about Darin's life has been discussed and rumored since 1982. Finally, in 2003, production began on *Beyond The Sea*, a biopic directed by and starring Kevin Spacey. The film was scheduled for release in late 2004.

Since Darin's death, a number of rare or previously unreleased recordings have been released, further enhancing his legacy. However, record label interest in releasing Darin product was very fallow for a long period of time. There was only one significant release in the first dozen years following his death, and it was a quick one – Motown's *Darin 1936-1973*. Released in February 1974, the album was assembled by Bob Crewe.

"Someone from Motown had me go in and cull whatever I could find to put together an album," Crewe recalled. "There wasn't much that was around. I put together an album of what was available."

After recording "Happy" (which made its album debut posthumously), Crewe and Darin had talked about further work together, and two tracks were recorded in Los Angeles: Darin and Tommy Amato's "Another Song On My Mind" and The Carpenters' hit "I Won't Last A Day Without You."

Both were included on *1936-1973*, along with a few Darin-produced tracks which sounded like demos – covers of "Blue Monday," "The Letter" and Dylan's "Don't Think Twice." Two tracks planned for the scrapped Desert Inn live album also surfaced: "Mack The Knife" and "If I Were A Carpenter."

By the late 1970s, the only Bobby Darin album in print was Atco's 12-track *The Bobby Darin Story*. For fans that did not catch Darin's discs during his heyday, looking for the old albums in collectors shops became the only option.

The CD boom of the mid-'80s finally resulted in some new Darin product hitting the marketplace. By the end of the decade, both Atlantic and Capitol released hits collections of 17 and 20 tracks respectively. Capitol's *Collectors Series* CD made standout tracks such as "When I Get Home" and "As Long As I'm Singing" (which had never even appeared on a Darin LP) available for the first time since their original 45 rpm release.

(Capitol also released a Wayne Newton *Collectors Series* CD in 1989 which contained tracks produced by T.M. Music. Again, many of these Darin-involved tracks had been unavailable for decades.)

Motown finally got around to releasing its shelved 1971 Darin live album, *Live At The Desert Inn*, on CD in 1987.

Still, as of the early 1990s, the vast majority of Darin's catalog remained unreleased on CD. The tide began to turn by mid-decade. By 2003, almost all of the original Atco/Atlantic and Capitol albums had trickled out (either domestically or via import) and the release of additional compilations filled in many holes.

Collections such as *Spotlight On Bobby Darin: Great Gentleman Of Song* (Capitol) and *The Unreleased Capitol Sides* (Collectors Choice) unearthed great previously-unreleased Darin renditions of standards such as "Just In Time," "I Left My Heart In San Francisco" and "You're Nobody Till Somebody Loves You." In all, studio recordings of 35 "new" songs have been released since 1995, as have over 20 tracks which previously only appeared on 1960s singles. Additionally, Darin's live magic has received greater exposure through releases such as *The Curtain Falls – Live At The Flamingo* which documents Darin's brilliant 1963 nightclub act.

[Please note that posthumous releases are covered in greater detail in the Discography section of this book.]

As of this writing, 46 Darin tracks (roughly 10% of his recordings) remain unreleased on legitimate CD. While there are still a few Atco B-sides which remain vinyl-only rarities, the majority of the non-CD recordings consist of Darin's early Decca recordings, most of the '68-'70 tracks recorded for Darin's own label, Direction, and nine Motown tracks.

This author had the privilege and pleasure to serve as a co-producer (along with Nik Venet and James Austin) of the 1995 Rhino Records four-CD box set *As Long As I'm Singing:*

The Bobby Darin Collection. The collection's 96 tracks were chosen to showcase Darin's entire career and present the "best of the best" of Darin's recordings in each of the styles he tackled – rock'n'roll, popular standards, Brill Building pop, jazz, country, folk, and protest songs. The collection put some lost or previously-overlooked gems front and center, as well as displaying Darin's talents as a songwriter and producer.

The box set gave a boost to the critical reassessment of Darin which occurred in the 1990s. As the years went by, Darin's reputation grew, and he was finally being recognized not only as a fine crooner, consummate showman, or appealing pop star, but as a true and utterly unique artist. The reviews the box set received displayed ever-growing consensus on Darin's greatness.

USA Today: "If Darin were alive today, he'd be radio's poster boy, a superb pop singer with a kaleidoscopic range of styles."

New York Times: "If Bobby Darin hadn't died at 37, he would probably be rapping today – and rapping well."

Newsday: "Was there ever a more versatile vocalist?"

Los Angeles Times: "In many ways, he may have been the most versatile, ambitious, and misunderstood artist of his time."

28

"After You've Gone"

What Might Have Been

The death of any artist always leads to the inevitable "What might have been if he had lived" questions. While answers about any deceased artist are speculative, in Darin's case, even speculation is difficult. As he died at so young an age, one must answer that question with another question – Had he lived how long? Three years? Ten years? Twenty years?

Consider the triumphant comebacks that Darin contemporaries like The Everly Brothers or Dion made well into the 1980s. Or consider how completely irrelevant to the music scene the traditional "Las Vegas entertainer" became in the '70s and '80s.

Speculating about Darin is also more difficult because, unlike almost all of the pop greats who were lost before their time, Darin was alone in knowing his time was short. By most accounts, Darin's decisions about the directions his career and music were going to take were made with consideration of the fact he would not be around too long.

In one span of only eight years, Darin moved from Broadway show tunes to gentle folk; from four-piece band protest rock back to Vegas and network TV variety. Some of these "phases" might have been explored at more length, or some might never have occurred at all, if Darin himself figured on a long and full life.

Still, the exercise of speculating what might have happened is so inviting that it shouldn't be passed upon after examining Darin's career so closely. First, it's likely that Bobby Darin would have had another hit.

In the early '70s, the public and radio became kinder to acts that had started in the '50s. If the Darin-Richard Perry pairing would have come to fruition, some degree of commercial success would likely have resulted. In 1973, Perry was the hottest producer in the business, the first "star" producer since Phil Spector. Barbra Streisand, Carly Simon and Ringo Starr had all achieved Top 10 success with Perry-produced releases.

Even though Darin's voice seemed to have lost a little power on the Bob Crewe sessions, its hard to believe that a Perry-Darin combination wouldn't have struck a little gold. Perhaps only six more months would have given us one more Bobby Darin album, and a Top 10 swan song.

To mount his comeback, Darin probably would have had to resume songwriting activities. Not that his hit would necessarily have to have been self-written. But part of Darin's comeback build-up would likely have been how well "Dream Lover," "Splish Splash," "Queen Of The Hop" and "Early In The Morning" stood the test of time – and how, with "Mack The Knife" and subsequent MOR standards, Darin's reputation as a songwriter got buried.

Keep in mind the big comebacks that two Darin contemporaries (and friends), Neil Sedaka and Paul Anka, made within a year of Darin's death. Their reputations as songwriters saved them from teen-idol/oldies relic oblivion. While the *Rolling Stone* crowd would never exactly embrace them, neither would they be vilified (*a la* Fabian and Frankie Avalon).

While neither Anka nor Sedaka had gone as far into Sinatra/Vegas territory as Darin, their rock'n'roll hits were not as fondly remembered as Darin's. Therefore, "Hello, Dolly!" and the like not withstanding, Darin still retained some instant rock'n'roll credibility. With quality material, Darin might have been welcomed back with more open arms – and with a wider audience – than either Anka or Sedaka.

A case could be made that Darin was heading back to rock'n'roll based on the 1973 "Midnight Special" performance. With the rock'n'roll revival in full bloom, Darin probably saw the value of aligning himself with his high-quality '50s hits, not only as a singer, but as a songwriter and musician. It's hard to imagine that Darin would have gone all the way in this direction – Richard Nader's oldies shows, etc. – but he went through 20 episodes of his TV show without singing "Dream Lover," then surprised observers by dusting it off on "The Midnight Special." Maybe Darin was about to proudly rescue his rock'n'roll oldies from the closet. With Paul Revere & The Raiders, Sonny & Cher, and others moving into the showrooms, Las Vegas was finally ready for rock'n'roll by the mid-'70s, so Darin would not have had to alter a more rock-oriented repertoire if he continued to play there.

Would Darin have been happy as an oldies act? Probably not in the long term, but in the short term, he may have thrown himself into it with the same verve as he did the protest phase or the TV variety show phase. He might have seen it as a shot to secure his place in the music's history. And if he would have had the chance to do that before he died, he might be more acknowledged in rock circles today.

More than 15 years after Darin's death, two of his closest musical associates – Bobby Scott and Nik Venet – pondered the question of what would have become of Darin. Neither saw Darin as aging rocker or Vegas remnant.

"Had he lived today," Scott said, "he would probably be doing what a guy like Tony Bennett is doing: Doing a lot of things that are considered jazzier. And he would bring interpretive things to songs, and a different look at them, so that people would happily pay their money to hear him."

Venet saw Darin as rising to the upper echelons of the non-performing end of the business: "He'd probably have his own film company and his own record company, and he'd be the executive like Francis Ford Coppola."

Probably the safest prediction is that Darin would have continued to keep everyone guessing, just as he did throughout his career. His death deprived the entertainment world of one of its most fascinating professionals, and denied younger audiences the chance to see a performer whose repertoire encompassed nearly a century of music and show business tradition – from vaudeville and the Broadway musical to rock'n'roll and folk songs.

The supreme combination of versatility, professionalism, taste, and artistry exhibited by Bobby Darin has been all too rare in the history of American popular music. His 18-year body of work – on records, on film, on television, and on the concert stage – is a legacy of quality that few performers of any age can match.

Chronology

A Summary of Important Dates
in the Life and Career of Bobby Darin

1936

May 14: Walden Robert Cassotto (Bobby Darin) born.

1956

January 17: Bobby Darin and Don Kirshner copyright their first song.

March 10: Darin makes TV debut on "Stage Show," singing "Rock Island Line."

1957

May: Darin records first two Atco Records singles in Nashville.

July 19: Darin appears (with Chuck Berry, Frankie Lymon, and Andy Williams) on Alan Freed's TV show "The Big Beat."

October: Darin appears at The Apollo Theatre.

December 16: Darin makes first appearance on "American Bandstand."

1958

April 10: Darin records "Splish Splash" and "Queen Of The Hop" in New York.

August 4: "Splish Splash" reaches #3 on the *Billboard* chart.

September: Darin's composition "This Little Girl's Gone Rockin'," written with Mann Curtis, becomes a pop and R&B hit for Ruth Brown.

December 19-24: Darin records tracks for his *That's All* album, including "Mack The Knife."

1959

March 5: Darin records "Dream Lover" in New York.

May 7-17: Darin opens for George Burns at Harrah's, Lake Tahoe.

July: "Dream Lover" hits #2 on the *Billboard* charts.

August 7: Darin debuts in Hollywood at The Cloister; George Burns introduces him.

September 25: Darin guests on Jimmy Durante's TV special, singing "Mack The Knife" and two duets with Durante.

October 5: "Mack The Knife" hits #1, stays there for nine weeks.

October 5: *That's All* enters *Billboard*'s LP chart, eventually reaching #7, charting for 52 weeks.

October 6: Darin becomes youngest artist ever to headline at The Sands, Las Vegas.

November 17: Darin guests on George Burns' TV special "The Big Time."

November 29: Darin wins two Grammy Awards. "Mack The Knife" is named Record Of The Year, and Darin is chosen as Best New Artist.

November 30: Infamous UPI story appears, quoting Darin as saying he hopes "to surpass Sinatra in everything he's done."

December 2: Darin appears on TV's "This Is Your Life."

December 4: Darin is questioned about payola and his radio appearances on Alan Freed's show by the New York District Attorney. He denies paying Freed.

December 26: *TV Guide* profiles Darin ("Hottest Singer Since Elvis").

1960

January 3: Darin and Connie Francis sing together on "The Ed Sullivan Show."

January 11: Darin is profiled by Shana Alexander in *Life* magazine.

March: Darin plays Britain with Duane Eddy, Clyde McPhatter; some audience members boo Darin's non-rock'n'roll material.

March 7: *This Is Darin* enters LP chart, will eventually reach #6.

May 12: Darin featured in a cover story in the jazz magazine *Down Beat* ("Bobby Darin And The Turn From Junk Music").

June: Darin debuts at The Copacabana; records *Darin At The Copa* LP June 15-16.

October 3: Darin sings "Lazy River" on Bob Hope's TV special; duets with Hope and Patti Page on "Mack The Knife."

October 17: *Darin At The* Copa LP enters chart; will eventually reach #9.

December 1: Darin marries actress Sandra Dee.

December: Darin appears briefly in his first movie, *Pepe*.

1961

January 31: "Bobby Darin And Friends" special airs on NBC.

April 17: Darin and Dee make first public appearance as husband and wife at the Academy Awards ceremony held at the Santa Monica Civic Auditorium. They present the awards for "Best Music, Scoring of a Dramatic or Comedy Picture" and "Best Music, Scoring of a Musical Picture."

August 9: *Come September*, starring Darin and Dee, opens.

December 16: Dodd Mitchell Darin born at Cedars of Lebanon Hospital, Hollywood.

1962

March 5: Darin receives a "New Star of the Year" Golden Globe Award for his performance in *Come September*.

April 4: *State Fair*, starring Darin, Pat Boone, and Ann-Margret, opens.

May: Darin introduces "folk" segment into his act, accompanying himself on guitar on "Cottonfields" at The Copa.

July: Darin signs with Capitol Records.

August: "Things" hits #3 on the *Billboard* charts.

September 19: *Pressure Point*, starring Darin and Sidney Poitier, opens.

November 29: Darin guests on Bob Hope's TV special with Ethel Merman, Jack Benny.

1963

January 23: Darin receives a Golden Globe Award nomination in the category "Actor in a Leading Role – Drama" for his performance in *Pressure Point*

February: Darin purchases T.M. Music for $500,000.

March 23: "You're The Reason I'm Living" hits #3.

July: Wayne Newton's "Danke Schoen," produced by Darin, enters chart.

October: Darin announces decision to leave nightclub performing to devote more time to T.M. Music, movies; opens last Vegas performance October 24 at The Flamingo.

December 25: *Captain Newman, M.D.* opens.

December 29: Darin guests on Judy Garland's TV show; performs folk material and duets with Garland.

1964

January 27: Darin receives a Golden Globe Award nomination in the category "Actor in A Supporting Role" for his performance in *Captain Newman, M.D.*

February 24: Academy Award nominations announced; Darin nominated for Best Supporting Actor for his role in *Captain Newman, M.D.*

April 13: Academy Awards ceremony held; Melvyn Douglas wins Best Supporting Actor award.

October 9: Darin and Janet Leigh star in TV drama "Murder In The First."

1965

March 24: Darin participates in demonstration protesting voting discrimination in Montgomery, Alabama.

August 25: *That Funny Feeling*, third and final Darin-Dee film, opens.

1966

January: Darin returns to nightclub performing after two-and-a-half-year hiatus; appears at The Flamingo in Las Vegas.

March 7: Darin appears on TV's "Run For Your Life" in a pilot for a projected fall series, "It's A Sweet Life" (with Eve Arden).

April: Darin returns to The Copa for the first time since May 1963.

August 12: Sandra Dee sues for divorce, asking for custody of Dodd (five).

August 15: Darin records "If I Were A Carpenter" in Los Angeles.

August 16: Darin appears with Richard Pryor (making his Las Vegas debut) at The Flamingo.

October 8: "If I Were A Carpenter" enters Top 40.

1967

March 2: "Rodgers & Hart Today" airs on ABC, with Darin, Petula Clark, The Supremes, The Mamas & The Papas, Count Basie.

March 7: Sandra Dee awarded a default divorce from Darin.

May 20: The British television special "Bobby Darin In London" airs on the BBC.

August 25: Darin performs at Princess Grace's annual Red Cross Gala in Monte Carlo.

October 4: Darin stars in Kraft Music Hall's "Give My Regards To Broadway," playing George M. Cohan.

1968

January 10: Darin hosts Kraft Music Hall's "A Grand Night For Swinging."

May: Darin campaigns for Robert F. Kennedy.

May 30: Darin is first performer at new San Francisco supper club Mr. D's. Here, he receives news that RFK is shot, June 4.

June 8-9: Darin attends RFK memorial service in New York and funeral at Arlington Cemetery.

July: Darin announces formation of his own label, Direction Records.

August: Commonwealth United Corp. buys Darin's T.M. Music.

October 30: Darin debuts new protest song, "Long Line Rider," at The Cocoanut Grove; changes from tuxedo to denim jacket mid-show.

1969

January 2: Darin returns to The Copacabana with four-piece rock band.

January 22: Darin (with mustache, without toupee) hosts the television special "Kraft Music Hall: Sounds Of The Sixties." He performs "Splish Splash" and "Long Line Rider" and duets with Judy Collins and Stevie Wonder.

January 31: Darin prohibited from singing "Long Line Rider" on "The Jackie Gleason Show"; walks off set.

May 13-18: Darin plays The Troubadour, L.A., with four-piece band; sings songs from Direction LPs and debuts "Simple Song Of Freedom."

July 16: "Bob" Darin appears at The Bonanza, Las Vegas, performing protest material and "Simple Song Of Freedom" solo on guitar.

August 2: Tim Hardin's recording of "Simple Song Of Freedom" enters *Billboard* chart; will peak at #50.

October 2: "Bob" Darin makes TV debut; sings "Distractions" on Tom Jones' TV show.

December 2: "Bob" Darin plays Sahara in Las Vegas, turns down requests for "Mack The Knife."

1970

May: Darin takes out newspaper ads denouncing U.S. invasion of Cambodia.

May 12: Darin speaks at anti-war demonstration at City Hall in Los Angeles. He announces "Phone For Peace," urges crowd to phone White House.

May 21: "Bobby" Darin back at The Landmark, Las Vegas; returns "Mack The Knife" into show.

June 17: Darin performs concert at London's Albert Hall.

July 27-31: Darin co-hosts on "The Mike Douglas Show."

1971

February 6: Darin records Desert Inn act for possible live album.

February 9: Darin enters hospital for heart operation.

April: "Melodie," Darin's first single for Motown, released.

September 1: Darin performs for first time since heart surgery, opening at Harrah's in Reno.

October 5: Darin appears on TV's "Ironside."

1972

January 13: Darin sings "Mack The Knife" and "Simple Song Of Freedom" on "The Flip Wilson Show."

February 7: Darin returns to Desert Inn, Las Vegas.

February 9: Darin appears on TV's "Night Gallery."

July: Darin performs concert in Central Park.

July 27: "The Bobby Darin Amusement Company" debuts for seven-week run on NBC; Burt Reynolds, George Burns guest on first show.

August: *Bobby Darin* (first Motown LP) is released.

November: NBC announces that Darin's TV show will return in January.

November: "Happy," Darin's last single, is released.

1973

January 16: Plans for "Bobby Darin Invitational Chess Classic" announced in New York; to be "richest chess tournament ever."

January 19: "The Bobby Darin Show" debuts on NBC.

April 3: NBC announces cancellation of Darin's show.

April 27: Last episode of Darin's show airs

June 25: Darin marries Andrea Joy Yaeger in Walnut Grove, California.

July 18: Darin opens at The Hilton, Las Vegas.

August: *Happy Mother's Day...Love, George*, Darin's final film, opens.

August 26: Concert at The Hilton, Las Vegas, is Darin's final live performance.

December 11: Darin enters Cedars of Lebanon Hospital, L.A., to repair two artificial heart valves received in a previous operation.

December 20: After eight hours on the operating table, Bobby Darin dies at the age of 37.

1990

January 17: Bobby Darin is inducted into the Rock and Roll Hall of Fame.

1995

November: Rhino Records releases the four-CD box set *As Long As I'm Singing: The Bobby Darin Collection.*

1999

June 9: Darin is inducted into the National Academy of Popular Music's Songwriters Hall of Fame.

Discography

U.S. Albums

Bobby Darin
Atco 33-102

Released July 1958
Produced by Herb Abramson, Ahmet Ertegun

Splish Splash; Just In Case You Change Your Mind; Pretty Betty; Talk To Me Something; Judy, Don't Be Moody; (Since You're Gone) I Can't Go On; I Found A Million Dollar Baby (In A Five And Ten Cent Store); Wear My Ring; So Mean; Don't Call My Name; Brand New House; Actions Speak Louder Than Words

That's All
Atco 33-104

Recorded December 19, 22, 24, 1958
Released March 1959
Produced by Ahmet Ertegun, Nesuhi Ertegun, Jerry Wexler
Arrangements by Richard Wess

Mack The Knife; Beyond The Sea; Through A Long And Sleepless Night; Softly As In A Morning Sunrise; She Needs Me; It Ain't Necessarily So; I'll Remember April; That's The Way Love Is; Was There A Call For Me; Some Of These Days; Where Is The One; That's All

This Is Darin
Atco 33-115

Recorded May 19-21, 1959
Released January 1960
Produced by Ahmet Ertegun, Nesuhi Ertegun
Arrangements by Richard Wess, Buddy Bregman

Clementine; Have You Got Any Castles Baby; Don't Dream Of Anybody But Me; My Gal Sal; Black Coffee; Caravan; Guys And Dolls; Down With Love; Pete Kelly's Blues; All Nite Long; The Gal That Got Away; I Can't Give You Anything But Love

Darin At The Copa
Atco 33-122

Recorded June 15-16, 1960
Released July 1960
Produced by Ahmet Ertegun, Nesuhi Ertegun
Arrangements by Richard Behrke, Buddy Bregman, Bobby Scott, Richard Wess

Swing Low Sweet Chariot/Lonesome Road; Some Of These Days; Mack The Knife; Love For Sale; Clementine; You'd Be So Nice To Come Home To; Dream Lover; Bill Bailey; I Have Dreamed; I Can't Give You Anything But Love; Alright, O.K., You Win; By Myself/When Your Lover Has Gone; I Got A Woman; That's All

For Teenagers Only
Atco SP-1001

Released September 1960
Produced by Ahmet Ertegun, Jerry Wexler

I Want You With Me; Keep A Walkin'; You Know How; Somebody To Love; I Ain't Sharin' Sharon; Pity Miss Kitty; That Lucky Old Sun; All The Way Home; You Never Called; A Picture No Artist Could Paint; Hush, Somebody's Calling My Name; Here I'll Stay

The 25ᵗʰ Day Of December
Atco 33-125

Recorded August 19-21, 1960
Released October 1960
Produced by Ahmet Ertegun
Arrangements by Bobby Scott

O Come All Ye Faithful; Poor Little Jesus; Child Of God; Baby Born Today; Holy Holy Holy; Ave Maria; Go Tell It On The Mountain; While The Shepherds Watched Their Flocks; Jehovah Hallelujah; Mary, Where Is Your Baby; Silent Night, Holy Night; Dona Nobis Pacem; Amen

Bobby Darin & Johnny Mercer: Two Of A Kind
Atco 33-126

Recorded August 13-22, 1960
Released February 1961
Produced by Ahmet Ertegun
Arrangements by Billy May

Two Of A Kind; Indiana; Bob White; Ace In The Hole; East Of The Rockies; If I Had My Druthers; I Ain't Gonna Give Nobody None Of My Jellyroll; Lonesome Polecat; My Cutey's Due At Two-To-Two Today; Medley: Paddlin' Madelin' Home/Row Row Row; Who Takes Care Of The Caretaker's Daughter; Mississippi Mud; Two Of A Kind

Love Swings
Atco 33-134

Recorded March 21-23, 1961
Released July 1961
Produced by Ahmet Ertegun
Arrangements by Torrie Zito

Long Ago And Far Away; I Didn't Know What Time It Was; How About You; The More I See You; It Had To Be You; No Greater Love; In Love In Vain; Just Friends; Something To Remember You By; Skylark; Spring Is Here; I Guess I'll Have To Change My Plan

Twist With Bobby Darin
Atco 33-138

Released December 1961
Produced by Ahmet Ertegun, Jerry Wexler

Bullmoose; Early In The Morning; Mighty Mighty Man; You Know How; Somebody To Love; Multiplication; Irresistible You; Queen Of The Hop; You Must Have Been A Beautiful Baby; Keep A Walkin'; Pity Miss Kitty; I Ain't Sharin' Sharon

Bobby Darin Sings Ray Charles
Atco 33-140

Recorded November 7, 8, 10, 14, 1961
Released March 1962
Produced by Ahmet Ertegun
Arrangements by Jimmy Haskell

What'd I Say; I Got A Woman; Tell All The World About You; Tell Me How Do You Feel; My Bonnie; The Right Time; Hallelujah I Love Her So; Leave My Woman Alone; Ain't That Love; Drown In My Own Tears; That's Enough

Things And Other Things
Atco 33-146

Released July 1962
Produced by Ahmet Ertegun

Things; I'll Be There; Lost Love; Look For My True Love; Beachcomber; Now We're One; You're Mine; Oo-Ee-Train; Jailer Bring Me Water; Nature Boy; Theme From "Come September"; Sorrow Tomorrow

Oh! Look At Me Now
Capitol 1791

Recorded July 1962
Released October 1962
Produced by Tom Morgan
Arrangements by Billy May

All By Myself; My Buddy; There's A Rainbow 'Round My Shoulder; Roses Of Picardy; You'll Never Know; Blue Skies; Always; You Made Me Love You; A Nightingale Sang In Berkeley Square; I'm Beginning To See The Light; Oh! Look At Me Now; The Party's Over

You're The Reason I'm Living
Capitol 1866

Recorded January 1963
Released February 1963
Produced by Nik Venet
Arrangements by Shorty Rogers, Gerald Wilson, Jimmy Haskell

Sally Was A Good Old Girl; Be Honest With Me; Oh Lonesome Me; (I Heard That) Lonesome Whistle; It Keeps Right On A-Hurtin'; You're The Reason I'm Living; Please Help Me I'm Falling; Under Your Spell Again; Here I Am; Who Can I Count On; Now You're Gone; Release Me

It's You Or No One
Atco 33-124

Recorded January 25-27, 1960
Released June 1963
Arrangements by Torrie Zito, Bobby Scott

It's You Or No One; I Hadn't Anyone Till You; Not Mine; I Can't Believe That You're In Love With Me; I've Never Been In Love Before; All Or Nothing At All; Only One Little Item; Don't Get Around Much Anymore; How About Me; I'll Be Around; All I Do Is Cry; I Guess I'm Good For Nothing But The Blues

18 Yellow Roses
Capitol 1942

Released July 1963
Produced by Nik Venet
Arrangements by Jack Nitzsche, Bobby Scott, Bert Keyes, Walter Raim

18 Yellow Roses; On Broadway; Ruby Baby; Reverend Mr. Black; End Of The World; Not For Me; Walk Right In; From A Jack To A King; I Will Follow Her; Our Day Will Come; Can't Get Used To Losing You; Rhythm Of The Rain

Earthy! Capitol 1826

Recorded July 1962
Released July 1963
Produced by Tom Morgan
Arrangements by Walter Raim

Long Time Man; Work Song; La Bamba; I'm On My Way Great God;
The Sermon Of Samson; Strange Rain; Why Don't You Swing Down;
Everything's Okay; Guantanamera; When Their Mama Is Gone;
Fay-O; The Er-i-ee Was A'Rising

Golden Folk Hits Capitol 2007

Released November 1963
Produced by Nik Venet
Arrangements by Walter Raim

Mary Don't You Weep; Where Have All The Flowers Gone?; If I Had A
Hammer; Don't Think Twice; Greenback Dollar; Why Daddy Why;
Michael Row The Boat Ashore; Abilene; Green, Green; Settle Down
(Goin' Down That Highway); Blowin' In The Wind; Train To The Sky

Winners Atco 33-167

Recorded February 1-2, 1960
Released June 1964
Produced by Ahmet Ertegun, Nesuhi Ertegun
Arrangements by Bobby Scott

Milord; Between The Devil And The Deep Blue Sea; Anything Goes; Do
Nothin' Till You Hear From Me; Golden Earrings; When Day Is Done;
I've Found A New Baby; What A Difference A Day Made; What Can I
Say After I Say I'm Sorry; Hard Hearted Hannah; Easy Living; They All
Laughed

From Hello Dolly To Goodbye Charlie Capitol 2194

Recorded September 17-18, 1964
Released November 1964
Produced by Jim Economides
Arrangements by Richard Wess

Hello, Dolly!; Call Me Irresponsible; The Days Of Wine And Roses;
More; The End Of Never; Charade; Once In A Lifetime (Only Once);
Sunday In New York; Where Love Has Gone; Look At Me; Goodbye,
Charlie

Venice Blue   Capitol 2322
Recorded March 1965
Released May 1965
Produced by Steve Douglas
Arrangements by Richard Wess, Ernie Freeman

Venice Blue; I Wanna Be Around; Somewhere; The Good Life; Dear Heart; Softly, As I Leave You; You Just Don't Know; There Ain't No Sweet Gal That's Worth The Salt Of My Tears; Who Can I Turn To?; A Taste Of Honey; In A World Without You

Bobby Darin Sings The Shadow Of Your Smile   Atlantic 8121
Recorded December 1965, March 1966
Released April 1966
Produced by Bobby Darin
Arrangements by Richard Wess, Shorty Rogers

The Shadow Of Your Smile; The Sweetheart Tree; I Will Wait For You; The Ballad Of Cat Ballou; What's New Pussycat?; Rainin'; Lover Come Back To Me; Cute; After You've Gone; It's Only A Paper Moon; Liza

In A Broadway Bag   Atlantic 8126
Recorded May 10, 1966
Released June 1966
Produced by Bobby Darin
Arrangements by Shorty Rogers, Perry Botkin, Jr.

Mame; I Believe In You; It's Today; Everybody Has The Right To Be Wrong; Feeling Good; Don't Rain On My Parade; The Other Half Of Me; Once Upon A Time; Try To Remember; I'll Only Miss Her When I Think Of Her; Night Song

If I Were A Carpenter   Atlantic 8135
Recorded August 15, October 31, November 1, 1966
Released December 1966
Produced by Charles Koppelman and Don Rubin
Arrangements by Donald Peake, Bob Halley

If I Were A Carpenter; Reason To Believe; Sittin' Here Lovin' You; Misty Roses; Until It's Time For You To Go; For Baby; The Girl That Stood Beside Me; Red Balloon; Amy; Don't Make Promises; Daydream

Inside Out   Atlantic 8142
Recorded March 7, 10, 1967
Released May 1967
Produced by Charles Koppelman and Don Rubin

The Lady Came From Baltimore; Darling Be Home Soon; Bes' Friends; I Am; About You; I Think It's Gonna Rain Today; Whatever Happened To Happy; Black Sheep Boy; Hello Sunshine; Lady Fingers; Back Street Girl

Bobby Darin Sings Doctor Dolittle   Atlantic 8154
Recorded July 25, 1967
Released August 1967
Produced by Ahmet Ertegun
Arrangements by Roger Kellaway

At The Crossroads; When I Look In Your Eyes; I Think I Like You; Where Are The Words; Something In Your Smile; Fabulous Places; My Friend, The Doctor; Beautiful Things; After Today; Talk To The Animals

Bobby Darin Born Walden Robert Cassotto   Direction 1936
Released September 1968
Produced by Bobby Darin
Arrangements by Bobby Darin

Questions; Jingle Jangle Jungle; The Proper Gander; Bullfrog; Long Line Rider; Change; I Can See The Wind; Sunday; In Memoriam

Commitment   Direction 1937
Released July 1969
Produced by Bob Darin
Arrangements by Bob Darin

Me & Mr. Hohner; Sugar-Man; Sausalito (The Governors Song); Song For A Dollar; The Harvest; Distractions (Part 1); Water Color Canvas; Jive; Hey Magic Man; Light Blue

Bobby Darin   Motown M753L
Released August 1972
Produced by Joe Porter
Arrangements by Jimmy Haskell, Michael O'Martian

Sail Away; I've Already Stayed Too Long; Something In Her Love; Who Turned The World Around; Shipmates In Cheyenne; Let It Be Me; Hard Headed Woman; Average People; I Used To Think It Was Easy; My First Night Alone Without You

British Only Release

Something Special   Atlantic 587073
Released May 1967

Don't Rain On My Parade; About A Quarter To Nine; Once Upon A Time; I Wish I Were In Love Again; Mack The Knife; If I Were A Carpenter; One For My Baby (Impersonations); The Girl Who Stood Beside Me; Funny What Love Can Do; What'd I Say; That's All

Posthumous Releases
(Consisting of Entirely- or Mostly-Unreleased Material)

Darin 1936-1973   Motown 813V1
Released February 1974
Produced by Bob Crewe, Bobby Darin, Joe Porter, Jerry Marcellino, Mel Larson
Arrangements by Charles Fox, Dave Watkins, Bill Holman, Jimmy Haskell, Ben Lanzarone, Art Freeman, Quitman Dennis

I Won't Last A Day Without You; Wonderin' Where It's Gonna End; Sail Away; Another Song On My Mind; Happy (Love Theme From Lady Sings The Blues); Blue Monday; Don't Think Twice, It's All Right; The Letter; If I Were A Carpenter; Moritat (Mack The Knife)

Live At The Desert Inn   Motown MCD 09070MD
Recorded February 6, 1971
Released 1987
Produced by Jerry Marcellino and Mel Larson
Arrangements by Quitman Dennis

Save The Country; Moritat (Mack The Knife); Fire And Rain; Hi-De-Ho (That Old Sweet Roll); Beatles Medley: Hey Jude/Elanor Rigby/Blackbird/A Day In The Life/Something; (Your Love Keeps Lifting Me) Higher And Higher; I'll Be Your Baby Tonight; Simple Song Of Freedom; Encore Medley: Chain Of Fools/Respect/Splish Splash/Johnny B. Goode

The Unreleased Capitol Sides
Collectors' Choice Music CCM-079-2

Released 1999

Produced by Nik Venet, Tom Morgan, Steve Douglas

I Got Rhythm; Alabamy Bound; I Wonder Who's Kissing Her Now; When My Baby Smiles At Me; Beautiful Dreamer; When You Were Sweet Sixteen; I Ain't Got Nobody; My Melancholy Baby; You're Nobody 'Til Somebody Loves You; What Kind Of Fool Am I?; Moon River; This Nearly Was Mine; Tall Hope; The Sweetest Sounds; Standing On The Corner; Stop The World (And Let Me Off); Whispering; Somebody Stole My Gal; Two Tickets; Love Letters; Gyp The Cat; Just Bummin' Around; On The Street Where You Live; Red Roses For A Blue Lady; If I Ruled The World

The Curtain Falls – Live At The Flamingo
Collectors Choice Music CCM-171-2

Recorded November 9, 1963

Released 2000

Intro/Hello Young Lovers; Ace In The Hole; You're Nobody 'Til Somebody Loves You; Medley: Splish Splash/Beyond The Sea/Artificial Flowers/Clementine; My Funny Valentine; I Walk The Line (Parody); 18 Yellow Roses; Mack The Knife; Comedy Routine; Work Song; Michael (Row The Boat Ashore); Mary Don't You Weep; I'm On My Way Great God; The Curtain Falls

Noteworthy Compilation Albums

Darin's recordings have appeared in numerous compilation collections, "greatest hits" and otherwise. Most noteworthy are the following:

The Bobby Darin Story   Atco 33-131

Released 1961

Darin's first 12 hit singles, from "Splish Splash" through "Lazy River," eight of which were making their first appearance on an album at the time of this compilation's release. Also includes brief Darin narration at the beginning and end. Reached #18 on *Billboard*'s album chart.

The Best Of Bobby Darin   Capitol 2571
Released 1966
> This release included only three of Darin's eight charting Capitol singles, but did contain both sides of the non-LP "That Funny Feeling/Gyp The Cat" single, and a previously-unreleased recording of "Fly Me To The Moon."

The Ultimate Bobby Darin   Warner Special Products 9-27606-2
Released 1986
> The first Darin CD, covering 17 of his Atco hit singles from "Splish Splash" through "Things."

The Capitol Collectors Series   Capitol CDP 791625 2
Released 1989
> A great 20-track collection which included nine Capitol A- or B-sides which had not previously appeared on an album.

Splish Splash: The Best Of Bobby Darin, Volume 1
Atco 91794-2

Released 1991
> Twenty-one rock/pop-oriented tracks, including 16 hits, plus both sides of the rare 1960 single "Moment Of Love/She's Tanfastic" and the 1964 B-side "Similau."

Mack The Knife: The Best Of Bobby Darin, Volume 2
Atco 91795-2

Released 1991
> Another 21 tracks, all of the "standards" variety. Includes six hit singles; the remaining 15 tracks became available on CD for the first time with this release.

Spotlight On Bobby Darin – Great Gentlemen Of Song
Capitol CDP 724382851226

Released 1995
> Twenty standards-style recordings from the Capitol era, including ten tracks from the *Oh! Look At Me Now* album. Most noteworthy for the inclusion of six previously unreleased tracks recorded in 1962-63 – "Alabamy Bound," "Standing On The Corner," "Just In Time," "All Of You," "I Got Rhythm," and "I'm Sitting On Top Of The World."

As Long As I'm Singing: The Bobby Darin Collection
Rhino R272206

Released 1995

A 96-track, 4-CD box set which covered the hits, key album tracks, and 20 rarities: four previously-unreleased studio recordings ("Easy Rider," "Everywhere I Go," "I'm Going To Love You," "Long Time Movin'"); four songs recorded live at The Flamingo in Las Vegas in November, 1963 ("My Funny Valentine," "You're Nobody 'Til Somebody Loves You," "The Curtain Falls," and "I'm On My Way Great God"); a live version of "I'll Be Your Baby Tonight" recorded at The Bonanza in Las Vegas in 1969; Darin's demos for "Dream Lover" and "Simple Song Of Freedom"; "This Isn't Heaven" from the *State Fair* soundtrack; and eight single A- or B-sides previously unavailable on album ("We Didn't Ask To Be Brought Here," "Funny What Love Can Do," "She Knows," "Minnie The Moocher," "Silver Dollar," "Walking In The Shadow Of Love," Sweet Reasons," and the alternate single version of "Simple Song Of Freedom").

A&E Biography: A Musical Anthology Capitol 72434 94752-0-5
Released 1998

A 14-track collection tied to the episode of the cable series that focused on Darin's life. Included three previously-unreleased live tracks recorded on March 11, 1973 for Darin's NBC television series – "Beyond The Sea," "If I Were A Carpenter," and "(Your Love Keeps Lifting Me) Higher And Higher."

Ultra-Lounge: Wild, Cool & Swingin' Capitol CDP-520333
Released 1999

Another 20 tracks from the Capitol years, ten of which originated from the *From Hello Dolly To Goodbye Charlie* and *Venice Blue* albums. Included previously unreleased recordings of "The Sweetest Sounds," "I Left My Heart In San Francisco," and "This Nearly Was Mine," as well as an earlier (1964) recording of "Gyp The Cat," and "Hello Young Lovers" which had only been available on the rare *Capitol Sings Rodgers & Hammerstein* various-artist compilation.

The Capitol Years EMI 97147
Released 1999

A three-CD set containing 63 tracks.

If I Were A Carpenter: The Very Best Of Bobby Darin 1966-1969   Varese 6007
Released 1999
> Eighteen tracks; 15 from Atlantic and three from Direction, including the previously unavailable on CD "Jive" and "Distractions (Part 1)."

Swingin' The Standards   Varese 6004
Released 1999
> Eighteen tracks, mostly from Darin's *The Shadow Of Your Smile* and *In A Broadway Bag* albums. Includes the 1966 A-side "The Breaking Point" and two tracks from the *Doctor Dolittle* album.

The Hit Singles Collection   Rhino 78386
Released 2002
Twenty out of Darin's 22 Top 40 hits in chronological order.

Singles

All singles released under the name Bobby Darin unless otherwise noted.

Rock Island Line / Timber	Decca 9-29883	1956
Silly Willie / Blue Eyed Mermaid *Bobby Darin and The Jaybirds*	Decca 9-29922	1956
Hear Them Bells / The Greatest Builder	Decca 9-30031	1956
Dealer In Dreams / Help Me	Decca 9-30235	1957
I Found A Million Dollar Baby / Talk To Me Something	Atco 6092	1957
Don't Call My Name / Pretty Betty	Atco 6103	1957
Just In Case You Change Your Mind / So Mean	Atco 6109	1958
Splish Splash / Judy, Don't Be Moody	Atco 6117	1958
Early In The Morning / Now We're One *The Rinky-Dinks* (originally issued on Brunswick 55073 by The Ding Dongs)	Atco 6121	1958
Queen Of The Hop / Lost Love	Atco 6127	1958

Mighty Mighty Man / You're Mine *The Rinky-Dinks*	Atco 6128	1958
Plain Jane / While I'm Gone	Atco 6133	1959
Dream Lover / Bullmoose	Atco 6140	1959
Mack The Knife / Was There A Call For Me	Atco 6147	1959
Beyond The Sea / That's The Way Love Is	Atco 6158	1960
Clementine / Tall Story	Atco 6161	1960
Moment Of Love / She's Tanfastic	Atco SPD	1960
Won't You Come Home Bill Bailey / I'll Be There	Atco 6167	1960
Beachcomber / Autumn Blues *Bobby Darin at the Piano*	Atco 6173	1960
Artificial Flowers / Somebody To Love	Atco 6179	1960
Christmas Auld Lang Syne / Child Of God	Atco 6183	1960
That's How It Went All Right / (non-Darin flip)	Colpix PC-1	1960
Lazy River / Oo-Ee-Train	Atco 6188	1961
Nature Boy / Look For My True Love	Atco 6196	1961
Theme From "Come September" / Walk Bach To Me *A-side by Bobby Darin & His Orchestra* *B-side also notes "Bobby Darin at the Harpsichord"*	Atco 6200	1961
You Must Have Been A Beautiful Baby / Sorrow Tomorrow	Atco 6206	1961
Ave Maria / O Come All Ye Faithful	Atco 6211	1961
Irresistible You / Multiplication	Atco 6214	1961
What'd I Say (Part 1) / What'd I Say (Part 2)	Atco 6221	1962
Things / Jailer Bring Me Water	Atco 6229	1962

If A Man Answers / A True, True Love	Capitol 4837	1962
Baby Face / You Know How	Atco 6236	1962
I Found A New Baby / Keep A Walkin'	Atco 6244	1962
You're The Reason I'm Living / Now You're Gone	Capitol 4897	1963
18 Yellow Roses / Not For Me	Capitol 4970	1963
Treat My Baby Good / Down So Long	Capitol 5019	1963
Be Mad Little Girl / Since You've Been Gone	Capitol 5079	1963
I Wonder Who's Kissing Her Now / As Long As I'm Singing	Capitol 5126	1964
Milord / Golden Earrings	Atco 6297	1964
Swing Low Sweet Chariot/ Similau	Atco 6316	1964
The Things In This House / Wait By The Water	Capitol 5257	1964
Hello, Dolly! / Goodbye, Charlie	Capitol 5359	1965
Venice Blue / In A World Without You	Capitol 5399	1965
When I Get Home / Lonely Road	Capitol 5443	1965
That Funny Feeling / Gyp The Cat	Capitol 5481	1965
Minnie The Moocher / Hard Hearted Hannah	Atco 6334	1965
We Didn't Ask To Be Brought Here / Funny What Love Can Do	Atlantic 2305	1965
The Breaking Point / Silver Dollar	Atlantic 2317	1966
Mame / Walking In The Shadow Of Love	Atlantic 2329	1966
Who's Afraid Of Virginia Wolf / Merci Cherie	Atlantic 2341	1966
If I Were A Carpenter / Rainin'	Atlantic 2350	1966
The Girl That Stood Beside Me / Reason To Believe	Atlantic 2367	1966
Lovin' You / Amy	Atlantic 2376	1967

The Lady Came From Baltimore / I Am	Atlantic 2395	1967
Darling Be Home Soon / Hello Sunshine	Atlantic 2420	1967
She Knows / Talk To The Animals	Atlantic 2433	1967
Long Line Rider / Change	Direction 350	1969
Me & Mr. Hohner / Song For A Dollar	Direction 351	1969
Jive / Distractions (Part 1) *Bob Darin*	Direction 352	1969
Baby May / Sweet Reasons *Bob Darin*	Direction 4001	1969
Maybe We Can Get It Together/ Rx-Pyro (Prescription: Fire) *Bob Darin*	Direction 4002	1970
Melodie / Someday We'll Be Together	Motown 1183	1971
Simple Song Of Freedom / I'll Be Your Baby Tonight (Promo only release)	Motown 1193	1971
Sail Away / Hard Headed Woman	Motown 1203	1972
Average People / Something In Her Love	Motown 1212	1972
Happy (Love Theme From "Lady Sings The Blues")/ Something In Her Love	Motown 1217	1972

Darin in Pressure Point
(United Artists publicity photo)

Bobby Darin On Film

From 1960 through 1973, Bobby Darin appeared in 13 motion pictures. He played significant roles in 11 of them, and was the star or co-star of six movies. He received an Academy Award nomination for Best Supporting Actor for his role in Captain Newman, M.D. *Below is a list of Darin's movies, in chronological order. Information on opening dates and locations is taken from the* American Film Institute Catalog.

"PEPE"

Opening: December 1960
Darin's billing: Cameo
Cast: Cantinflas, Dan Dailey, Shirley Jones, Carlos Montalban
Darin's role: himself
Director: George Sidney
Producer: George Sidney

"COME SEPTEMBER"

Opening: August 9, 1961, Minneapolis
Darin's billing: Fourth
Cast: Rock Hudson, Gina Lollobrigida, Sandra Dee, Bobby Darin, Walter Slezak, Joel Grey
Darin's character: Tony
Director: Robert Mulligan
Producer: Robert Arthur

"TOO LATE BLUES"

Opening: January 1962, Detroit

Darin's billing: First

Cast: Bobby Darin, Stella Stevens, Everett Chambers, Cliff Carnell, Seymour Cassel

Darin's character: John "Ghost" Wakefield

Director: John Cassavetes

Producer: John Cassavetes

"STATE FAIR"

Opening: April 4, 1962, Dallas

Darin's billing: Second

Cast: Pat Boone, Bobby Darin, Pamela Tiffin, Ann-Margret, Tom Ewell, Alice Faye

Darin's character: Jerry Dundee

Director: Jose Ferrer

Producer: Charles Brackett

"HELL IS FOR HEROES"

Opening: May 30, 1962, Los Angeles

Darin's billing: Second

Cast: Steve McQueen, Bobby Darin, Fess Parker, Harry Guardino, Bob Newhart, James Coburn

Darin's character: Private Corby

Director: Don Siegel

Producer: Henry Blanke

"PRESSURE POINT"

Opening: September 19, 1962, Los Angeles

Darin's billing: Co-top billing (with Sidney Poitier)

Cast: Sidney Poitier, Bobby Darin, Peter Falk, Carl Benton Reid, Mary Munday

Darin's character: The Patient

Director: Hubert Cornfield

Producer: Stanley Kramer

"IF A MAN ANSWERS"
Opening: October 10, 1962, Chicago
Darin's billing: Co-top billing (with Sandra Dee)
Cast: Sandra Dee, Bobby Darin, Michelle Presle, John Lund, Cesar Romero, Stefanie Powers
Darin's character: Eugene Wright
Director: Henry Levin
Producer: Ross Hunter

"CAPTAIN NEWMAN, M.D."
Opening: December 25, 1963, Los Angeles
Darin's billing: "Co-starring"
Cast: Gregory Peck, Tony Curtis, Bobby Darin, Eddie Albert, Angie Dickinson, Robert Duvall, Dick Sargent
Darin's character: Corporal Jim Tompkins
Director: David Miller
Producer: Robert Arthur

"THAT FUNNY FEELING"
Opening: August 25, 1965, Los Angeles
Darin's billing: Co-top billing (with Sandra Dee)
Cast: Sandra Dee, Bobby Darin, Donald O'Connor, Nita Talbot, Larry Storch
Darin's character: Tom Milford
Director: Richard Thorpe
Producer: Harry Keller

"GUNFIGHT IN ABILENE"
Opening: May 1967
Darin's billing: First
Cast: Bobby Darin, Emily Banks, Leslie Nielsen, Donnelly Rhodes, Don Galloway, Michael Sarrazin
Darin's character: Cal Wayne
Director: William Hale
Producer: Howard Christie

"COP-OUT"

Opening: January 5, 1968, New Orleans (Released in Great Britain with the title "Stranger In The House" in July 1967)

Darin's billing: Third

Cast: James Mason, Geraldine Chaplin, Bobby Darin, Paul Bertoya, Ian Ogilvy

Darin's character: Barney Teale

Director: Pierre Rouve

Producer: Dimitri de Grunwald

"THE HAPPY ENDING"

Opening: December 21, 1969, New York

Darin's billing: Seventh (as "Robert Darin")

Cast: Jean Simmons, John Forsythe, Lloyd Bridges, Teresa Wright, Dick Shawn, Nanette Fabray, Robert Darin, Tina Louise

Darin's character: Franco

Director: Richard Brooks

Producer: Richard Brooks

"HAPPY MOTHER'S DAY...LOVE, GEORGE"

Opening: August 1973

Darin's billing: Third

Cast: Patricia Neal, Cloris Leachman, Bobby Darin, Tessa Dahl, Ron Howard

Darin's character: Eddie

Director: Darren McGavin

Producer: Darren McGavin

Television Appearances

This section chronicles Bobby Darin's appearances on television, including his own 1972-73 variety series, his own specials, and his guest appearances on musical, variety, and drama programs. The majority of the information on air dates, guests, and musical numbers has been gathered from TV Guide. *The listing of guest appearances, based on information gathered during the author's research, is not intended to be comprehensive.*

Bobby Darin's Own Variety Series (1972-73)

"The Bobby Darin Amusement Company" aired as a summer replacement for the "The Dean Martin Show" for seven weeks in the summer of 1972. It returned, as "The Bobby Darin Show," for 13 weeks in early 1973. The seven 1972 episodes aired Thursdays at 10:00 p.m. The thirteen 1973 episodes aired Fridays at 10:00 p.m.

The information on the songs and guests was gathered from *TV Guide*, with the exceptions of seven shows (numbers 4, 9, 11, 14, 16, 18, and 19) which were viewed by the author. It is quite likely that song lists are incomplete for some episodes and that additional songs were performed.

Each show closed with Darin performing "Mack The Knife" as the credits rolled.

The Bobby Darin Amusement Company
Show #1
Air Date: July 27, 1972

Guests: George Burns, Burt Reynolds, Bobbie Gentry

Darin's Songs: "Can't Take My Eyes Off You," "You Are My Sunshine/ Got My Mojo Working," "Medley: Proud Mary/Polk Salad Annie/ Never Ending Song Of Love" (duet with Bobbie Gentry)

Show #2

Air Date: August 3, 1972

Guests: Debbie Reynolds, Charles Nelson Reilly

Darin's Songs: "Charade," "Beyond The Sea," "Love Story" (duet with Debbie Reynolds)

Show #3

Air Date: August 10, 1972

Guests: Pat Paulsen, Joan Rivers, Dusty Springfield

Darin's Songs: "I'll Be Your Baby Tonight," "You've Got A Friend" (duet with Dusty Springfield)

Show #4

Air Date: August 17, 1972

Guests: Donald O'Connor, Dionne Warwick, Phil Ford & Mimi Hines

Darin's Songs: "If I Were A Carpenter," "Spinning Wheel," "Bridge Over Troubled Water" (duet with Dionne Warwick), "I'll Never Fall In Love Again" (duet with Donald O'Connor)

Show #5

Air Date: August 24, 1972

Guests: Carl Reiner, Claudine Longet

Show #6

Air Date: August 31, 1972

Guests: Florence Henderson, Pat Paulsen

Darin's Songs: "That's All," "Artificial Flowers," "Work Song," "Happy Together" (duet with Florence Henderson)

Show #7

Air Date: September 7, 1972

Guests: The Smothers Brothers, Joanie Sommers

Darin's Songs: "Brother Can You Spare A Dime?," "Talk To The Animals," "Side By Side By Side" (with The Smothers Brothers)

The Bobby Darin Show

Show #8

Air Date: January 19, 1973

Guests: Burl Ives, Dyan Cannon, Mimi Hines, Flip Wilson

Darin's Songs: "Once In A Lifetime," "Sweet Caroline," "About A Quarter To Nine," "Happy," "Something" (duet with Dyan Cannon)

Show #9

Air Date: January 26, 1973

Guests: Helen Reddy, David Steinberg

Darin's Songs: "Born Free," "Caravan," "Bridge Over Troubled Water," "I'll Be Your Baby Tonight," "St. Louis Blues," "If Not For You" (duet with Helen Reddy), "Meet Me In St. Louis" (with Helen Reddy and ensemble)

Show #10

Air Date: February 2, 1973

Guests: Flip Wilson, Petula Clark

Darin's Songs: "Hello Young Lovers," "Artificial Flowers," "Happy," "All I Have To Do Is Dream" (duet with Petula Clark)

Show #11

Air Date: February 9, 1973

Guests: Redd Foxx, Nancy Sinatra, Seals & Crofts

Darin's Songs: "Lover Come Back To Me," "King Of The Road," "Lonesome Road," "If," "Light My Fire" (duet with Nancy Sinatra); "My Kind Of Town" (duet with Nancy Sinatra)

Show #12

Air Date: February 16, 1973

Guests: Charles Nelson Reilly, Taj Mahal, Freda Payne

Darin's Songs: "Dreidel," "This Could Be The Start Of Something Big," "Ain't No Mountain High Enough" (duet with Freda Payne)

Show #13

Air Date: February 23, 1973

Guests: Cloris Leachman, Tim Conway

Darin's Songs: "Don't Rain On My Parade," "A Nightingale Sang In Berkeley Square," "Song Sung Blue," "Alone Again (Naturally)," "Never My Love" (duet with Cloris Leachman)

Show #14

Air Date: March 2, 1973

Guests: Elke Sommer, Donald O'Connor

Darin's Songs: "It's Today," "Mame," "Once Upon A Time," "Two Of A Kind" (duet with Donald O'Connor), "Let's Fall In Love" (duet with Elke Sommer), "Give A Little Whistle" (duet with Charlene Wong)

Show #15

Air Date: March 23, 1973

Guests: Sid Caesar, Dusty Springfield, Jackie Joseph, The Persuasions

Darin's Songs: "Some People," "Help Me Make It Through The Night," "I Get A Kick Out Of You," "Climb Every Mountain," "Baby I Need Your Lovin'" (duet with Dusty Springfield)

Show #16

Air Date: March 30, 1973

Guests: Andy Griffith, Connie Stevens, Eric Weissberg & Steve Mandell

Darin's Songs: "As Long As I'm Singing," "Brooklyn Roads," "I've Got You Under My Skin," "If I Were A Carpenter," "You've Got A Friend" (duet with Connie Stevens)

Show #17

Air Date: April 6, 1973

Guests: Phyllis Diller, Leslie Uggams, David Bromberg

Darin's Songs: "Charade," "I'll Remember April," "Here's That Rainy Day," "I'll Be Seeing You," "Happy Together" (duet with Leslie Uggams)

Show #18

Air Date: April 13, 1973

Guests: Artie Johnson, Bread

Darin's Songs: "There's A Rainbow 'Round My Shoulder," "Let The Good Times Roll," "Cry Me A River"

Show #19

Air Date: April 20, 1973

Guests: Carol Lawrence, Pat Buttram, Bill Withers

Darin's Songs: "Get Me To The Church On Time," "Shilo," "Guys And Dolls," "Come Rain Or Come Shine," "Volare," "Words" (duet with Carol Lawrence), "There's A Hole In The Bucket" (duet with Carol Lawrence), "It's De-Lovely" (duet with Carol Lawrence), "High Hopes" (duet with Charlene Wong)

Show #20

Air Date: April 27, 1973

(All-music show featuring Bobby Darin and Peggy Lee in concert)

Songs Performed by Bobby Darin: "For Once In My Life/Once In A Lifetime," "Help Me Make It Through The Night," "Can't Take My Eyes Off You," "Bridge Over Troubled Water," "Midnight Special," "(I Heard That) Lonesome Whistle," "Medley: You Are My Sunshine/ Bo Diddley/Splish Splash"

Songs Performed by Bobby Darin and Peggy Lee: "Just Friends," "Something To Remember You By," "Skylark," "Spring Is Here," "Long Ago and Far Away"

Bobby Darin's Own TV Specials

BOBBY DARIN & FRIENDS
Air Date: January 31, 1961
Guests: Joanie Sommers, Bob Hope
Darin's Songs: "I Got Rhythm/I Got Plenty Of Nothing," "I Have Dreamed," "Some People," "Lucky Pierre," "I've Had It," "I Wish I Were In Love Again" (duet with Joanie Sommers), "Bill Bailey" (with Joanie Sommers and Bob Hope)

BOBBY DARIN IN LONDON
(BBC special broadcast in the UK only)
Air Date: May 20, 1967
Darin's Songs: "Don't Rain On My Parade," "About A Quarter To Nine," "Once Upon A Time," "I Wish I Were In Love Again," "Mack The Knife," "If I Were A Carpenter," "The Girl Who Stood Beside Me," "Funny What Love Can Do," "What'd I Say," "That's All"

THE DARIN INVASION
(Canadian TV special, syndicated in the U.S. in 1971)
Air Date: October 1971 (air date in New York)
Guests: George Burns, Pat Carroll, Linda Ronstadt, The Poppy Family
Darin's Songs: "Higher And Higher," "Reviewing The Situation," "Hi-De-Ho," "If I Were A Carpenter," "Simple Song Of Freedom"

Darin Guest Appearances On Musical/Variety Programs

STAGE SHOW (series episode)
Air Date: March 10, 1956
Host/Star: The Dorsey Brothers
Darin's Songs: "Rock Island Line"

THE BIG BEAT (series episode)
Air Date: July 19, 1957
Host/Star: Alan Freed
Guests: Chuck Berry, Frankie Lymon, Andy Williams, Bobby Darin
Darin's Songs: "Talk To Me Something"

DICK CLARK SATURDAY NIGHT BEECHNUT SHOW (series episode)
Air Date: July 19, 1958
Host/Star: Dick Clark
Guests: Bobby Darin, George Hamilton IV, Jack Scott
Darin's Songs: "Splish Splash"

BOB CROSBY SHOW (series episode)
Air Date: August 23, 1958
Host/Star: Bob Crosby
Guests: Bobby Darin, Allen & DeWood, The Modernaires
Darin's Songs: "Splish Splash"

DICK CLARK SATURDAY NIGHT BEECHNUT SHOW (series episode)
Air Date: November 1, 1958
Host/Star: Dick Clark
Guests: Bobby Darin, The Everly Brothers, The Olympics, The Elegants
Darin's Songs: "Queen Of The Hop"

DICK CLARK SATURDAY NIGHT BEECHNUT SHOW (series episode)
Air Date: January 10, 1959
Host/Star: Dick Clark
Guests: Bobby Darin, LaVern Baker, Morton Downey, Jr.
Darin's Songs: unknown

PERRY COMO SHOW (series episode)
Air Date: April 18, 1959
Host/Star: Perry Como
Guests: Julie London, Bobby Darin, Lou Carter, Art Wall, Jr.
Darin's Songs: unknown

DICK CLARK SATURDAY NIGHT BEECHNUT SHOW (series episode)
Air Date: May 2, 1959
Host/Star: Dick Clark
Guests: Bobby Darin, Connie Francis, Wilbert Harrison, The Crests
Darin's Songs: "Dream Lover"

ED SULLIVAN SHOW (series episode)
Air Date: May 31, 1959
Host/Star: Ed Sullivan
Guests: Bobby Darin, Edith Piaf, Wayne & Shuster, Trude Adams, Rex Ramer
Darin's Songs: "Mack The Knife," "Dream Lover"

DICK CLARK SATURDAY NIGHT BEECHNUT SHOW (series episode)
Air Date: August 22, 1959
Host/Star: Dick Clark
Guests: Bobby Darin, Fabian, Dodie Stevens
Darin's Songs: "Mack The Knife," "Dream Lover"

ED SULLIVAN SHOW (series episode)
Air Date: September 6, 1959
Host/Star: Ed Sullivan
Guests: Bobby Darin, others
Darin's Songs: unknown

AN EVENING WITH JIMMY DURANTE (Special)
Air Date: September 25, 1959
Host/Star: Jimmy Durante
Guests: Lawrence Welk, Sal Mineo, Bobby Darin, Gisele MacKenzie
Darin's Songs: "Mack The Knife," "That's All," "Bill Bailey" (with Durante), "Personality" (with Durante)

THE LOUIS JOURDAN TIMEX SPECIAL (Special)
Air Date: November 11, 1959
Host/Star: Louis Jourdan
Guests: Jerry Lewis, Abbe Lane, Xavier Cugat, Bobby Darin, Jane Morgan
Darin's Songs: unknown

GEORGE BURNS IN THE BIG TIME (Special)
Air Date: November 17, 1959
Host/Star: George Burns
Guests: Jack Benny, Eddie Cantor, George Jessel, Bobby Darin, The Kingston Trio
Darin's Songs: "Clementine," "I Ain't Got Nobody" (with Burns)

THE BIG PARTY (series episode)
Air Date: December 3, 1959
Host/Star: Douglas Fairbanks, Jr.
Guests: Danny Thomas, Mike Nichols & Elaine May, Chuck Connors, Bobby Darin, Harold Arlen & Johnny Mercer
Darin's Songs: unknown

ED SULLIVAN SHOW (series episode)
Air Date: January 3, 1960
Host/Star: Ed Sullivan
Guests: Bobby Darin, Connie Francis, Edgar Bergen
Darin's Songs: "Beyond The Sea," "That's The Way Love Is," "You Make Me Feel So Young" (with Connie Francis), "You're The Top" (with Connie Francis)

ED SULLIVAN SHOW (series episode)
Air Date: February 28, 1960
Host/Star: Ed Sullivan
Guests: Bobby Darin, Connie Francis, Della Reese, Senor Wences
Darin's Songs: "Clementine," "By Myself/When Your Lover Has Gone"

DICK CLARK SATURDAY NIGHT BEECHNUT SHOW (series episode)
Air Date: March 19, 1960
Host/Star: Dick Clark
Guests: Bobby Darin, Freddy Cannon, Dorsey Burnette, The Coasters
Darin's Songs: "Beyond The Sea"

DICK CLARK SATURDAY NIGHT BEECHNUT SHOW (series episode)
Air Date: June 11, 1960
Host/Star: Dick Clark
Guests: Bobby Darin, The Skyliners, The Crests
Darin's Songs: "I'll Be There," "Bill Bailey"

COKE TIME (Special)
Air Date: June 27, 1960
Host/Star: Pat Boone
Guests: Frankie Avalon, Bobby Darin, Annette Funicello, Paul Anka,
    Edward Byrnes, Bob Denver, Anita Bryant
Darin's Songs: "All I Need Is The Girl," "Amapola"

BOB HOPE BUICK SHOW (Special)
Air Date: October 3, 1960
Host/Star: Bob Hope
Guests: Patti Page, Bobby Darin, Joan Crawford
Darin's Songs: "Artificial Flowers," "Lazy River," "Two Different
    Worlds" (with Patti Page), "Medley: Thanks For The Memory/Mack
    The Knife/Two Sleepy People" (with Bob Hope)

JACKIE GLEASON SHOW (series episode)
Air Date: March 17, 1961
Host/Star: Jackie Gleason
Guests: Bobby Darin
Darin's Songs: "When Irish Eyes Are Smiling"

AT THIS VERY MOMENT (Special)
Air Date: April 1, 1962
Host/Star: Burt Lancaster
Guests: Harry Belafonte, Bobby Darin, Jimmy Durante, Connie
    Francis, Charlton Heston, Bob Hope, Dinah Shore, Lena Horne,
    The Kingston Trio
Darin's Songs: "Bill Bailey" (with Jimmy Durante)

ED SULLIVAN SHOW (series episode)
Air Date: May 6, 1962
Host/Star: Ed Sullivan
Guests: Diahann Carroll, Bobby Darin, The Amazing Ballantine
Darin's Songs: unknown

MERV GRIFFIN SHOW (series episode)
Air Date: October 4, 1962
Host/Star: Merv Griffin
Guests: Bobby Darin
Darin's Songs: unknown

BOB HOPE SHOW (Special)
Air Date: November 29, 1962
Host/Star: Bob Hope
Guests: Ethel Merman, Jack Benny, Bobby Darin
Darin's Songs: "All By Myself," "Hit Parade Medley (parody): Ahab The
    Arab/They Call The Wind Maria/Speedy Gonzales/Monster Mash/
    Papa-Oom-Mow-Mow" (with Bob Hope)

DINAH SHORE SPECIAL (Special)
Air Date: April 14, 1963
Host/Star: Dinah Shore
Guests: Bobby Darin, Andre Previn
Darin's Songs: "Blue Skies," "Long Time Man," "Work Song," "Bidin'
    My Time," "Everybody's Doin' It/Let's Do It (Let's Fall In Love)" (with
    Dinah Shore), "If I Had My Druthers" (with Dinah Shore)

JUDY GARLAND SHOW (series episode)
Air Date: December 29, 1963
Host/Star: Judy Garland
Guests: Bobby Darin, Bob Newhart
Darin's Songs: "I'm On My Way Great God," "Michael Row The Boat
    Ashore," "Railroad Medley" (with Judy Garland)

JACK BENNY SHOW (series episode)
Air Date: January 28, 1964
Host/Star: Jack Benny
Guests: Bobby Darin
Darin's Songs: "As Long As I'm Singing"

EDIE ADAMS SHOW (series episode)
Air Date: February 6, 1964
Host/Star: Edie Adams
Guests: Bobby Darin
Darin's Songs: "This Nearly Was Mine," "Kurt Weill Medley: Mack
    The Knife/Moon-Faced And Starry Eyed/Surabaya Johnny/Here
    I'll Stay/Bilbao Song/Alabama Song" (duet with Edie Adams)

ANDY WILLIAMS SHOW (series episode)
Air Date: January 11, 1965
Host/Star: Andy Williams
Guests: Bobby Darin, Vic Damone, Henry Mancini
Darin's Songs: "Once In A Lifetime," "To Be A Performer/Three Of A Kind/Broadway Medley" (with Andy Williams and Vic Damone), "Leader Of The Pack" (with Vic Damone and The Osmonds)

ANDY WILLIAMS SHOW (series episode)
Air Date: September 13, 1965
Host/Star: Andy Williams
Guests: Bobby Darin, Robert Goulet, Woody Allen
Darin's Songs: "That Funny Feeling," "Girls Medley" (with Andy Williams and Robert Goulet), "You Can't Cheat An Honest Man" (with Andy Williams and Robert Goulet), "Here's To Us" (with Andy Williams and Robert Goulet)

RED SKELTON SHOW (series episode)
Air Date: September 21, 1965
Host/Star: Red Skelton
Guests: Bobby Darin, Jackie and Gayle
Darin's Songs: "Sunday In New York," "That Funny Feeling"

STEVE LAWRENCE SHOW (series episode)
Air Date: October 11, 1965
Host/Star: Steve Lawrence
Guests: Bobby Darin
Darin's Songs: unknown

ANDY WILLIAMS SHOW (series episode)
Air Date: January 10, 1966
Host/Star: Andy Williams
Guests: Bobby Darin, Eddie Fisher, Herb Alpert & The Tijuana Brass
Darin's Songs: unknown

ANDY WILLIAMS SHOW (series episode)
Air Date: October 9, 1966
Host/Star: Andy Williams
Guests: Anthony Newley, Bobby Darin, Nancy Wilson
Darin's Songs: "Mame"

(Left to Right) Eddie Fisher, Andy Williams, and Darin on "The Andy Williams Show," 1966
(NBC publicity photo)

RODGERS & HART TODAY (Special)
Air Date: March 2, 1967

Host/Star: None

Guests: Bobby Darin, The Supremes, Petula Clark, The Mamas & The Papas, Count Basie

Darin's Songs: "The Lady Is A Tramp," "I Wish I Were In Love Again" (with the Basie Band), "Any Old Place" (with Petula Clark), "Falling In Love With Love" (with The Supremes and the Basie Band), "Mountain Greenery" (with Petula Clark, The Supremes, and the Basie Band)

KRAFT MUSIC HALL: "GIVE MY REGARDS TO BROADWAY" (Special)
Air Date: October 4, 1967

Host/Star: Bobby Darin

Guests: Liza Minnelli, Kaye Stevens, Dennis Day, Max Morath, Jack Benny

Darin's Songs: "Yankee Doodle Dandy," "Always Leave 'Em Laughing"

AND DEBBIE MAKES SIX (Special)
Air Date: November 19, 1967

Host/Star: Debbie Reynolds

Guests: Bobby Darin, Bob Hope, Jim Nabors, Donald O'Connor, Frank Gorshin

Darin's Songs: "Always" (with Debbie Reynolds), "Jackson" (with Debbie Reynolds), "Medley: It Takes Two/Where Did Our Love Go/There Is A Mountain/You Keep Runnin' Away/Hold On, I'm Comin'" (with Debbie Reynolds)

KRAFT MUSIC HALL: "A GRAND NIGHT FOR SWINGING" (Special)
Air Date: January 10, 1968

Host/Star: Bobby Darin

Guests: Bobbie Gentry, Bobby Van, George Kirby

Darin's Songs: "Talk To The Animals," "Mack The Knife," "Drowning In My Own Tears," "Long Time Movin'" (with Bobbie Gentry), "Nothing Can Stop Us Now" (with Bobbie Gentry and Bobby Van)

ROWAN & MARTIN'S LAUGH-IN (series episode)
Air Date: October 14, 1968

Host/Star: Rowan & Martin

Guests: Bobby Darin

Darin's Songs: "Mack The Knife" (parody) (duet with Artie Johnson)

KRAFT MUSIC HALL: "THE SOUND OF THE SIXTIES" (Special)
Air Date: January 22, 1969
Host/Star: Bobby Darin
Guests: Buddy Rich, Judy Collins, Stevie Wonder, Laura Nyro
Darin's Songs: "Let The Good Times Roll," "Splish Splash," "Honey Take A Whiff On Me," "Long Line Rider," "If I Were A Carpenter" (with Stevie Wonder), "I'll Be Your Baby Tonight" (with Judy Collins)

THIS IS TOM JONES (series episode)
Air Date: October 2, 1969
Host/Star: Tom Jones
Guests: Bobby Darin, others
Darin's Songs: "Distractions," "A Worried Man/Aquarius/Let The Sunshine In" (with Tom Jones)

THE MIKE DOUGLAS SHOW (Daily talk show)
Air Date: Week of July 27, 1970 (July 27-31)
Host/Star: Mike Douglas
Guest Host: Bobby Darin
Darin's Songs: unknown

ANDY WILLIAMS SHOW (series episode)
Air Date: September 19, 1970
Host/Star: Andy Williams
Guests: Martin Landau, Barbara Bain, The Supremes, Bobby Darin
Darin's Songs: "Mack The Knife"

FLIP WILSON SHOW (series episode)
Air Date: September 24, 1970
Host/Star: Flip Wilson
Guests: Bobby Darin, Denise Nichols, Roy Clark
Darin's Songs: "Melodie," "Who Takes Care Of The Caretaker's Daughter" (with Flip Wilson and Roy Clark)

FLIP WILSON SHOW (series episode)
Air Date: November 20, 1970
Host/Star: Flip Wilson
Guests: Ella Fitzgerald, Bobby Darin, Charlie Pride
Darin's Songs: "Higher And Higher," "Country-Western Medley" (with Flip Wilson and Charlie Pride)

FLIP WILSON SHOW (series episode)
Air Date: December 17, 1970
Host/Star: Flip Wilson
Guests: Bobby Darin, Sid Caesar, B.B. King
Darin's Songs: "Gabriel," "Paddlin' Madelin' Home/Row Row Row" (with Flip Wilson), "Noises In The Street" (with Flip Wilson and Sid Caesar)

FLIP WILSON SHOW (series episode)
Air Date: January 21, 1971
Host/Star: Flip Wilson
Guests: Muhammad Ail, Bobby Darin, Lily Tomlin
Darin's Songs: "Lazy River," "If I Were A Carpenter," "Toot Toot Tootsie" (with Flip Wilson)

GOIN' BACK TO INDIANA (special)
Air Date: September 19, 1971
Host/Star: The Jackson Five
Guests: Tommy Smothers, Rosie Grier, Diana Ross, Bill Cosby, Bobby Darin
Darin's songs: None (non-singing cameo role)

FLIP WILSON SHOW (series episode)
Air Date: January 13, 1972
Host/Star: Flip Wilson
Guests: Bobby Darin, Redd Foxx, Tim Conway
Darin's Songs: "Mack The Knife," "Simple Song Of Freedom," "One Of Those Songs" (with Flip Wilson)

THE TONIGHT SHOW (series episode)
Air Date: March 6, 1972
Host/Star: Johnny Carson
Guests: Bobby Darin, Buffy St. Marie
Darin's Songs: unknown

THE DAVID FROST SHOW (series episode)
Air Date: Syndicated; aired in New York on March 19, 1972
Host/Star: David Frost
Guest: Bobby Darin
Darin's Songs: "For Once In My Life," "If I Were A Carpenter," "Mack The Knife," "A Worried Man/Splish Splash"

SONNY & CHER COMEDY HOUR (series episode)
Air Date: November 10, 1972
Host/Star: Sonny & Cher
Guests: Bobby Darin
Darin's Songs: "Sail Away"

THE TONIGHT SHOW (series episode)
Air Date: February 6, 1973
Host/Star: Johnny Carson
Guests: Bobby Darin, Orson Bean, Seals & Crofts, Joan Embrey
Darin's Songs: "You Are My Sunshine/Splish Splash"

THE MIDNIGHT SPECIAL (series episode)
Air Date: March 16, 1973
Host/Star: Paul Anka
Guests: Bobby Darin, Tammy Wynette, George Jones, The Doobie
  Brothers, Fanny, Edwin Hawkins Singers
Darin's Songs: "If I Were A Carpenter," "Dream Lover/Splish Splash"

Darin Appearances On Drama Programs

HENNESEY
Air Date: October 5, 1959
Episode Title: "Hennesey Meets Honeyboy"
Darin's Character: Honeyboy Jones

DAN RAVEN
Air Date: September 23, 1960
Episode Title: "The High Cost Of Fame"
Darin's Character: Bobby Darin

WAGON TRAIN
Air Date: October 4, 1964
Episode Title: "The John Gillman Story"
Darin's Character: John Gillman

BOB HOPE CHRYSLER THEATRE
Air Date: October 9, 1964
Episode Title: "Murder In The First"
Stars: Janet Leigh, Bobby Darin
Darin's Character: Brad Kubec

BURKE'S LAW
Air Date: April 7, 1965
Episode Title: "Who Killed Hamlet"

RUN FOR YOUR LIFE
Air Date: March 7, 1966
Episode Title: "Who's Watching The Fleshpot"
Stars: Bobby Darin, Eve Arden
Darin's Character: Mark Shepherd

DANNY THOMAS HOUR
Air Date: January 15, 1968
Episode Title: "The Cage"
Stars: Bobby Darin, Dean Stockwell, Sugar Ray Robinson

IRONSIDE
Air Date: October 5, 1971
Episode Title: "The Gambling Game"

CADE'S COUNTY
Air Date: November 28, 1971
Episode Title: "A Gun For Billy"
Darin's Character: Billy Dobbs

NIGHT GALLERY
Air Date: February 9, 1972
Episode Title: "Dead Weight"
Stars: Bobby Darin, Jack Albertson

Darin Guest Appearances On Game Shows

PASSWORD
Air Date: January 6, 1963
Host: Allen Ludden
Guests: Bobby Darin, Rosemary Clooney

WHAT'S MY LINE
Air Date: February 9, 1964
Host: John Charles Daly
Guests: (Panelists) Bobby Darin, Arlene Francis, Dorothy Kilgallen, Bennett Cerf

I'VE GOT A SECRET
Air Date: February 17, 1964
Host: Gary Moore
Guest: Bobby Darin

MATCH GAME
Air Date: February 1-5, 1965
Host: Gene Rayburn
Guests: Bobby Darin, Joan Fontaine

Songs Written By Bobby Darin

The following list, derived from an examination of copyright records at the Library of Congress, consists of songs written or co-written by Bobby Darin. The majority of these compositions are copyrighted under the name Bobby Darin, although some are credited to "Bob Darin," and a few others to "Bob Cassotto." The list is arranged alphabetically by song title.

Title	Co-writer	Copyright Date
After School Rock And Roll	Don Kirshner	03/21/56
	George M. Shaw	
All Your Friends Are Here		04/14/67
Amy		01/27/67
Another Song On My Mind	Tommy Amato	03/11/74
As Long As I'm Singing		08/28/62
Autumn Blues		08/09/60
Baby I Miss You		09/15/65
Baby May		12/29/69
Bad Girl		04/04/63
Ballet Dance		04/14/67
Barb'ry Ann	Claire Kaufman	04/02/58
Be Mad Little Girl		09/18/63
Beachcomber		08/09/60
Bi-aza-ku-sasa	Rudi Trailor	07/11/58
Boss Barracuda	Terry Melcher	05/22/64

Title	Co-writer	Copyright Date
Brand New House	Woody Harris	07/30/58
Broken Up Inside	David Hill	03/17/60
Bubble Gum Pop	Don Kirshner	01/17/56
Bullfrog		09/10/68
Bullmoose		04/09/59
By My Side	Don Kirshner	07/22/57
Can't You See Me		04/14/67
Casey, Wake Up!		03/12/64
Change		08/09/68
Chantal's Theme		06/21/62
Coffee Perkin' Time		10/07/64
Come		04/14/67
Come September (Instrumental Theme)		06/01/61
Come September (with added lyrics)	Cy Coben	11/02/66
Comin' Down With A Heartache	Rudy Clark	04/15/63
Daydreamer	Jimmy Boyd	05/01/62
Dealer In Dreams	Don Kirshner	04/24/56
Delia	Don Kirshner	04/03/57
Distractions		06/06/69
Don't Call My Name	Don Kirshner	10/21/57
Down So Long		07/25/63
Dream Baby	Arthur Resnick	09/25/63
Dream Lover		04/09/59
Early In The Morning	Woody Harris	06/09/58
Eighteen Yellow Roses		04/22/63
Elizabeth		12/13/63
The End Of Never	Francine Forest	07/31/64

AMERICA'S
MOST VERSATILE
YOUNG
SHOWMAN

BOBBY DARIN

In A Fabulous Piano Hit!

BEACHCOMBER

AND

Autumn Blues

Atco 6173

With Orchestra Conducted by
Shorty Rogers

A T C O
R E C O R D S

Title	Co-writer	Copyright Date
Everywhere I Go		01/18/68
Face To Face		04/14/67
The Feelin'	David Hill	03/17/60
Fourteen Pairs Of Shoes	Russell Alquist	04/09/65
Freedom To Love	Arthur Resnick	02/12/64
Funny What Love Can Do		09/15/65
Gone		12/26/62
The Great Society		02/03/65
The Greatest Lover In The World		04/14/67
Gyp The Cat	Don Wolf	07/29/65
The Harvest		06/06/69
Hello Sunshine		04/07/67
Hey Magic Man		06/06/69
Hot Rod U.S.A.	Terry Melcher	04/13/64
I Am		04/07/67
I Can See The Wind		08/09/68
I Can't Believe A Word You Say	Rudy Clark	04/15/63
I Want To Spend Christmas With Elvis	Don Kirshner	11/29/56
I Got My Own Thing Going	Rudy Clark	07/29/65
I'll Be There		10/20/59
I'm Gonna Love You		01/18/68
If You Love Him		03/12/64
If A Man Answers		06/21/62
In Memoriam		08/09/68
It's Him I Wanna Go With Mama	Arthur Resnick	04/20/64
It's What's Happening Baby		06/14/65
Jailer Bring Me Water		06/12/62
Jingle Jangle Jungle		08/09/68

Title	Co-writer	Copyright Date
Jive		06/06/69
Keep A-Movin' Mama	Don Kirshner	02/11/57
Light Blue		06/06/69
The Lively Set		03/23/64
Long Time Movin'		01/18/68
Long Line Rider		08/09/68
Look At Me	Randy Newman	06/25/64
Look For My True Love		06/24/60
Los Angeles	Francine Forest	08/04/66
Lost Love	Don Kirshner	08/06/58
Love Me Right	Don Kirshner	07/23/57
Made In The Shade		05/01/62
Maybe We Can Get It Together		03/02/70
Me And Mr. Hohner		05/12/69
Mighty Mighty Man		10/24/58
Moment Of Love		10/08/59
Monkey	Rudy Clark	06/18/63
Mountain Of Love	Don Kirshner	02/07/58
Multiplication		08/15/61
My First Real Love	Don Kirshner George M. Shaw	02/15/56
My Dog Got A Tag On Her		11/19/64
My Mom	Terry Melcher	08/22/64
Not For Me		04/22/63
Now We're One		06/09/58
O.K. Girl (aka "O.K. Boy")	Russell Alquist	04/26/65
Oo-ee Train		02/02/62
Peck-A-Cheek	Cy Coben	03/17/58
Prescription-Fire (Rx-Pyro)		03/02/70

Title	Co-writer	Copyright Date
Pretty Betty	Don Kirshner	10/21/57
Prison Of Your Love		01/18/68
The Proper Gander		08/09/68
Queen Of The Hop	Woody Harris	08/29/58
Questions		08/09/68
Rainin'		04/07/66
Real Love	Woody Harris	06/11/58
The Rest Of My Life		04/02/58
Revolution Of The Goats	Norman Strassberg	08/06/58
Rock Pile	Don Kirshner George M. Shaw	03/14/56
The Rogers Cha Cha	Don Kirshner	02/06/56
Run, Little Rabbit		04/13/64
Sausalito (The Governors Song)		06/06/69
Save A Sinking Heart	Al Byron	01/26/61
School's Out	Woody Harris	06/11/58
She's Tanfastic		05/06/60
Shirl Girl	Rudy Clark	09/25/63
Silly Willie	Don Kirshner George M. Shaw	03/14/56
Simple Song Of Freedom		06/12/69
So Mean	Don Kirshner	07/03/57
Somebody To Love		10/20/59
Something In Her Love	Tommy Amato	10/31/72
Somewhere Out There		04/14/67
Song For A Dollar		05/12/69
Soul City		08/07/64
Splish Splash	Jean Murray	06/06/58
Sugar Man		12/05/66

Title	Co-writer	Copyright Date
Sugar Man		06/06/69
Summertime Symphony		06/22/59
Sunday		08/09/68
Sweet Reasons		12/29/69
Talk To Me Something	Don Kirshner	02/14/57
That Funny Feeling		10/12/64
That's The Way Love Is		04/02/58
Things		09/08/61
The Things In This House		08/26/64
This Little Girl's Gone Rockin'	Mann Curtis	04/25/58
Three To Get Ready		03/23/61
Timber	Don Kirshner George M. Shaw	03/12/56
Treat My Baby Good		07/25/63
A True True Love		08/28/62
Turbine Montage		10/07/64
Turned Down Theme		03/02/64
Two Of A Kind	Johnny Mercer	12/08/60
Two Tickets		10/12/64
Wait A Minute	Don Kirshner	01/12/61
Wait By The Water		08/26/64
Walk Bach To Me		07/11/61
Water Color Canvas		06/06/69
We Didn't Ask To Be Brought Here		09/15/65
Wear My Ring	Don Kirshner	04/30/57
Wendy		12/03/64
Wha'ch You Mean	Rudi Trailor	07/11/58
When I Get Home	Russell Alquist	05/12/65

Title	Co-writer	Copyright Date
While I'm Gone		02/18/63
Whomp Be Omp Bomp		06/13/58
Why Oh You	Don Kirshner	02/21/57
Wilco Jingle	Don Kirshner	02/06/56
A World Without You	Rudy Clark	03/22/65
You Just Don't Know		03/22/65
You Know How		10/08/59
You Got Me		04/14/67
You're The Reason I'm Living		12/26/62
You're Mine		10/24/58
Zoom-A-Roo	Arthur Resnick	03/09/64

Bobby Darin Songs
Recorded By Other Artists

This is a partial listing of songs written (or co-written) by Bobby Darin which have been recorded by other artists

Song	**Artist**
As Long As I'm Singing	Brian Setzer Orchestra
	Freddy Cole
	Matt Monro
Bad Girl	Johnny Cymbal
Beachcomber	? and the Mysterians
	Johnny Gibson Trio
Boss Barracuda	Surfaris
Brand New House	Otis Spann
Bullmoose	'68 Comeback
	Jimmy Gilmer and the Fireballs
	Wild Angels
By My Side	Davy Hill
Delia	Bobby Short
Down So Long	Roosevelt Grier

Song	Artist
Dream Baby	Wayne Newton
Dream Lover	Astronauts
	Bobby Rydell
	Debbie Elam
	Duane Eddy
	Gary Lewis and the Playboys
	Johnny Burnette
	Manhattan Transfer with James Taylor
	Mary Hopkins and Sundance
	Plasmatics
	Ronnie Hawkins
	Santo and Johnny
	Spider Turner
	Billy "Crash" Craddock
	Dion
	Don McLean
	Glen Campbell & Tanya Tucker
	Johnny Nash
	Paris Sisters
	Peter McCann
	Rick Nelson
	Susie Brading
	Tony Orlando
Early In The Morning	Bobby Vee
	Connie Francis
	Freddie and the Dreamers
	Joe Brown
	Mamaicans
	Z.Z. Hill
	Buddy Holly
	Mac Curtis
	Tommy Roe

Song	Artist
Eighteen Yellow Roses	Steve Goodman
	Texas Tornados
	C.L. Goodson
Hello Sunshine	Gary Lewis and the Playboys
Hot Rod USA	Catalinas
	Fantastic Baggys
	The Knights
	Rip Chords
I Want To Spend Christmas With Elvis	Little Lambsie Penn
I'll Be There	Cass Elliot
	Cissy Houston
	Clint Holmes
	Elvis Presley
	Gerry and The Pacemakers
	Tony Orlando
Jailer Bring Me Water	Bachelors
	Freddie and the Dreamers
	Johnny Rivers
	Trini Lopez
Love Me Right	LaVern Baker
Monkey (aka Do The Monkey)	King Curtis
Multiplication	Johnny Rivers
	Showaddywaddy
My First Real Love	Connie Francis
My Mom	Osmond Brothers

Song	Artist
Now We're One	Buddy Holly
Queen Of The Hop	Dave Edmunds
	Dion
Real Love	Jaye Sisters
Run Little Rabbit	Catalinas
School's Out	Jaye Sisters
Shirl Girl	Wayne Newton
Simple Song of Freedom	Della Reese
	Mystic Moods Orchestra
	Spirit Of Us
	Tim Hardin
Soul City	Roosevelt Grier
Splish Splash	Barbra Streisand
	Charlie Drake
	Conway Twitty
	Dee Dee Sharp
	Hank Williams Jr.
	Johnny Cash
	Lindisfarne
	Loggins & Messina
	Sandy Nelson
	Sha Na Na
	Steve Goodman
Sweet Reasons	Judy Mayhan
Theme From "Come September"	Billy Vaughan & His Orchestra
	Dick Jacobs
	Santo and Johnny
	John Severson

Song	**Artist**
Things	Alan Price
	Anne Murray
	Billy Walker
	Buddy Alan
	Daniel O'Donnell
	Dean Martin and Nancy Sinatra
	Jerry Lee Lewis
	Robbie Williams
This Little Girl's Gone Rockin'	Glenda Collins
	Ruth Brown
Wait A Minute	Coasters
Wear My Ring	Gene Vincent
When I Get Home	Searchers
You Just Don't Know	Mary K. Miller
	Wayne Newton
You're The Reason I'm Living	Elvis Presley
	Gary Stewart
	Lamar Morris
	Price Mitchell
	Ronnie Dove
	Sonny James
	Wanda Jackson

Unreleased Tracks

This list consists of never-released tracks recorded by Bobby Darin during his stints at Atco (1957-62) and Atlantic (1965-67). Information was gathered from Atlantic Records: A Discography *by Michel Ruppli. "Session Notes" are included when the unreleased track was recorded at the same session as a released Darin single or LP.*

Although additional unreleased material is reported to exist from Darin's Capitol and Motown periods, specific information regarding unreleased tracks recorded for these labels was unavailable.

Song Title	Session Date	Session Notes
Some Of These Days (early version)	10/29/58	—
Didn't It Feel Good	12/05/58	Plain Jane 45
The Breeze And I	05/19/59	This Is Darin LP
Sunday Kind Of Love	05/20/59	This Is Darin LP
Since My Love Was Gone	05/20/59	This Is Darin LP
The Lamp Is Low	05/21/59	This Is Darin LP
A Game Of Poker	02/01/60	Winners LP
I Got A Woman	02/02/60	Winners LP
Birth Of The Blues (Live)	06/15-16/60	Darin At Copa LP
My Funny Valentine (Live)	06/15-16/60	Darin At Copa LP
Splish Splash (Live)	06/15-16/60	Darin At Copa LP

Song Title	Session Date	Session Notes
Lily Of Laguna	08/14/60	Johnny Mercer LP
Back In Your Own Backyard	08/17/60	Johnny Mercer LP
Cecilia	08/22/60	Johnny Mercer LP
Bobby's Blues	03/25/61	—
Special Someone	06/06/61	Come September 45
Teenage Theme	06/06/61	Come September 45
Movin' On	06/06/61	Come September 45
Sweet Memories Of You	08/19/65	We Didn't Ask 45
Ain't That A Bunch Of Nonsense	08/19/65	We Didn't Ask 45
Baby I Miss You So	08/23/65	—
Ace In The Hole	12/13/65	Shadow Of LP
The Best Is Yet To Come	12/13/65	Shadow Of LP
The Sheik Of Araby	12/14/65	Shadow Of LP
This Could Be The Start Of Something	12/14/65	Shadow Of LP
I Got Plenty Of Nothing	12/15/65	Shadow Of LP
Baby Won't You Please Come Home	12/15/65	Shadow Of LP
Weeping Willow	02/04/66	Rainin' 45
Strangers In The Night	03/23/66	Shadows Of LP
True Love Are Blessing	04/21/66	—
Merry Go Round In The Rain	06/21/66	—
LA	08/01/66	Unreleased LP
I Can Live On Love	08/01/66	Unreleased LP
Manhattan In My Heart	08/01/66	Unreleased LP
Lulu's Back In Town	08/01/66	Unreleased LP
Mountain Greenery	08/01/66	Unreleased LP
For You	08/01/66	Unreleased LP

Song Title	Session Date	Session Notes
What Now My Love	08/01/66	Unreleased LP
It's Magic	08/01/66	Unreleased LP
Danke Schoen	08/01/66	Unreleased LP
My Own True Love	08/01/66	Unreleased LP
On A Clear Day	08/01/66	Unreleased LP
Quarter To Nine	08/01/66	Unreleased LP
Seventeen	08/01/66	Unreleased LP
Funny What Love Can Do (alt version)	11/01/66	Carpenter LP
Good Day Sunshine	11/01/66	Carpenter LP
Younger Girl	11/01/66	Carpenter LP
Saginaw Michigan	03/28/67	—
Biggest Night Of Her Life	07/19/67	She Knows 45
All Strung Out	11/13/67	—
Tupelo Mississippi Flash	11/18/67	—
Natural Soul Loving Big City Countryfied Man	11/19/67	—

Darin at The Landmark Hotel, September 1970
(Las Vegas News Bureau)

Unrecorded Songs Performed
Live By Bobby Darin

The following is a partial list of songs that Bobby Darin performed live, but never recorded. The list includes numbers from his concert and TV appearances; duets are not included. Songs included on official live albums are not listed here, even if Darin never recorded a studio version. The list clearly exhibits the wide range of popular music embraced by Bobby Darin.

After I've Gone Away

All I Need Is The Girl

All Of Me

Alone Again (Naturally)

Always Leave 'Em Laughing

Bidin' My Time

Bo Diddley

Boil That Cabbage Down

Born Free

Bridge Over Troubled Water

Brooklyn Roads

Brother, Can You Spare A Dime?

Can't Take My Eyes Off You

Climb Ev'ry Mountain

Come A Rum Rum

Come Rain Or Come Shine

Cottonfields

Cry Me A River

Danny Boy

Don't Worry 'Bout Me

Dreidel

The Erie Canal

Everybody's Talkin'

For Once In My Life

Gabriel

Get Me To The Church On Time

Got My Mojo Working

Gotta Travel On

He's Got The Whole World In His Hands

Help Me Make It Through The Night

Here's That Rainy Day

Honey Take A Whiff On Me

I Ain't Nobody

I Get A Kick Out Of You

I Got Plenty Of Nothing

I'll Be Seeing You

I'm A Fool To Want You

I've Got The World On A String

I've Got You Under My Skin

If

King Of The Road

The Lady Is A Tramp

Lady Madonna

Let The Good Times Roll

Meditation

Midnight Special

My Kind Of Town

My Tears

One Of Those Songs

Pass Me By

Reviewing The Situation

Shilo

Short Fat Fannie

Sing Sing Song

(Sittin' On) The Dock Of The Bay

Sixteen Tons

Some People

Someone To Watch Over Me

Song Sung Blue

Spinning Wheel

Spirit In The Dark

St. Louis Blues

Sweet Caroline

This Could Be The Start Of Something Big

This Is The Life

Toot Toot Tootsie

Try A Little Tenderness

Volare

What Now My Love

When Irish Eyes Are Smiling

When The Saints Go Marching In

When You Wore A Tulip

Yankee Doodle Dandy

Yesterday

You Are My Sunshine

You've Lost That Lovin' Feelin'

Bibliography

Bianco, David. *Heat Wave: The Motown Fact Book*. Ann Arbor, MI: Popular Culture, Ink., 1988.

Bronson, Fred. *The Billboard Book Of Number One Hits*. New York: Billboard Publications, Inc., 1985

Brooks, Tim and Earle Marsh. *The Complete Directory To Prime Time Network TV Shows 1946-Present*. New York: Ballantine Books, 1992.

Clark, Dick and Richard Robinson. *Rock, Roll & Remember*. New York: Thomas Y. Crowell Company, 1976.

Darin, Dodd and Maxine Paetro. *Dream Lovers: The Magnificent Shattered Lives of Bobby Darin and Sandra Dee*. New York: Warner Books, 1994.

DiMucci, Dion and Davin Seay. *The Wanderer: Dion's Story*. New York: Beech Tree Books, 1988.

DiOrio, Al. *Borrowed Time: The 37 Years Of Bobby Darin*. Philadelphia: Running Press, 1986.

Francis, Connie. *Who's Sorry Now?* New York: St. Martin's Press, Inc., 1984

Gambaccini, Paul, Tim Rice and Jonathan Rice. *British Hit Singles*. Enfield: Guinness Publishing, 1991.

Gillett, Charlie. *Making Tracks: Atlantic Records And The Growth Of A Multi-Billion Dollar Industry*. London: W.H. Allen, 1975.

Howar, Barbara. *Laughing All The Way*. New York: Stein and Day, 1973

Irvin, Jim (editor). *The Mojo Collection*. Edinburgh: Mojo Books, 2000.

Kaplan, Mike (editor). *Variety International Showbusiness Reference*. New York: Garland Publishing Inc., 1981.

Katz, Ephraim. *The Film Encyclopedia*. New York: Thomas Y. Crowell Publishers, 1979.

Lee, Peggy. *Miss Peggy Lee: An Autobiography*. New York: Donald I. Fine, Inc., 1989.

Miller, Jim (editor). *The Rolling Stone Illustrated History of Rock & Roll*. New York: Rolling Stone Press, 1980.

Munden, Kenneth W. (executive editor). *The American Film Institute Catalog Of Motion Pictures Produced In The United States*. New York: R.R. Bowker, 1971.

Nash, Jay Robert and Stanley Ralph Ross. *The Motion Picture Guide*. Chicago: Cinebooks, 1985.

Newfield, Jack. *Robert Kennedy: A Memoir*. New York: E.P. Dutton & Co., Inc., 1969.

Newton, Wayne with Dick Maurice. *Once Before I Go*. New York: William Morrow and Company, Inc., 1989.

O'Neil, Thomas. *The Grammys*. New York: Penguin Books, 1993.

Parish, James Robert. *Actors Television Credits 1950-1972*. Metuchen, NJ: The Scarecrow Press, Inc., 1973

Ribowsky, Mark. *He's A Rebel*. New York: E.P. Dutton, 1989.

Ruppli, Michel (compiled by). *Atlantic Records: A Discography*. Westport, CT: Greenwood Press, 1979.

Sedaka, Neil. *Laughter In The Rain: My Own Story*. New York: Putnam's, 1982.

Shale, Richard. *Academy Awards*. New York: Frederick Ungar Publishing Co., 1978.

Shore, Michael with Dick Clark. *The History Of American Bandstand*. New York: Ballantine Books, 1985.

Smith, Joe. *Off The Record: An Oral History Of Popular Music*. New York: Warner Books, 1988.

Terrace, Vincent. *Encyclopedia Of Television Series, Pilots And Specials 1937-1973*. New York: New York Zoetrope, 1986.

— *Television Specials*. Jefferson, NC: McFarland & Company, 1995.

Warner, Jay. *Billboard's American Rock'n'Roll In Review*. New York: Schirmer Books, 1997.

Whitburn, Joel. *Top Pop Albums 1955-1985*. Menomonee Falls, WI: Record Research Inc., 1985.

— *Pop Memories 1890-1954*. Menomonee Falls, WI: Record Research Inc., 1986.

— *Top 1000 Singles 1955-1987*. Milwaukee: Hal Leonard Books, 1988.

— *Top Country Singles 1944-1988*. Menomonee Falls, WI: Record Research Inc., 1989.

— *Bubbling Under Singles & Albums*. Menomonee Falls, WI: Record Research Inc., 1998.

— *Top Pop Singles 1955-1999*. Menomonee Falls, WI: Record Research Inc., 2000.

— *Top Adult Contemporary 1961-2001*. Menomonee Falls, WI: Record Research Inc., 2002.